ANALYZING POVERTY AND POLICY REFORM

For Karen Chandler

Analyzing Poverty and Policy Reform

The Experience of Côte d'Ivoire

CHRISTIAAN GROOTAERT
The World Bank

With contributions from
LIONEL DEMERY and RAVI KANBUR

Avebury

Aldershot • Brookfield USA • Hong Kong • Singapore • Sydney

Published by
Avebury
Ashgate Publishing Limited
Gower House
Croft Road
Aldershot
Hants GU11 3HR
England

Ashgate Publishing Company
Old Post Road
Brookfield
Vermont 05036
USA

A CIP catalogue record for this book is available from the British Library

ISBN 1 85972 378 0

Library of Congress Catalog Card Number: 96-84407

Printed and bound by Athenaeum Press, Ltd.,
Gateshead, Tyne & Wear.

Contents

Figures and Tables

Acknowledgements

The majority of findings reported in this volume were obtained through research project *Poverty and the Social Dimensions of Structural Adjustment in Côte d'Ivoire, 1985-88 - A Policy Oriented Analysis* co-sponsored by the World Bank and the Commission of the European Communities.

The author would like to thank Philippe Callier, Michael Cohen, Lionel Demery, Jean-Luc Dubois, Ravi Kanbur, Michel Noel, Chris Scott, Ismail Serageldin, Antoine Simonpietri, Roger Sullivan, Jack Van Holst-Pellekaan for their contributions and support during the writing of this work.

Thanks are also due to the National Institute of Statistics of Côte d'Ivoire which made available the data of the Côte d'Ivoire Living Standards Surveys for this research. At the World Bank, the data were managed by Gi-Taik Oh and Meera Venkataraman.

The technical production of this document was undertaken by Mary Abuzeid, Susan Assaf and Elena Vitanov.

Any views expressed in this work are those of the authors only, and should not be attributed to the World Bank, its affiliated organizations, or any of the other institutions which supported or were affiliated with this research.

Introduction and outline

Since the start of structural adjustment programs in the 1980s, a growing debate has emerged as to the efficiency of these programs to bring about sustainable economic growth and as to their impact on poverty and basic needs fulfillment. Most evidence accumulated to date suggests that 'adjusting' countries have experience more improvement (or less decline) in their macroeconomic performance than 'non-adjusting' countries particularly if the adjustment effort is sustained (Corbo et al., 1992; World Bank, 1994). However, it is also recognized that progress has been much slower than anticipated originally and that structural adjustment and associated policy change is a long term endeavor in most countries.

It is much less clear what the impact of the adjustment process has been on the poor. Initial claims of a strong negative impact (Cornia et al., 1987) were based on insufficient empirical evidence and a too limited conceptual approach, which failed to distinguish adequately between the effects of economic recession and those of adjustment – itself a policy response to the recession and the concomitant internal and external imbalances. Recent work (World Bank, 1990; Demery et al., 1993) has provided a more refined framework to describe the transmission mechanism between macroeconomic events and the microeconomy of households and individuals. This work has emphasized the role of labor and commodity markets and of economic and social infrastructure, and described in some detail the relevant factors in the transmission process in the case of the social sectors (education, health) and in the case of important target groups (women, rural smallholders, the poor). One emerging conclusion form this work is that the poverty and social impacts of adjustment can only rarely be predicted on purely theoretical and a priori ground. The reasons are (at least) twofold. First, a typical adjustment package consists of many different macroeconomic and sectoral measures. These measures do not necessarily have converging impacts. Second, the impact of a given single policy action is usually difficult to predict, even when considered in isolation. For example, how an exchange rate devaluation will impact the poor depends upon the consumption and income patterns of the poor, the composition of imports and exports, associated tariffs and subsidies, etc. Moreover, the impact of a given measure can depend upon which other components are in the package.

What all this means is that the determination of what happens to household welfare and poverty under conditions of structural change is largely an empirical matter. And this presents a serious problem, because in many developing countries, especially in Africa, the needed social and economic data base is nonexistent or out of date. It is therefore potentially very instructive to undertake detailed case studies in those rare countries where the needed data do exist. One such case is Côte d'Ivoire over the period 1985-88. To our knowledge, this case is unique in Africa, because the available data meet two essential conditions. First, any analysis of the impact of macroeconomic change requires comparable data for at least two points in time, situated appropriately relative to the adjustment phase so that they can reflect its impact. Second, the concern with household welfare and poverty requires the availability of micro-level data which cover the different dimensions of household welfare. In Côte d'Ivoire, both conditions have been met by the Côte d'Ivoire Living Standards Survey (CILSS) which was undertaken for four consecutive years, 1985-88. The CILSS asked detailed information on income, expenditure, employment, health, education, housing and other socioeconomic characteristics of household and individuals. The period 1985-88 represents a particularly critical phase in Côte d'Ivoire's process of structural change. Adjustment efforts in Côte d'Ivoire started in 1981, and were sustained for six years. After showing signs of improvement in 1985-86, the economy nosedived in 1987-88 and the government abandoned the structural adjustment program (it was resumed in late 1989). The initial years of CILSS data (1985-86) are thus able to pick up the effects of sustained adjustment, while the latter years (1987-88) will reflect the abandonment of the effort and rapid economic decline – in effect, a period of destabilization. Even recognizing the existence of lagged effects, this feature is particularly important, because it provides a 'natural' way to disentangle adjustment from recession effects.[1]

The objective of this book is to chart the evolution of household welfare and poverty in Côte d'Ivoire between 1985-88 and to try to understand this evolution in the context of the macroeconomic change which occurred over the period. We are concerned to find out how the overall incidence and depth of poverty has evolved, and what changes may have occurred in the regional and socioeconomic patterns of poverty. It stands to reason that the macroeconomic swings will have benefited some groups and hurt other, and it is clearly of interest for policy to know who they are. It is to be expected that the economic decline in 1987-88 will have had a negative impact on household welfare, but the question is by how much and where the impact was concentrated.

In trying to address these questions, we selected a methodology centered around a double decomposition of a poverty index. First, a decomposition along regional and socioeconomic lines will be used to try to relate specific policy measures to the welfare of subgroups of the population. Second, the change in the poverty index over time will be decomposed into its growth and distribution components, in order to assess the relative role played by each.

As we hope this book will demonstrate, this approach can provide policy-makers with much relevant information for the assessment of past policies and for the design of new ones, in the area of poverty and basic needs. It will be clear though, and must be explicitly stated from the outset, that our approach will not permit to prove causality in a formal way, neither between macroeconomic policies and macroeconomic performance, nor between the latter and changes at the micro level. Strictly speaking, only a general equilibrium model of the economy, suitably disaggregated, would be capable of doing so. And while such model could be one of several useful areas of follow-up research, we did not think it was the most fruitful starting point. In fact, the design itself of such a model requires a good prior understanding of the factual patterns of changes in the economy, both at macro and micro levels, and the findings in this study may contribute to the eventual construction of such a model.

While the main purpose of the book is to present empirical evidence of changes in welfare and poverty in Côte d'Ivoire, we do aim to go beyond the specifics of the case study and to derive some lessons with general relevance and applicability to other countries as well. First, we shall try to assess the general usefulness of our methodology as a tool to analyze poverty. Second, the experience gained during the analysis of the data will permit to draw specific conclusions regarding the optimal type of data collection for the monitoring and policy-oriented analysis of poverty.

However, most importantly, we recognize that Côte d'Ivoire's macroeconomic experience is not unique in Africa. Many African countries experienced solid growth during the 1960s and 1970s, only to see the gains wiped out during the 1980s. What sets Côte d'Ivoire apart is that it was one of the best performers in Sub-Saharan Africa in the first two decades after independence. Consequently, there was a high level of expectations among the population and its leaders that the upward trend would continue – and also a lot of room for decline when the economic boom did end.

Many of the external shocks and policy failures which characterized Côte d'Ivoire's experience were also present in other countries. We argue, therefore, that the types of social and poverty impacts which we shall demonstrate in this book for Côte d'Ivoire are likely to have occurred in many other countries as well – where unfortunately the data do not exist to demonstrate this directly. While of course we have attempted to present the most precise results for Côte d'Ivoire in this volume, what matters most for extracting policy lessons is not the exact magnitude of increases in poverty or declines in basic needs fulfillment. What matters most is the awareness that these impacts can be very severe and can occur very rapidly, and that they are likely to hurt the most disadvantaged among the population. This is the main message this book wants to convey. However, it also wants to say that these impacts are neither inevitable nor irreversible. We hope that this book may serve as a loud alert to countries undergoing structural change and economic recession as to the importance of taking the social and poverty impacts into account from the very beginning, so that some of the severe impacts can be avoided.

At the end of the volume, a poverty alleviation strategy is suggested which can be a guide for the future but which can also serve to buffer the shocks *en route*. The evidence in this book also underlines the vitality and entrepreneurship of poor people, many of whom manage to escape poverty on their own means, even in a general climate of economic adversity. An important lesson is that government action should support such initiatives to increase earnings, rather than replace them by ill-conceived transfer programs.

Outline

The *first chapter* in this volume sets the macroeconomic stage for the changes in level of living and poverty which occurred in Côte d'Ivoire in the 1980s. In a sense, the chapter picks up where *Ivory Coast – The Challenge of Success* (Den Tuinder, 1978) left off. That work detailed the economic success story of Côte d'Ivoire in the first fifteen years of independence, and directed a major challenge to the policy makers of the country: the challenge to continue economic growth by diversifying the export base, to share growth more equally among the population, and to reduce reliance on foreign factors. Chapter 1 begins in 1975, and describes the onset of destabilization, the collapse of the world prices of coffee and cocoa, the severe recession of the eighties, and the government's efforts at adjustment. The chapter focuses on the constraints which caused adjustment at first to succeed only partially, but then to fail altogether to regenerate sustainable growth in the latter part of the decade.

After describing the relevant institutional set up in the country, Chapter 1 identifies four main factors which lay behind macroeconomic destabilization: unsustainable investment, a decline in savings, appreciation of the real exchange rate, and market distortions. Ironically, the initial destabilizing event derived from a favorable shock – the commodity price boom in the late 1970s. This led to an ambitious public expenditure program which proved unsustainable. When export revenues fell, the government maintained the investment program through external borrowing. Rising interest rates made the debt service more burdensome, and the debt overhang dominated the macroeconomic accounts throughout the 1980s. Macroeconomic imbalances were made more severe by falling domestic savings. Although the nominal exchange rate could not change, the real rate fell because of domestic inflation fueled by rapid monetary expansion. The resulting overvalued exchange rate was however only one of several market distortions which were pervasive during the eighties. A system of import tariffs and export taxes distorted the market for tradeable commodities, and this distortion was aggravated by the state's interventions in the marketing of agricultural commodities.

Faced with growing internal and external imbalances, the government turned to the International Monetary Fund and the World Bank for assistance. In 1981, an Extended Arrangement was agreed to with the Fund, followed by five Stand-by Arrangements over the course of the decade. At the same time the World Bank provided support through three Structural Adjustment Loans (SALs) over the period 1981-86. After a two-year interruption of Bank support, a series of Sectoral Adjustment Loans (SECALs) was initiated in 1989. There were four main adjustment policies: contractionary monetary and fiscal policy, agricultural price reforms, liberalization in trade policy, and public enterprise reform. The main feature of the adjustment programs of the 1980s in Côte d'Ivoire was their reliance on internal adjustment. Given the limited room to manoeuver to change relative prices, especially the real exchange rate, absorption reduction was one of the few options available to the government to restore macroeconomic balance. Public investment expenditure was cut from 18 percent of GDP in 1978-83 to just three percent in 1987-91. However, wages and salaries were not cut in line with other expenditure components, and debt service commitments resulted in no closing of the overall fiscal deficit. Contractionary monetary policy was applied more successfully. In the early part of the decade, producer prices of major export crops were raised to bring them closer to world prices. In later years, prices were maintained, and the persistence of real exchange rate overvaluation continued to effectively tax agriculture. In 1989, producer prices of coffee and cocoa were cut in half. The weakness of Ivorian agriculture is a serious outcome of the failure of the adjustment effort. Finally, trade policy was liberalized in a limited way (mainly by replacing quantitative import restrictions with tariffs) in an effort to mimic a real exchange rate depreciation, and some reform of public enterprises was attempted but without much policy focus.

In reviewing macroeconomic indicators at the beginning and the end of the decade, Chapter 1 concludes that imbalances were as much in evidence at the end as at the beginning, with the sole exception of monetary instruments and the rate of inflation. In general, the adjustment efforts of the 1980s failed to correct the imbalances. In so far as there was some success, it was attributable mainly to contractionary macroeconomic policies, which led to import compression and a decline in GDP. Chapter 1 argues that this policy response might have been sufficient to restore balance had the unsustainably high level of public investment been the only source of destabilization. An indicator of this is the measure of success achieved up to 1986. But thereafter, the deterioration in the international terms of trade and the appreciation of the real exchange rate required additional policy measures. In addition, many of the distortions from trade and price interventions and direct government involvement in productive activities were never adequately addressed. The failure to regenerate economic growth has meant a high cost in terms of declines in levels of living and increased poverty among the people of Côte d'Ivoire. To document this cost and to suggest corrective policies is the main objective of the remainder of this volume.

Before presenting the empirical findings in Chapters 3 and following, *Chapter 2* presents the data sources for the analysis and addresses methodological issues. The primary data source is the Côte d'Ivoire Living Standards Survey (CILSS) which was conducted annually from 1985 to 1988. The sample size each year was 1,600 households and the sample design was a rotating panel – that is, 50 percent of the households were revisited the following year, and the other half was replaced with new households. The survey thus yielded a sequence of four cross-sectional data sets (each of which is representative of the country as a whole), as well as three overlapping panels of approximately 800 households each (1985-86, 1986-87, and 1987-88). The survey collected detailed information on employment, income, expenditures, assets, basic needs, and other socioeconomic characteristics of the households. Over the four years, coverage and methodology of the data collection were held constant so that results are comparable over time.

The fact that data were collected for four consecutive years is important to the analysis in this volume. The 1985-88 period represents a particularly critical phase in Côte d'Ivoire's process of structural change. As discussed in Chapter 1, adjustment efforts in Côte d'Ivoire started in 1981 and were sustained for six years. Both as a result of these efforts and favorable harvests and increases in the world prices for coffee and cocoa, the Ivorian economy showed signs of improvement in 1985-86. In contrast, in 1987-88 the economy nosedived and the government abandoned the adjustment program. The initial years of CILSS data (1985-86) are thus able to pick up the effects of the adjustment effort, while the later years (1987-88) reflect the abandonment of the effort and rapid economic decline – in effect, a period of destabilization. This is a particularly important feature of the data, because it help to disentangle adjustment from recession effects.

Chapter 2 describes the investigations we have done to assure us of the quality and reliability of the CILSS data. We paid special attention to the sample design and developed a set of corrective weights to compensate for certain deficiencies in the representativeness of the sample. In general, we concluded that the data are of high quality, consistent with other data sources, and provide a valuable basis for analyzing the evolution of levels of living and poverty in Côte d'Ivoire.

The methodology for doing this is based on the recognition that the level of living of households is a multidimensional concept which includes direct consumption of goods and services as well as the fulfillment of basic needs. Separate chapters (three and four, respectively) are devoted to the analysis of these two ingredients. We considered it very important to take regional price differences into account in assessing level of living and poverty, and to do this we drew upon the extensive price data base collected under the auspices of the International Comparisons Project. This yielded a more accurate price index than what was previously available in Côte d'Ivoire (see Chapter 6).

Chapter 2 further discusses the selection of two poverty lines and a poverty index. The key analytic feature we rely on is that the index be decomposable along policy-relevant dimensions, which makes it possible to relate macroeconomic events to the changing regional and socioeconomic composition of poverty. The selected index also makes it possible to decompose the observed changes in poverty in components due to growth and to changes in distribution. This volume explicitly does not aim to construct an economywide model. This choice was made for two reasons. First, it was our ambition to show that relatively simple analytic tools could be used to derive policy relevant conclusions, directly helpful to policy makers concerned with the alleviation of poverty. We consider it a distinct benefit if such tools can be used quickly in the country which collects the data. Second, economy-wide models have heavy data requirements both of the macroeconomy and at the household level, their construction is time-consuming, and experience with them is mixed. We would argue therefore, that even if countries have the capacity to construct and run such models, they are a second-stage research objective.

In *Chapter 3*, the presentation of empirical results begins. This chapter concentrates on the direct consumption component of household welfare and charts the evolution of household expenditure and expenditure-based poverty. The main finding is that during the 1985-86 adjustment phase, the overall incidence of poverty did not change and the incidence of extreme poverty was reduced. During the 1987-88 destabilization phase, poverty rose sharply, and in 1988, the incidence of poverty was 50 percent higher than in 1985. There were clear regional and socioeconomic patterns to this increase. Urban poverty rose faster than rural poverty, especially among civil servants. The salary freeze in the public sector is likely to have affected the lowest paid civil servants the most. In rural areas, poverty rose rapidly among export crop farmers. This was traced to falling crop yields, suggesting that price protection for producers was not a sufficient condition to ensure poverty protection.

The chapter also presents the results of the dynamic decomposition of the poverty index, which indicates that the entire increase in poverty can be attributed to negative economic growth. Redistribution effects contributed to reducing poverty and especially extreme poverty. Our calculations show that a return to pre-1980 'miracle' growth rates would be needed to successfully reduce poverty through economic growth alone. To the extent that this is not likely to happen, an argument may exist for targeted poverty alleviation policies. Our results indicate which regions and socioeconomic groups should be priority targets.

The analysis of income and expenditure composition suggests that there are no goods which are predominantly produced or consumed by the poor. This implies that commodity-specific price supports or subsidies are not an effective way to help the poor in Côte d'Ivoire. We found that the overall share of tradeable items in the consumption basket is not very different between the poor and nonpoor. However, for the poor the tradeables consist mainly of food, especially import substitutes such as rice, while for the nonpoor two thirds of consumed tradeables were imported nonfood items.

Finally, Chapter 3 argues that similar increases in poverty as those experienced by Côte d'Ivoire in 1985-88 may have occurred in other African countries as well. Indeed, Côte d'Ivoire's record of macroeconomic decline is not unique in Africa, but in other countries the effects are not likely to be documented by virtue of the lack of household surveys. This implies a strong call for regular monitoring of poverty at the household level. Similarly, one of the most striking findings is the speed with which the destabilization in Côte d'Ivoire in 1987-88 'trickled down' to households, and the magnitude of the effect. There is no reason to assume that such effect could not occur in other countries as well. The contrast with the adjustment years provides dramatic evidence of the costs in terms of increased poverty that can stem from even one or two years of unchecked economic decline and destabilization. The important lesson is that it is much more feasible to protect the poor with a managed adjustment program than under conditions of destabilization.

Chapter 4 turns to the basic needs dimension of poverty. Three key basic needs are investigated: education, health, and housing. Housing has been affected directly by the structural adjustment program in Côte d'Ivoire, by the government's withdrawal from providing public housing. The provision of education and health services has been affected indirectly, mainly through the fiscal restraint stemming from the adjustment program. The chapter's main finding is that during structural adjustment as well as destabilization in the 1980s, the poorest population groups in Côte d'Ivoire suffered deep setbacks in their fulfillment of basic needs. This happened even though the government maintained the overall level of social expenditure and even though, on a countrywide basis, more basic needs indicators (literacy, school enrollment, use of health care facilities, access to safe water, housing amenities) changed little over the period 1985-88. In itself, this is an encouraging finding, in that the deterioration in expenditure-based welfare was not matched by a deterioration in the fulfillment of basic needs. This finding underscores the importance of looking separately at the different dimensions of the level of living, since they clearly need not all move in the same direction.

The key point, however, is that the countrywide results masked very wide differences between the poor and the nonpoor. Basic needs indicators declined systematically for the poorest households, almost regardless of the average trend of a given indicator. The declines were especially dramatic in education, and, as the chapter argues, this may have jeopardized significantly the prospects of the poorest people in Côte d'Ivoire to rely on education to escape from poverty in the next generation.

The chapter argues strongly that the focus of policy reform, and of indicators to monitor its social impact, should not be on aggregate levels of public spending – in contrast to what has often been suggested in the literature. Instead, the focus should be on the intrasectoral and functional allocation of expenditure, but even more so on the distribution of service delivery. When monitoring this, the poor should not be considered as a homogeneous group. The Côte d'Ivoire results presented in Chapter 4 clearly show that the condition of the poorest can be quite different from that of the poor as a group, and so can the evolution of that condition. Likewise, the policy recommendations can be very different, since the very poor represent a more urgent target group. Policies like selective subsidies for school meals and books may be needed for the poorest, but may not be appropriate for the poor as a group, if for no other reason than that the total cost would be forbidding.

The results discussed in Chapters 3 and 4 indicate that the consequences for poverty of the economic decline in Côte d'Ivoire in the 1980s were severe and not to be doubted. But the question remains as to how widespread the collapse in welfare was, and whether a lucky few escaped the decline. *Chapter 5* turns to these questions by exploiting the panel feature of the CILSS data. This provides information on the welfare level of the *same* households over *two* periods of time. As we said earlier, the CILSS contains three overlapping two-year panels. Such data are quite rare in Africa, and among developing countries in general, and thus they give a unique opportunity to understand better the dynamics of poverty.

Two key findings emerged from the analysis. First, 'two-period poverty' (i.e. poverty based on a discounted sum of per capita expenditure assessed against a discounted sum of poverty lines over the two years of the panel) confirms the trends in poverty observed from the yearly cross-sectional data. Second, and more interestingly, two-year poverty is generally less than the one-year snapshot poverty figures. This suggests that mobility in the panels is considerable, particularly across poverty classes. Indeed, the results in the chapter show that as many as 30 percent of households changed their poverty status from one year to the next. In the worst two-year period, 1987-88, when poverty incidence increased from 35 percent to 46 percent, there were 6.3 percent of households who *improved* their poverty class, moving from the extreme poor to midpoor or nonpoor categories, or from midpoor to nonpoor. These upward movements were not the same everywhere, but displayed distinct regional and socioeconomic patterns.

The results in Chapter 5 provide a note of optimism in what is otherwise a bleak picture of poverty in Côte d'Ivoire. They show that even in conditions of severe economic distress, there is a dynamism among many poor which allows them to escape poverty on their own means. It is very important that government programs to alleviate poverty look into these spontaneous efforts, especially by facilitating the startup or expansion of informal sector enterprises from which many poor derive the bulk of their income. Government programs should especially avoid to become substitutes for the poor's own efforts, e.g. through ill-targeted transfer programs.

The last analytic chapter, *Chapter 6*, looks in more details at an often overlooked aspect of poverty measurement, namely the consideration of regional price differences. This is not usually an omission of neglect, but a forced omission due to the absence of suitable price data in many developing countries. The customary situation is that price collection for the Consumer Price Index (CPI) covers only the capital city, or, at best, urban areas. Such indexes are particularly inappropriate for the study of structural adjustment policies, which aim to alter price relativities, most of which have a significant effect on rural households.

The price information in Côte d'Ivoire is better than in most African countries in that separate CPI series exist for African and European households in the country, and since 1985, for 'workers and traditional craftsmen' and for 'professional and managerial occupations'. Yet, every one of these CPI series excludes rural households. The designers of the CILSS attempted to compensate for this shortcoming by including a limited amount of collection of price data as part of the survey. Unfortunately, the results, especially prices for nonfood items, proved insufficient for the construction of an adequate regional price index.

Chapter 6 draws attention to the price data which have been collected in many countries as part of the International Comparisons Project (ICP). The ICP data are customarily used to calculate purchasing power parities across different currencies, but Chapter 6 shows that they can also be used for price analysis *within* a country. This is a novel use of such data. A Paasche price index was constructed, based on ICP prices for 260 product categories, which were matched with 27 food categories and 25 nonfood categories from the CILSS. The index shows that relative to Abidjan prices in other cities are seven percent lower and in rural areas from 13 percent to 24 percent lower. Clearly, the inclusion of such price differences is crucial for correct measurement of poverty incidence, and the chapter illustrates the errors that can occur if price differences are not or incorrectly included. Finally, the detailed price data are also used to construct price indexes for each poverty and socioeconomic category in Côte d'Ivoire.

The *final chapter* in this book proposes a poverty strategy for Côte d'Ivoire based on the earlier findings, and highlights the lessons relevant for other countries as well. The starting point is the finding that the main cause of rising poverty during the eighties was the absence of economic growth. Changes in the distribution of welfare in fact contributed to reducing poverty. The remedy must thus in the first place lie in the generation of sustainable economic growth in such a way that all groups in Ivorian society participate. The encouraging lesson of the early part of the eighties is that even when growth is moderate, it is possible to improve the conditions of the poor. The experience of this period also teaches that managed structural change should be the underlying framework for effective poverty alleviation.

The chapter sets out ten major orientations, based on the empirical findings, which should be embodied in an effective poverty strategy. The orientations cover the generation of economic growth, the regional and socioeconomic targets, the support to the agricultural sector, the rising urban poverty, and the basic needs priorities. The ensuing strategy which is proposed rests on three pillars: income generation for the poor, targeted delivery of those basic needs services most lacking to the poor, and the provision of selected safety nets to the most destitute.

Income generation for the poor must focus on the two sectors with the greatest potential to help the poor: rural agriculture and the urban informal sector. In rural areas, the priority is to promote more diversification in the export crops grown and to provide a full support package for farmers through an enhanced extension system, focused on the farming system as a whole rather than on selected crops. Poverty impact will be maximized by focusing on the Savannah and West Frost zones. In urban areas, employment creation in the tradeable goods sectors needs to be promoted. The realities of population growth in Côte d'Ivoire are such that a growing number of labor market entrants will have to be absorbed by the informal sector, and this sector will have to take the lead in employment creation. An important precondition for such strategy is the upgrading of urban infrastructure serving the informal sector.

In basic need provision, the poor have suffered the greatest setbacks in education, and a number of actions are needed to promote primary school enrollment among poor families. These could include increased scholarships allocated on a needs criterion, especially for girls, and needs-targeted subsidies for textbooks, uniforms and school meals at the primary level. The cost recovery burden needs to be shifted from the primary to the higher levels. Long-term efforts to improve the access of the poor to health services require a fundamental reorientation of Côte d'Ivoire's health system away from urban-based curative facilities toward more rural and primary care. Recurrent expenditures need to be reallocated especially toward medications. In housing, the priority is to improve access of the urban poor to piped water, either through house connections or public standpipes.

Lastly, a program of cash transfers may be needed for the most destitute households who lack the means to take advantage of the income generation programs because of age, disability, etc.

The successful implementation of a poverty alleviation strategy in Côte d'Ivoire will require parallel action on several fronts: regulatory reform to remove market distortions, increased and better-targeted cost recovery, continued decentralization of responsibility and means of financing towards local governments, and increased popular participation. A new poverty monitoring system, based on the CILSS experience, but with a simplified survey instrument, would provide the empirical basis for targeting the program, and measuring its impact.

Finally, Chapter 7 discusses a number of lessons from Côte d'Ivoire's experience which are likely to be relevant for other African countries as well. First, as we have seen, the effects of the 1987-88 recession/destabilization trickled down to households very rapidly and very severely. The same can happen in other countries experiencing similar declines in macroeconomic performance. The contrast with the adjustment period indicates that it is much more feasible to protect the poor with a managed adjustment program, and that the cost of not doing so can be very high and demand a long period to reverse the damage. Second, Côte d'Ivoire's experience underlines that effective poverty alleviation is not likely to be possible without the foundation of sustainable economic growth.

A third general lesson pertains to the fulfillment of basic needs. The poor and especially the poorest may suffer serious setbacks, even when average

xxiii

conditions remain the same or even improve. It is thus not sufficient to monitor basic needs trends at the national level, but disaggregation by region, socioeconomic group, and poverty status are essential. As a corollary, a fourth lesson is that basic needs should be monitored directly, by looking at the distribution of beneficiaries, and not by looking at aggregate levels of public spending. Policy reform needs to focus on the intrasectoral and functional allocation of resources. Fifth, this study's results confirm the importance of not considering the poor as a homogeneous group. The condition of the very poor can deteriorate much faster than that of the poor as a group, and special targeting and program design may be needed to reach them effectively.

Lastly, and most generally, the use in this study of a multidimensional poverty profile, in combination with a decomposable poverty index, proved to be an effective tool to link macroeconomic change to welfare of households and individuals. Such tools could readily be used in the planning offices in many developing countries and help in the design of poverty alleviation policies. We hope that the following chapters constitute a useful guide towards that objective.

Notes

1   The ideal data set would describe the economy from some point in time before the start of structural adjustment, through the period of implementation, and afterwards. In the case of Côte d'Ivoire, this would require annual data from the late seventies to the early nineties. The CILSS data thus cover only a relative brief time in this longer period of structural change. Inevitably this limits the policy conclusions that can be drawn. Nevertheless, the CILSS data are situated as well as possible within the period of structural change to capture its effects.

1 The macroeconomic setting

Lionel Demery[1]

The 1980s proved extremely difficult for Côte d'Ivoire. Whereas rising world commodity prices and international finance on favorable terms kept growth expectations high during the 1970s, the harsher realities facing primary-goods-producing countries had now to be dealt with. The record shows that little changed after ten years of adjustment. The government faced macroeconomic imbalances of roughly the same order at the end of the decade as at the beginning. And policy-induced distortions in trade and exchange persisted. Côte d'Ivoire thus illustrates some repercussions of not adjusting and offers insights into what the counterfactual to structural adjustment might entail. Several adjustment operations in Côte d'Ivoire – involving Structural Adjustment Facilities from the IMF and Structural Adjustment Loans (SALs) and Sector Adjustment Loans (SECALs) from the World Bank – achieved some measure of policy reform. But what they achieved was too little, too late. The fundamental problems remained unaddressed.

Early attempts at adjustment were made during 1981-86, and partial adjustment was achieved, due in part to more favorable external circumstances. But the adjustment impetus failed, and later efforts at adjustment during 1987-91 (through the last SAL in 1987-88 and the SECALs during 1989-91) did not achieve the macroeconomic policy reforms needed. There are thus three periods in Côte d'Ivoire's adjustment experience: 1975-80 is the destabilizing period, when macroeconomic imbalances grew to crisis proportions; 1981-86 can be termed a period of partial adjustment; 1987-91 is a period of inadequate or fettered adjustment. The key difference between the partial and fettered adjustment phases is the movement in the real exchange rate. After having depreciated, it appreciated, thus fettering any attempt at structural adjustment.

The analysis in this chapter emphasizes the constraints that fettered the adjustment effort and in large measure explained why so little was achieved during the decade. The country experienced negative economic growth for six years of the 1980s, and its per capita income fell enough to make the country eligible once more for IDA financing. In explaining the transformation from buoyant growth to a dismal and uncertain outlook, this chapter highlights the main constraints that prevented adjustment:

- The severity and recurrence of economic shocks, evident in the continued decline in the terms of trade, due in part to an undue concentration on coffee and cocoa in the country's foreign exchange earnings.

- The persistence of rigidities and distortions, which constrained the adjustment effort significantly. These include the pegging of the CFA franc to the French franc (which undermined the country's competitiveness), a tendency toward nominal rigidity in domestic wages, a similar tendency toward domestic price rigidity (due to the oligopolistic structure of the country's product markets), and the pervasive influence of the state in the domestic economy.

- The reluctance of the government to take the need for adjustment seriously, and to identify itself with the adjustment programs supported by the World Bank. This lack of ownership was a significant problem in gaining enough political commitment to the reform process. But the government was also reluctant to revise its expectations fast enough in the face of rapidly changing external circumstances.

The institutional setting

Institutional characteristics, in part responsible for the macroeconomic destabilization, seriously constrained the ability of the country to undertake effective adjustment with minimal social cost. This section briefly describes the main economic institutions, identifying how they circumscribed policy choice.

The fiscal system

Fiscal policy in Côte d'Ivoire operates through a fairly complex set of government financial arrangements. The financial operations of the government are carried out by six principal agencies of the central government, several centrally operated special purpose funds, and 137 local authorities. Because few data are available about local activities, this chapter is based on the fiscal accounts of the central government and its other central funds. The six main agencies responsible for financial operations of the central government are:

- The Direction Générale du Budget is in charge of the budget, with the Direction des Budgets et Comptes responsible for the Budget Général de Fonctionnement, which concerns mainly the current budget (revenue and expenditure other than debt service). It also deals with the part of the government investment program financed by earmarked tax revenue and domestic borrowing. The Direction des Investissements Publics is responsible for the Budget Spécial des Investissements de l'Etat (BSIE). The aim of the government in 1993 was to unify the budget process into a Budget Unique within two years.

- The Caisse Autonome d'Amortissement or Autonomous Amortization Fund (CAA) has two departments, dealing with public debt and banking. The first deals with all financial arrangements concerned with the government's investment program that is wholly or partly financed by foreign borrowing.

- The Agricultural Price Stabilization Fund (CSSPPA) was set up to stabilize producer prices of important export crops – cocoa, coffee, and cotton (and also rice, which is relatively unimportant). Whether the CSSPPA generates revenue for the central government depends on the relationship between the government-determined producer price and the world price for the commodity. As a stabilization fund, the CSSPPA should not generate revenues over a prolonged period, since gains during periods of high world prices would be expected to be counteracted by losses from below-average world prices. The CSSPPA generated large surpluses for the central government until 1986, which were either invested or transferred to other government departments.

- The Price Equalization Fund for Staple Products (CGPPGC) was established to stabilize consumer prices of imported rice and sugar. Its scale of operations is much smaller than that of the CSSPPA, so the macroeconomic implications are less significant.

- Social security has two funds: the National Social Security Fund and the Pension Fund for Government Employees.

In addition the central government includes agencies dedicated to specific funds, including the National Sewerage Fund, the National Hydraulics Fund, the National Investment Fund, the National Office for Vocational Training, the Oil Palm Fund, and various petroleum funds. The allocation of revenues to these various agencies is generally inflexible, with systematic earmarking of tax revenues preventing cross-agency transfers.

The main source of financial flexibility lies in the CSSPPA, which in times past was used to finance some major items of central government expenditure. But this source of more flexible financing is also the most variable, the least transparent, and the least planned. Its share in government revenue ranged from highs of 40.7 percent in 1977 and 28.8 percent in 1985 (high world prices) and lows of 4.7 percent in 1981 and 1.2 percent in 1987 (low world prices). World prices have of late remained low, keeping the contribution of the stabilization funds to government revenue modest. This fundamental change in the flow of funds between the government and the agricultural economy is a key to understanding macroeconomic destabilization during the decade. An important characteristic of the CSSPPA is that its activities are not part of the routine budget process of central government (involving, for example, parliamentary approval). The net budgetary implications of CSSPPA activities affect other central government budgeting only in an *ex post* sense. Reforms of the CSSPPA were undertaken in 1991.

The tax base of central government (traditionally about 20 percent of GDP) relies heavily on indirect taxes, with about a third of the revenue from domestic indirect taxes, another third from taxes on imports, and just under 10 percent from taxes on exports. The remaining 25 percent of tax revenues are from direct taxes. In general, the Ministry of Economy and Finance collects taxes through its tax and customs department and allocates them to ministries and agencies. Attempts were made during the 1980s (especially in 1987-88) to increase tax revenue, especially indirect (trade) taxes. The details and limits of these policies are spelled out below.

The monetary setting

Côte d'Ivoire belongs to the West African Monetary Union (WAMU), established in 1962. Other members are Benin, Burkina Faso, Mali, Niger, Senegal, and Togo.[2] The Banque Centrale des Etats de l'Afrique de l'Ouest (BCEAO) has responsibility for conducting WAMU's monetary affairs. The Council of the Heads of State (of WAMU) decides on issues of membership and resolves issues of conflict among member states. The Council of Ministers of Finance has ultimate authority for the policy of the BCEAO. These two councils take only unanimous decisions. The Board of Administrators, consisting of two representatives from each member country and France, is responsible for its daily operations. Each member country has a National Credit Committee, consisting of the Minister of Finance, other country representatives of the Board of Administrators, and four other officials appointed by the government. The Committees submit targets for money supply growth and credit to BCEAO and until 1989 were responsible for the sectoral allocation of credit.[3]

4

WAMU has a common currency – the CFA franc (franc de la Communauté Financière d'Afrique), pegged to the French franc. Until January 1994, the parity (of CFAF 50 = FF 1) had not changed for more than 40 years (since 1948). The free convertibility between the CFAF and the French franc at this fixed parity was maintained through an Operations Account (Compte d'Opérations) of the WAMU with the French Treasury, and an obligation by France to support WAMU in maintaining unlimited and full convertibility of the CFA franc. France provides an overdraft facility through the Operations Account, and WAMU in return agrees to rules governing its credit policy and the management of the external accounts of members. When gross reserves are positive, the BCEAO deposits the equivalent of at least 65 percent of its foreign exchange reserves with the Operations Account. Interest payments on positive balances are equal to the rediscount rate of the Bank of France. Convertibility can also be supported through use of overdraft facilities on the Operations Account, the case for WAMU for much of the 1980s. The interest applied to the overdraft rises progressively to the Bank of France rediscount rate.

Although the Operations Account is a pooling of the individual countries' external balances (or overdrafts) with the French Treasury, the BCEAO maintains separate accounts for each country and credits or charges each according to its contribution to the pooled account.[4] The guarantee of convertibility is subject to rules that apply to the BCEAO and its management of the Operations Account. Whenever the pooled external reserves of the BCEAO fall below 20 percent of its sight liabilities over three consecutive months, the Board of Administrators must meet to take appropriate monetary action. These decisions are reached through simple majority.

Within the constraints of the fixed parity of the CFA franc, the BCEAO decides on credit policy. The most important instrument of the BCEAO is setting annual credit ceilings in each member country. Until 1989, there were two discount rates: the regular rate (taux d'escompte normal, or TEN) and a preferential rate (taux d'escompte préférentiel, or TEP). The second rate applied to crop credit, housing loans, and loans to small and medium-size enterprises. The margin between the two rates was usually 2.5 percentage points. In a package of reforms in October 1989, the TEP was abolished. The money market rates in the Union are set by the BCEAO to keep domestic interest rates in line with those prevailing internationally, especially in France. Most interest rates, including the central bank discount rate, are set by the BCEAO for all member countries. As part of the 1989 reforms, interest rates were to be used as a more flexible instrument of policy.

Credit to the government in any given year is limited by statute to 20 percent of the country's total annual tax receipts collected two years previously. This limit on the borrowing the government can undertake in any year is an important feature of the fiscal and monetary scene in Côte d'Ivoire. It seriously restricts the opportunity for seignorage financing, and with favorable effects on the rate of inflation.

But there are three other major financing avenues for the government. First, it can use the public enterprise sector, which is not included in the BCEAO restrictions (public enterprise finances are treated as part of the private sector category in the BCEAO accounts). By reducing its direct financing to public enterprises, and forcing them to borrow within the banking system, the government can increase total public borrowing and circumvent to some extent the 20 percent limit. Second, the government can simply accumulate arrears to the private sector. This source of 'finance' can have serious effects on policy implementation (as with export subsidies, discussed in further detail below) and on the private sector in general. Third, the government (and public enterprises) can borrow externally without violating the guidelines of WAMU. The leverage that the BCEAO can exert on public sector financing in Côte d'Ivoire is thus greater when its access to external borrowing is limited. This explains why monetary control slipped somewhat during the late 1970s when external finance was available – and was restored in the 1980s when access to external finance was more difficult (see Lane 1989, for more detail on the effectiveness of monetary policy in Côte d'Ivoire).

At the beginning of the 1980s decade there were twenty deposit money banks – fourteen were commercial banks, of which five were branches of foreign banks. There were six specialized credit institutions, including the 'development banks' established to finance such specific sectors as agricultural and rural development, industry, housing, and public works. These development banks found it difficult to compete with the deposit banks, with which they were on an equal footing. The banking system faced problems throughout the 1980s.

The labor market

Given the pegging of the CFA franc to the French franc, and the limited scope for manipulating the nominal exchange rate, a greater onus was placed on adjustments in domestic prices to effect real exchange rate adjustments and to maintain external competitiveness. As in a two-sector dependent economy model, the real exchange rate is increased through relative declines in the prices of nontradeables rather than increases in the prices of tradeables (through nominal devaluations). To maintain competitiveness, domestic monetary policy has to be tight, keeping inflation in line with that of competitors. But if the nominal exchange rate is significantly overvalued and if the country's payments situation reaches a crisis so that discrete adjustments

6

are needed to restore competitiveness quickly, downward movements in domestic prices may be needed. This implies full wage flexibility for adjustment policies to be effective without creating unemployment and internal disequilibrium especially if inflation rates are low among the competitors. The labor market is therefore critical in determining the outcomes of adjustment policies in countries that face limited exchange rate policy options and a lack of international competitiveness, like Côte d'Ivoire in the 1980s.

The labor market in Côte d'Ivoire is predominantly rural, and wage labor is very uncommon in rural areas. The Côte d'Ivoire Living Standards Surveys, which cover the second half of the 1980s, report on average only about five percent of rural household income from wage employment (Demery, 1993). The rural labor market is generally unaffected directly by institutional and other rigidities.

The urban labor market, by contrast, is influenced by three types of distortion. First, it is subjected to labor legislation, much inherited from the colonial past. Minimum wage levels are specified for all categories of workers in medium-size and large firms. Legislation also places constraints on employers to provide fringe benefits and restricts their freedom to layoff workers. The government sets the minimum wage for both urban and rural labor markets. Minimum wages are not index linked, and so the government has some freedom to allow real values to fall. The urban real minimum wage fell through much of the 1980s.

Second, the wage system is also influenced by *Conventions Collectives*, periodic negotiations between firms, unions, and the government to agree on wage scales by skill and seniority. Average wages for unskilled workers have risen above the minimum urban wage as workers gain seniority. The evidence on urban wage trends is difficult to interpret because of this 'seniority' effect. Levy and Newman (1989) argue that the slight increase in real wages during 1980-87, despite a sharp fall in minimum wages (by 25 percent), is to some extent a statistical illusion. During the recession, many firms were liquidated. Those remaining in business were obliged to cut their workforces, generally affecting the lower half of the pay scale. This induced increase in seniority (caused by the recession) increased mean wages, despite the fall in real minimum wages.

The implications of these trends for the adjustment programs are difficult to determine. If the growth in seniority was reflected in higher productivity, the wage cost per unit of output would have fallen, improving the country's competitiveness. But if productivity gains from seniority are limited or absent, wage costs per unit of output may well have risen. It is also important to distinguish between the real *consumption* wage and the real *product* wage in assessing how much the real wage rigidity impaired the adjustment program.

The former deflates the nominal wage by a consumption-based cost of living index, while the latter takes the sectoral output price as the deflator. According to Berthélemy and Bourguignon (1992, p. 135), "while wage-earners experienced a drop in their real purchasing power, the 'real product wage' paid by employers *increased substantially*" (my emphasis). If so, real wage rigidity is likely to have impaired the adjustment process, at least for the formal sector.

Third, there is the influence of high public sector wages, more closely related to French civil service levels than to domestic conditions. Expatriate salaries and wages are also common in the private sector, especially at the executive level. Berthélemy and Bourguignon (1992, p. 74) conclude that 'there is probably considerable room for reductions in wages and salaries throughout the modern labor market that would make wages and salaries more competitive'. A similar conclusion was drawn by an internal World Bank assessment: 'Overall the evidence is clear that unit wages per unit of output as well as wages per employee are comparatively high in Côte d'Ivoire.' The study compared Ivorian wage levels with those of its main competitors. In textiles, wages in Côte d'Ivoire were estimated to be FF 46,300 per person in 1988, compared with FF 13,800 per person in Mauritius. Similar comparisons showing high wage costs in Côte d'Ivoire were made with Thailand (tuna production) and with India and South Korea (spinning activities). These distortions might also have influenced the urban informal sector, and even rural wages. Little is understood of these wage interrelationships, a subject in need of further research.

The product market

Three characteristics of the product market are central to understanding the events of the 1980s. First is the dominance of agriculture, and especially that of two key export crops, cocoa and coffee, and of forestry and timber products. With many planters in coffee and cocoa production and many logging companies in forestry, the product markets could be highly competitive. But given the government's role in the marketing these products outcomes seldom reflected this competitiveness.

Second is the public sector's dominance of product markets through marketing and through publicly owned enterprises. The government has historically maintained the right to control both prices and margins at all stages of distribution. This control has been generally evaded in the industrial sector, but was effective in agriculture, especially export agriculture. Although export crops were marketed by private companies, their activities were subject to close control by the Agricultural Price Stabilization Fund (CSSPPA). The companies were obliged to pay producers the CSSPPA-determined price –

and having sold the produce in world markets (following approval by the CSSPPA) were required to remit to the CSSPPA the difference between the export price and the producer price plus the exporters' margin. Because of the need to monitor carefully the activities of the marketing companies, those that trade in coffee and cocoa were required to renew their permits annually.

One influence of the state over economic activity in Côte d'Ivoire is through a network of public enterprises, wholly or partly owned by the state. During the 1970s, the number of public enterprises grew rapidly, directly involving the state in nearly every area of economic activity. In 1977, there were 113 state-owned and partly state-owned enterprises, with a third of the country's employment and a quarter of its value added. The activities of these enterprises covered a wide range of sectors – from basic infrastructure to major industrial undertakings.

Compared with private enterprises, the public enterprises were generally inefficient. During 1982-88, the government invested more than US $500 million (net cumulative investment) in the sector, but the return on this investment has been estimated to average only two percent a year. During the 1970s, these enterprises enjoyed operating surpluses. But for much of the 1980s they moved into deficit, partly a result of the economic downturn that dominated the decade, and partly a result of the failure by the government to pay out subsidies. Perhaps the most important factor has been economic mismanagement. In April 1983, President Houphouët-Boigny acknowledged publicly that mismanagement was mainly responsible for public enterprise losses of about 1.2 percent of GDP that year (Berthélemy and Bourguignon, 1992).

The third key characteristic of the Ivorian product market was the highly oligopolistic modern sector. More than half the manufacturing industrial sectors were dominated by one or two firms (Berthélemy and Bourguignon, 1992). Given the influence of the state, and the high protection accorded to manufacturing, the sector was highly oligopolistic. This led to price rigidity, which constrained how much the internal adjustment could correct external imbalances (given a fixed nominal exchange rate). It also undermined competition and allocative efficiency.

The nature and causes of macroeconomic destabilization

The destabilizing events of the late 1970s were a result of both external shocks and poor or delayed policy responses. This section traces these destabilizing events.

9

Terms of trade instability

The macroeconomic instability in the 1980s can be traced to the success of the previous decade. With an average GDP growth rate of eight percent a year between 1965 and 1975, Côte d'Ivoire was considered a notable success story among African economies, as reflected in the title of Den Tuinder's (1978) volume, *The Challenge of Success*. But from the mid 1970s onward, events took a different course. Ironically, a favorable external shock interrupted the growth path. A boom in coffee and cocoa prices in 1976 (brought about by a frost-induced failure of the Brazilian coffee harvest) turned the country's terms of trade dramatically in its favor – from 77.9 in 1975 to 100.5 in 1976 and 140.2 in 1977. The Agricultural Price Stabilization Fund (CSSPPA) kept producer prices stable during this period and so accumulated large surpluses (16 percent of GDP in 1977) available as government revenue. The government used these resources to embark on an ambitious investment program that would have significant implications for macroeconomic balances in the following decade. But given the strong growth already achieved and the expectation that commodity prices were on an upward trend, these events were viewed as the dawn of an era of self-sustained growth. Although not quite matching the earlier period, GDP grew by 5.3 percent a year on average from 1975 through 1980, with strong growth of 4.2 percent a year in agriculture and 13.4 percent in industry (Annex 1).

But the price boom was short-lived. Between 1977 and 1980, export prices fell by 30 percent, and the country's terms of trade declined from their peak of 140.2 (in 1977) to only 98.1 (Annex 1). The decline continued to 1983, but recovered somewhat in 1984 and 1985. Thereafter, the terms of trade continued their inexorable decline (from 101.8 in 1986 to only 61.2 in 1990 and 62.6 in 1992). For the 1980s as a whole, the terms of trade declined by 38 percent. This single shock dominated all macroeconomic accounting in Côte d'Ivoire during the 1980s. For 1980-85, the terms of trade improved by 14 percent of GDP. But between 1985 and 1990, the deterioration in the terms of trade amounted to 25 percent of GDP.[5]

The main reasons Côte d'Ivoire is particularly susceptible to terms of trade losses are its heavy dependence on two main export crops, cocoa and coffee, and the large share of its exports of these crops in world trade. Although this dependency increased rapidly over the past two decades, there is some evidence of recent diversification, especially from coffee. At the end of the 1970s, Ivorian exports of cocoa represented 16 percent of total world trade by volume, and coffee eight percent. By the end of the 1980s, the share of coffee exports has halved, but that of cocoa doubled (by volume to 33 percent).

The investment program which underpinned much of the macroeconomic imbalances of the early 1980s originated in a report of the Ministry of Planning, *Côte d'Ivoire 2000*, prepared in 1974 and finalized at the beginning of 1977, when the commodity price boom was under way. To understand why such serious macroeconomic problems were encountered in the 1980s, it helps to review this investment program and to establish its main weaknesses.

Ambitious, even by the favorable standards of the time, the *Côte d'Ivoire 2000* investment program was a significant attempt at reaching a consensus about the country's economic strategy. The original public sector investment projection that undergirded the plan amounted to CFAF 1,350 billion in 1975 prices, considered by the World Bank to be unsustainable. The final figure in the plan was CFAF 1,020 billion, lower than originally planned, but noticeably higher that the CFAF 800 billion the Bank considered to be sustainable. The plan assumed annual GDP growth of 8.7 percent, exceeding the 8.3 percent growth between 1965 and 1973. This high growth assumption was justified partly as being the outcome of the ambitious investment program. The main weaknesses in the implementation of the program were overspending, investment in tradeables, long gestation lags, and inefficient investments.

Tendency towards overspending   The investment targets were exceeded, indicating significant overspending, particularly in transport, energy, and housing but also in education, agriculture, trade, and tourism. Investment in manufacturing was far below that planned (Berthélemy and Bourguignon, 1992). The lack of budgetary discipline can be traced mainly to the fact that much expenditure (especially by public enterprises) is not subject to normal budgetary approval and procedure. The discretionary use of the revenues generated by the CSSPPA was another major factor in this poor management of public funds.

Underinvestment in tradeable   Much of the investment was in nontradeables, too little in activities that would diversify tradeables. Linked to this was a weak private response to *Côte d'Ivoire 2000*. Exports were way below target, particularly manufacturing exports, expected to grow at rate of 15.9 percent, compared with actual growth of only 7.4 percent.

Long gestation lags and inefficient investments   Poor selection of projects yielded low income streams, in part due to an emphasis on infrastructure investment, especially in the northern Savannah region. In some cases, the gestation periods were longer than expected because of incomplete implementation – as for example, bridge construction completed in the

Savannah region, but with delays in the construction of the connecting roads. But in other cases, the activities simply were not efficient. The SODESUCRE program absorbed 37 percent of the Plan's allocation to agricultural investment, but yielded little in return. Production costs in SODESUCRE factories were high and the capital-output ratio for these investments was 5.8 to 1. Some investment projects were selected for the prestige value, such as the construction of a new capital city at Yamoussoukro. The emphasis on infrastructure and the selection of low-yielding (especially prestige) projects combined to result in an incremental capital-output ratio for the investment program as a whole of about 4.1 (Berthélemy and Bourguignon, 1992). The planned ICOR was close to three (more in keeping with recent experience).

Decline in savings

A major destabilizer toward the end of the 1970s was a dramatic fall in savings. National savings declined from 25 percent of GDP in 1977 to only 10 percent in 1980 and 6.8 percent in 1981 (Table 1.1). Both private and public savings were significantly lower than planned under *Côte d'Ivoire 2000*. The fall in private savings was probably due to an increase in remittances by foreign workers (though it is not clear why remittances increased markedly in the second half of the 1970s). Berthélemy and Bourguignon (1992) also suggest that the increase in food prices at this time (from the shock-induced boom) affected aggregate savings because most saving in Côte d'Ivoire is by food-deficit (urban) households. But there are other explanations. During the destabilizing period, the temporary favorable commodity price shock may have induced agents to increase consumption, (Bevan and others, 1990).[6] The terms of trade decline and the recession and falling profits following the boom – combined with the emerging effect of debt service in the public sector – would then explain much of the downturn in national savings during the adjustment period.

Low domestic savings, combined with poor export performance, meant that a larger proportion of the investment program had to be financed through foreign borrowing, particularly by the public sector. External borrowing scheduled under the program amounted to CFAF 327 billion, but public sector external borrowing amounted to CFAF 438 billion – an overshoot of 34 percent. This accumulation of debt was to dominate future macroeconomic policy.

Increasing debt service

The increased external borrowing and a general increase in world interest rates meant that the Ivorian economy faced a significant increase in debt service, creating a financial crisis in 1980. *Côte d'Ivoire 2000* expected a debt service to export ratio of 7.5 percent, but that ratio increased from just under seven percent of exports in 1975-77 to just under 18 percent in 1978-80 and to 53 percent in 1987-89 (Table 1.1)

Real exchange rate appreciation

Both the favorable export price shock and the increased foreign borrowing to finance the investment program could be expected to lead to an appreciation of the real exchange rate, as reviewed in the Dutch-Disease literature (Devarajan and de Melo, 1987). The mechanism involved in such models usually entails a fixed nominal exchange rate and a real exchange rate appreciation driven by an acceleration in domestic inflation relative to world inflation. In Côte d'Ivoire, the movement of the real exchange rate is a result of changes in both the nominal rate (from fluctuations in the fortunes of the French franc) and the relative inflation index.

The real effective exchange rate (REER) appreciated over the crisis period 1975-1980 (Table 1.2). Since the nominal effective exchange rate was stable, (reflecting the stability of the French franc), the main cause of this appreciation was the movement in the Ivorian price level relative to inflation among its competitors. The relative price index based on the CPI rose from 103.7 in 1975 to 128.1 in 1980. So an acceleration in the rate of Ivorian inflation was the main factor behind the loss of international competitiveness recorded during the second half of the 1970s. And there can be little doubt that the acceleration in the inflation rate was a result of the commodity price boom and the concurrent investment boom. This boom was financed partly through borrowing internally – the money supply grew by 19 percent a year between 1975 and 1980, which inevitably increased domestic inflation.[7]

The REER depreciated somewhat after 1980 – in part because of an improvement in the relative inflation rate (which fell to 100 in 1985) but also because of a depreciation of the French franc (depreciating the NEER from 108.2 in 1980 to 85.8 in 1983). The first factor can be attributed to the early efforts at adjustment. The second was simply fortuitous. But after 1983 the movement of the REER was dominated by an *appreciation* of the French franc, causing the NEER to appreciate significantly (from 85.8 in 1983 to 166.3 in 1991). Also affecting the moves in the NEER were devaluations by trading partners – such as Ghana and Nigeria. Although its membership of the CFA franc zone kept inflation low, so that the relative inflation index fell from 100 in 1985 to 86.1 in 1991, the REER appreciated noticeably – from 97.4 in 1983 to 143.2 in 1991 (based on the domestic CPI). It is clear that the major misalignment in the real exchange rate occurred between 1983 and 1987.

Table 1.1
External debt, 1975-91 (million US$, current)

	1975-77	1978-80	1981-83	1984-86	1987-89	1990-91
A. Total external debt[a]	1,632.3	4,807.4	7,444.2	9,646.0	14,410.7	18,463.3
Use of IMF credit	18.8	41.3	545.5	653.6	494.1	401.4
Short term debt	159.3	881.7	1,052.5	725.3	2,011.1	3,198.2
Total long term debt	1,454.2	3,884.4	5,846.2	8,267.1	11,905.5	14,863.6
Public/publicly guaranteed long term debt	1,356.2	3,598.7	4,803.9	5,762.8	8,227.2	10,306.1
Official creditors	490.9	1,071.3	1,439.3	2,669.9	4,989.3	7,264.1
Multilateral	184.9	429.3	752.8	1,243.9	2,186.7	2,813.5
of which IDA	3.7	7.5	7.5	7.3	7.1	22.4
of which IBRD	92.7	236.4	533.3	995.6	1,740.2	1,949.6
Bilateral	306.0	642.1	686.5	1,426.0	2,802.6	4,450.6
Private creditors	865.3	2,527.5	3,364.6	3,092.9	3,238.0	3,042.0
Bonds	20.9	17.5	6.8	3.8	1.5	0.0
Commercial banks	450.3	1,358.5	2,106.7	2,194.1	2,606.6	2,694.2
Other private	394.0	1,151.4	1,251.1	894.9	629.9	347.8
Private non-guaranteed long term	98.0	285.7	1,042.3	2,504.3	3,678.3	4,557.5
B. Debt service payments as % of exports GNFS (cash basis)[b]						
Before rescheduling	6.7	17.7	33.4	38.8	53.3	27.4
After rescheduling	6.7	17.7	32.7	23.8	20.2	8.9

a World Bank data.
b IMF data, Report No. SM/85/146 and SM/91/84.

Table 1.2
Nominal and real effective exchange rates, 1975-91[a]

Year	NEER	Multilateral CPI/FWPI[b]	Multilateral REER (CPI)[a]	Bilateral REER[c]	Terms of trade	Resource balance[d] (% GDP)
1975	105.1	103.7	108.9	83.1	77.9	0.1
1976	101.1	104.2	105.3	86.6	100.5	5.5
1977	98.3	119.3	117.3	104.6	140.2	6.3
1978	101.5	124.3	126.1	113.1	126.4	-0.9
1979	108.4	126.5	137.1	116.5	112.7	-3.1
1980	108.2	128.1	138.5	122.7	98.1	-6.1
1981	97.2	123.6	120.2	120.3	85.4	-7.1
1982	89.9	121.3	109.0	116.4	83.4	-2.9
1983	85.8	113.5	97.4	111.0	84.9	-1.7
1984	95.2	104.6	99.5	102.2	97.0	11.5
1985	100.0	100.0	100.0	100.0	100.0	13.2
1986	120.5	105.0	126.6	110.4	101.8	7.5
1987	139.1	101.0	140.5	110.7	83.8	4.4
1988	141.9	99.3	140.9	112.5	76.4	2.8
1989	146.4	92.0	134.7	107.8	65.4	3.0
1990	163.3	87.6	143.0	108.3	61.2	4.4
1991	166.3	86.1	143.2	111.4	62.6	4.8

a   Multilateral nominal effective exchange rate (NEER) is a trade-weighted index of nominal exchange rates of Côte d'Ivoire's main trading partners. The multilateral real effective exchange rate (REER) is NEER adjusted for price changes in the home country relative to the trading partner. The home price index used in this adjustment is the Consumer Price Index (CPI), and the trading partner price index is the wholesale price index (WPI)l. The nominal effective exchange rate (NEER) reported in the first column is computed as a trade weighted index of the nominal exchange rates of Côte d'Ivoire's trading partners, where the nominal rate is the foreign currency price of the CFA franc. Two main adjustments in the weights are made to standard IMF calculations of the nominal and real effective exchange rates. First, higher weights are accorded to Nigeria, Ghana, and Zaire, to reflect the considerable unrecorded trade with these countries which is not reflected in the trade weights used by the IMF. Second, trade weights of zero are applied to Brazil and Argentina (because of the distorting effects of their high inflation rates) and also Hong Kong and Taiwan (because of a lack of data. An increase in NEER signifies a nominal appreciation. The multilateral *real effective exchange rate* is simply NEER adjusted for changing price levels in Côte d'Ivoire compared with its trading partners. The table reports two alternative methods for deflating NEER to obtain the estimates of REER. Both use the wholesale price index of Côte d'Ivoire's trading partners on the grounds that this reflects more closely the prices of tradeable. In one case, the Ivorian consumer price index (CPI) is used in computing the deflator. Since this index reflects nontradeable as well as tradable prices, it is preferable to use the CPI of Côte d'Ivoire and the WPI of its competitors in deflating the NEER to obtain the REER (see Edwards, 1989). This is because it measures more accurately the concept of the real exchange rate defined as P_t/P_n, where the t and n subscripts refer to tradable and non-tradeables prices. Taking the world price of tradeable as given (P_t^*), the real exchange rate under this definition becomes eP_t^*/P_n, e being the nominal exchange rate. This is then approximated by $e(WPI^w/CPI^d)$ (the w and d subscripts referring to trading partner and domestic indices respectively). In Table 1.2 REER is simply NEER multiplied by CPI/FWPI divided by 100. Again, an increase in the REER signifies an real exchange rate appreciation.

b The home country CPI divided by the trade-weighted WPI of trading partners.

c The bilateral real exchange rate index is CFAF/French franc rate multiplied by the relative CPIs of the two countries.

d Resource balance is measured in current prices.

Source: World Bank data.

After that domestic adjustment (in terms of monetary restraint and low price inflation) prevented further deterioration in competitiveness.

The attempt to restore competitiveness through domestic or internal adjustment, which seems to have been reasonably successful in the early 1980s when world inflation was high, failed to restore competitiveness later in the decade when world inflation has been low. Although the relative price index moved in the required direction (from 113.5 in 1983 to 86.1 in 1991, taking the CPI-based indicator), the adjustment was insufficient to compensate for the marked nominal appreciation of the CFA franc, the result of a strong French franc. This appreciation in the REER, combined with the sharp decline in the terms of trade, was the main destabilizing force in the second half of the 1980s, preventing the government from restoring competitiveness to an economy destabilized in the earlier years of the decade. This appreciation of the CFA franc during the latter half of the 1980s was a perverse response to economic shocks, for the declining terms of trade called for in REER depreciation.

Market distortions

The overvaluation of the exchange rate was one of several market distortions pervasive during the crisis period – and after. Two broad sources of market intervention distorted price signals and resource allocation. A system of import tariffs and export taxes on international trade created distortions within the tradeables category of commodities, increasing the domestic prices of protected goods and penalizing others. And the state's marketing of (especially agricultural) commodities was pervasive, with a plethora of state-run marketing boards and public enterprises engaged directly in economic activity.

At the beginning of the 1980s, Côte d'Ivoire relied on tariff and nontariff

16

barriers to provide protection to domestic producers. Berthélemy and Bourguignon (1992) report that the effective average tariff rate was about 25 percent (28 percent for manufactured products). Quantitative restrictions influenced the domestic price more than the tariff structure. A list of 310 foreign products (drawn up in 1975) either could not be imported at all or were subject to import licensing. By 1982, 426 manufactured items were on the list, accounting for 38 percent of imports (Berthélemy and Bourguignon, 1992). In addition to the granting of licenses, a system of prior authorization was introduced in 1984, which proved to be a serious impediment to trade.

The combination of tariffs, quantitative restrictions, exchange rate overvaluation, and direct price setting policies seriously distorted the domestic price and incentive structure in product markets. Estimates of the effects of these three policy-induced distortions on agricultural incentives during the crisis period (Schiff and Valdés, 1992)[8] show that price distortions in Côte d'Ivoire during 1960-82 were due as much to the indirect effects of exchange rate overvaluation as to the direct effects of tariffs and quantitative restrictions. Overall, agricultural producers were taxed at about 49 percent in nominal terms – 23.3 percent from exchange rate distortions and 25.7 percent from direct trade and other tax and price setting distortions (Table 1.3). But these nominal protection rates, differed across agricultural sectors. Importable commodities (particularly rice) received significant protection from external competition, with direct protection being of the order of 26 percent over 1960-82 (higher than the 14 percent average reported by Schiff and Valdés for all 16 developing countries covered). Although importables producers (as with all tradeables producers) were penalized by the overvalued exchange rate, their total protection rate was positive (just under three percent).

But trade policy interventions taxed the exportables sector – directly by 28.7 percent during 1960-82, and for a total tax (taking into account the effects of the exchange rate distortion) of 52 percent (Table 1.3). The tendency of trade policy to tax exportables and protect importables caused serious price and resource allocative distortions in Côte d'Ivoire. There were even higher distortionary effects of trade policy during the crisis period, 1976-82 – positive net protection of importables at just under seven percent, compared with highly negative protection for exportables (78 percent overall).

The adjustment programs of the 1980s

At the beginning of the 1980s, the government confronted serious economic problems. First it faced a financial crisis and was concerned that the commitments entered into during the destabilizing period could not be met. For this, urgent financial assistance was called for. Second, policy reforms

Table 1.3
Direct, indirect, and total rates of nominal protection
of Ivorian agriculture, 1960-82

	Indirect protection	Direct protection	Total protection
Côte d'Ivoire, 1960-82			
All agricultural products	-23.3	-25.7	-49.0
Importables	-	26.2	2.9
Exportables	-	-28.7	-52.0
Côte d'Ivoire, 1960-72			
All agricultural products	-17.5	-32.2	-49.7
Importables	-	27.3	9.8
Exportables	-	-35.7	-53.2
Côte d'Ivoire, 1976-82			
All agricultural products	-34.5	-39.6	-74.1
Importables	-	41.4	6.9
Exportables	-	-43.5	-78.0

Source: Schiff and Valdes (1992).

were required to reduce the serious macroeconomic imbalances from the overambitious programs of the previous years – imbalances that were both internal (budget deficit, monetary expansion, and inflation) and external (the trade deficit and an emerging debt service burden). Third, markets had become distorted by a plethora of policy interventions, so that resource allocation was generally inefficient. The real exchange rate was a key relative price in need of correction. Fourth, there was a serious deterioration in public sector management, particularly among public enterprises. These problems were an outgrowth of the easy spending that followed the boom years 1975-77.

In dealing with these problems, the government turned to the IMF and the World Bank. An Extended Arrangement was agreed with the Fund in February 1981 covering a three-year period, followed by five Standby Arrangements during the decade and another in 1991. In all, IMF support amounted to SDR 1 billion over the 10-year period (Table 1.4). At the same time, the World Bank provided support through three structural adjustment loans (SALs) during 1981-86 (involving US $650 million) and six sector adjustment loans (SECALs) over 1989-91 (providing US $780 million). Movements in the terms of trade (and particularly coffee and cocoa prices) and in the value of the dollar were to have important repercussions for the programs. In most cases, these changes could not have been anticipated, and program designs were therefore (with hindsight) found wanting. These changes in external events are the basis of the twofold division of the 1980s – the partial adjustment in 1981-86 and the fettered adjustment in 1987-91. During the first period, the real exchange rate depreciated in Côte d'Ivoire, and there was some recovery in the terms of trade (at least during 1984-86). During the second, the real exchange rate appreciated, and the terms of trade fell, thus fettering the adjustment effort. Figure 1.1 summarizes how the government sought to deal with the challenges it faced during the 1980s.

Table 1.4
World Bank and IMF support to structural adjustment
programs in Côte d'Ivoire

World Bank loans		US $ millions
1981	Structural Adjustment Loan I	150
1983	Structural Adjustment Loan II	250
1986	Structural Adjustment Loan III	250
1989	Agricultural Sector Adjustment Loan	150
1989	Energy Sector Adjustment Loan	100
1990	Water Supply Sector Adjustment Loan	80
1991	Financial Sector Adjustment Loan	200
1991	Competitiveness Adjustment Loan	100
1991	Human Resources Adjustment Loan	150
IMF support		SDR millions
1981	Extended Arrangement (3 years)	484.50
1984	Stand-by Arrangement (1 year)	82.75
1985	Stand-by Arrangement (1 year)	66.20
1986	Stand-by Arrangement (2 years)	100.00
1987	Stand-by Arrangement (16 months)	94.00
1989	Stand-by Arrangement (17 months)	175.80
1991	Stand-by Arrangement (1 year)	82.75

Source: Grootaert (1993a).

Partial adjustment, 1981-86

Adjustment during this period was supported by the initial IMF Extended Arrangement, by two IMF standby Arrangements, and by SALs I and II.

Policy area	Initial circumstances	Reforms	Assessment
1. Fiscal policy and economic management	Fiscal deficit in 1980 was 12% of GDP, contrasting with a small surplus in 1977. This was due to an expansion in investment spending, financed through foreign borrowing.	Attempts were made to reduce the fiscal deficit through: - limiting investment expenditures - introducing three-year rolling investment plan (loi programme) - bringing stabilization fund surpluses under the budget - improving reporting and appraisal procedures.	The overall fiscal deficit has not been closed during the decade. In 1991, it was 13% of GDP. Despite cuts in public investment from 18% (1978-83) to 3% (1987-91) the increase in debt service and wages/salaries have aggravated the fiscal deficit problem. However, the primary deficit has been successfully closed.
2. Monetary policy	As a member of the WAMU, monetary policy is governed by rules restricting seignorage. Despite this, the government engaged in expansionary monetary policy in early 1980s by borrowing from public enterprise and from abroad. Money supply grew by 19% per annum between 1975-80.	Credit ceiling tightened under IMF guidance. WAMU rediscount rate raised.	Monetary expansion was successfully arrested during the decade. The reduced availability of external borrowing meant that the WAMU rules tightened monetary discipline. Broad monetary growth fell to 10% pa between 1980-75 and to -1.45% during 1986-91.
3. Trade policy	Major distortions in incentives and resource allocation caused by trade policy (tariffs and quantitative restrictions, and exchange rate overvaluation) and direct price controls.	Adjustment attempted to: remove quantitative restrictions with temporary import surcharge; apply tariffs/export subsidies yielding uniform effective protection rates of 40%. In this way, trade policy involved a liberalization component and an attempt to mimic a depreciation.	The program only succeeded during its early years (especially 1985-87). Thereafter, implementation was weak. Effective rates of protection were not uniform, and quantitative restrictions were reimposed in 1987. System of incentives remains highly distorted.

Figure 1.1   Initial distortions and policy progress under structural adjustment programs

Policy area	Initial circumstances	Reforms	Assessment
4. Exchange rate policy	Nominal exchange rate fixed to FF remained stable during crisis period due to FF stability. But real exchange rate appreciated as a result of domestic inflation due to commodity windfall and investment boom.	No change in nominal change rate policy: CFA franc parity with FF to remain at FF1 = CFA 50. Real exchange rate changes to be achieved through internal adjustment.	Appreciation of French franc caused marked appreciation in real exchange rate after 1983; internal policy (fiscal/monetary restraint) unable to reverse appreciation. CFA franc therefore overvalued at end of decade.
5. Public enterprise reforms	During crisis period, public enterprises were well funded, but were inefficient and not subject to budget processes and accountability. Hence they became a serious drain on exchequer finance.	Policy reforms sought to bring public enterprise activities under the discipline of the budget, introduce proper audits and accountability, and restructure inefficient enterprises. Under SAL III resource flows to the para-public sector to be reduced by 30% (in 1986) and annually thereafter. Programs also sought to accelerate the privatization program, especially after 1990.	Incorporation of enterprise budgets into central government accounting generally achieved. Management audits conducted as planned. Management practices in several public enterprises improved, but they remain inefficient, and enterprises continue to absorb public funds. Four enterprises privatized by 1991, and program to expand to 20 enterprises in 1991-93, and a further 30 enterprises in a second phase.
6. Financial sector reforms	Real interest rates generally negative during 1975-80. Credit market controlled by credit ceilings. Multiple interest rates in operation: lower rates for crop credit (TEP). Over-expansion in the private banking sector.	Most financial sector reforms introduced in late 1980s. Interest rates raised. Less reliance on direct quantitative credit controls, more on indirect instruments; direct sector credit controls and favorable TEP rates to be abolished; development banks to be monitored, assisted and restructured, especially BNDA. Insurance also to be assisted.	Real interest rates positive throughout adjustment period; TEP effectively abolished, and interest rate structure simplified; attempts to rescue BNDS failed, and government arranging liquidation; other major commercial banks continue to be troubled, and require continued assistance; similarly, problems remain with insurance sector.

Figure 1.1   Initial distortions and policy progress under structural adjustment programs

21

Adjustment policies were partially successful, due in part to a depreciation of the French franc (and therefore the CFA franc) against the dollar and to the recovery in commodity prices. But the SAL documents and the World Bank audits of the operations saw the structural adjustment process as a medium term task. Initial adjustment policies were concerned with short run objectives – mainly stabilization through fiscal and monetary restraint. But more fundamental weaknesses in the Ivorian economy would take longer to address: the institutional weaknesses in government and the public enterprise sector, and the distortions in trade and exchange.

Contractionary fiscal policy The first priority of stabilization in Côte d'Ivoire at the beginning of the 1980s was controlling and reducing the fiscal deficit. The overall deficit had risen to 12 percent of GDP in 1980, averaging more than 10 percent of GDP during 1978-80. Even the primary deficit was nine percent of GDP in 1980. There were two broad policy responses: a contractionary fiscal policy and more fundamental efforts to improve economic management.

Given the low world coffee and cocoa prices and the recession, there was little opportunity to increase revenue, at least during 1981-83. Tax policy was contractionary – excise taxes were raised on petroleum products, alcoholic beverages, and tobacco. But these changes had little effect on tax revenue, which increased from 20.5 percent of GDP during 1978-80 to just 21.4 percent during 1981-83, and slipped back to 19.3 percent in 1984-86. Fluctuations on the revenue side were due mainly to changes in nontax revenues, especially revenues from coffee and cocoa, which fell markedly during 1981-83, and recovered just as dramatically during 1984-86.

The government was thus obliged to put greater emphasis on restricting expenditure, particularly investment expenditure, cut from its peak of 23 percent of GDP in 1978 to 13 percent in 1983 and to less than five percent in 1986.[9] Current expenditures were not cut as drastically under the fiscal contraction, hovering around 19 percent of GDP during 1979-83, contracting to 15 percent in 1985, but increasing to 20 percent in 1986 as a result of more favorable external circumstances. One aspect of the cut in current expenditure, with immediate impact on the welfare of households, was the government's decision in 1984 to freeze civil service wages. These remained frozen until January 1986 and rose only slightly in subsequent years.

With this policy, the primary deficit closed to just 2.2 percent of GDP in 1983 and went into surplus during 1984-86. But significant increases in interest rates and debt service meant that the overall fiscal deficit was not closed during 1981-83. It was reduced to manageable proportions (just under three percent of GDP) only in 1986 when the temporary improvement in commodity prices raised government revenues.

In short, contractionary fiscal policy succeeded in closing the fiscal deficit that had mushroomed during the destabilizing period – due to a more favorable revenue outcome in 1984-86 but also to dramatic cutbacks in investment spending. The revenue improvement did not come from any broadening of the tax base, since the revenue from standard taxes did not increase. The improvement came mostly from revenues on coffee and cocoa. On the expenditure side, little was achieved in reducing government consumption, despite efforts to curtail the rapid growth in wages and salaries.

Monetary and financial policy In the first half of the 1980s, there was a significant return to monetary discipline. Credit ceilings were set on net domestic assets of the banking system and on net claims on the public sector. These credit ceilings were met, in part because private demand for credit was low. Borrowers were cautious in view of uncertainty over the debt issue and its rescheduling – and because of the drought and the general recession. The ceilings were also met because of supply factors – the central bank followed an extremely tight credit policy, crowding out the private sector when the government increased its use of credit from the banking system (as opposed to external borrowing).

The monetary restraint reduced the growth of money supply dramatically in 1982-83, but monetary expansion returned during 1984-85, with M2 growth averaging 16.6 percent a year. Fueled mainly by the balance of payment surplus during these years, this expansion was also a result of an increase in time deposits (in part a response to increased real interest rates) and to a slow down in the velocity of circulation from historically high levels in 1981-84. With a return to an external deficit in 1986, monetary expansion continued to be constrained.

The BCEAO previously relied mainly on credit ceilings as the instrument of monetary control, with interest rates kept low to encourage private investment. As a result of reforms introduced in 1981, the BCEAO adopted a more flexible interest rate policy to control credit and prevent capital outflows. The basic rediscount rate was raised from eight percent to 10.5 percent between April 1980 and April 1982 and to 12.5 percent up to April 1983, when it fell back to 10.5 percent. This pushed real interest rates into double digits during 1982-85 (see Table 1.1). But the two-rate system continued, with the normal rate (the TEN rate) 2.5 percent higher than the preferential rate (the TEP rate), applied mainly to crop credit and to credit advanced to the government and local authorities, to small national enterprises, and to first home buyers for construction. Monetary policy relied less on quantitative credit constraints, with the associated sector-specific allocations, and increasingly on the use of indirect methods of control.

At the beginning of the decade, the banking system in Côte d'Ivoire comprised 21 deposit money banks, of which 15 were commercial banks and six were specialized credit institutions, most set up to finance specific sectors.[10] These institutions had serious difficulties competing with the commercial banks, mainly because of their large portfolios of bad debts. To avoid bankruptcy, the development banks relied mainly on arrears financing and on high-interest overdraft facilities with the BCEAO.

Agricultural policy reforms The benefits of the boom in world coffee and cocoa prices during the destabilizing period generally were not passed on to the farmer, and producer prices were not increased significantly. Under SALs I and II, several policy reforms were introduced to raise agricultural production incentives. First, there were substantial price increases in all major crops, including coffee and cocoa, in an effort to raise export production. Between 1981 and 1984, producer prices of major export crops were raised by 25-35 percent in current terms, bringing them closer to world prices. Second, the consumer price of rice was raised, in effect raising the producer prices of such foodcrops as yams, plantain, cassava, and maize. These price increases occurred under favorable external circumstances. Both the depreciation of the CFA franc against the dollar and the recovery in world commodity prices during 1984-86 meant that the CSSPPA could to maintain large surpluses while raising producer prices. Producer prices remained below world market prices, so producers continued to be taxed.

The new structure of price incentives in agriculture had a strong impact on cocoa and cotton, whose production increases were essentially due to higher producer prices and to a rebound of output after two years of drought. The response for coffee was weaker. Price parity with cocoa had induced farmers to plant more cocoa while neglecting coffee.

Trade policy Major reforms were needed to restore international competitiveness and lay the foundation for expanded (and diversified) exports. The adoption of an export subsidy scheme and a revision of the customs tariff were major thrusts of the Ivorian adjustment program. Duties on many products were reduced (but increased on intermediate goods), quantitative restrictions were replaced with temporary surcharges to be gradually reduced to zero over five years. The objective was a uniform 40 percent rate of effective protection. The export subsidy scheme involved a new subsidy on value added on exports to countries outside the West African Economic Community, applied first to 52 percent of industrial value added and then gradually extended to all industry. A further incentive to export was provided though accelerating reimbursement of the value added tax on exports.

24

Progress in the implementation was slow and effectively postponed to later operations.

Public enterprise reform   The sheer size and influence of the public enterprises, their general low efficiency, and the macroeconomic implications of this inefficiency made it inevitable that public enterprise reform would remain on the adjustment agenda for the whole decade. It has proved difficult. Steps taken during the period of partial adjustment included the introduction of a systematic and comprehensive financial and economic monitoring system (tableau de bord) in the Ministry of Finance. A rehabilitation program was implemented for several enterprises that had been audited. The emphasis of public expenditure policy during 1981-86 was to improve the management of enterprises, not to change ownership. Some were merged with others, and some liquidated. In 1984, parastatal wages were aligned with those in the regular civil service, which meant a significant wage cut for parastatal employees. But the program of public enterprise reform lacked clearly defined policy objectives.

Fettered adjustment, 1987-91

Any success during the partial adjustment can be attributed to three major factors: the implementation of some structural adjustment reforms that began the process of improving economic management and restoring production incentives; the depreciation of the French franc, which caused a real exchange rate depreciation, at least up to 1983; and the improvement in the terms of trade. But the economic crisis returned in 1987, as the terms of trade took another sharp downward turn, exposing the underlying weaknesses of the Ivorian economy and demonstrating the need for continued and intensified policy reform. Throughout the rest of the 1980s the terms of trade continued to decline. But the adjustment process was fettered by the appreciation of the real exchange rate, brought about by a stronger French franc and by currency devaluations in competitor countries, such as Nigeria and Ghana. The government was obliged to rely on internal adjustment, trying to restore competitiveness through reducing domestic absorption.

During this period, adjustment in Côte d'Ivoire was supported by a third SAL, which sought to intensify the policy initiatives of earlier years. But the government drew back from its commitment to adjustment and abandoned the program in 1987. This led to an interruption in Bank lending to Côte d'Ivoire for two years (1987-89). Then, following the conclusion of an agreement with the Fund in 1989 on a new Stand-by Arrangement, Bank lending was resumed with the approval of six sector adjustment operations, mobilizing US $730 million (Table 1.4). Under the Medium-Term Framework that undergirded the

25

last three of these SECALs, it was acknowledged that the competitiveness problem needed to be addressed in advance of second tranche releases. The SECALs should therefore be viewed not so much as attempts to replace macroeconomic policy reforms (aimed at competitiveness), but as necessary complements to such reforms. Without the needed adjustment in the real exchange rate, the SECALs could not be expected to restore sustainable growth.

Fiscal policy The sharp fall in commodity prices in 1987 revealed the fragility of the favorable fiscal outcomes during the partial adjustment. Because producer prices remained unchanged as world prices fell, the CSSPPA operating surplus of nine percent of GDP in 1985 fell dramatically to just 0.3 percent in 1987. Given the fact that investment and nonsalary expenditures had been trimmed to the bone earlier in the decade, fiscal policy required an even more austere taxation stance. Tax raising measures (mainly on indirect taxation) were taken in 1987 and 1988.[11] But the outcomes were disappointing, particularly for import taxes, which did not yield the expected revenue improvements. This was due to the elimination of revenue from the agricultural stabilization funds, the poor revenue outcomes of import tax increases, due in part to evasion and to declining imports, and a contraction in the tax base, mainly as a result of the recession.

With little room for maneuver on the revenue and expenditure fronts, the government found it difficult to reduce the fiscal deficit. The primary deficit, having improved during 1984-86, rose to 7.6 percent of GDP in 1989, while the overall deficit increased to 17.6 percent of GDP. Since then, further expenditure cuts, notably on current expenditures other than wages and salaries, reduced the deficit somewhat. Unable to close the fiscal deficit, and with external financing opportunities limited, the government had little alternative but to let arrears accumulate even further during the second half of the decade.

Monetary and financial policy Monetary and credit policies continued to be contractionary. Broad money growth was negative during 1987-91 (on average -2.2 percent a year). Credit to the private sector was constrained, with serious effects on the economy. The financial problems of the government and the sharp deterioration in commodity prices meant that the CSSPPA was obliged to finance its operating losses by accumulating arrears to exporters. This accumulation of crop credit crowded out noncrop or ordinary credit, aggravating the recession.

Interest rate policy also changed. The TEN interest rate had been cut from a peak of 12.5 percent in 1983 to just 8.5 percent in 1986. But upward adjustments increased it to 10 percent in 1989. The preferential rate (TEP) premium was reduced in March 1989 and abolished in October.

The banking system continued to face serious problems – arising in part from poor bank portfolios but also from a serious liquidity shortage, due to the credit squeeze, payments arrears,[12] and low deposits. The problems of the former development banks were particularly acute, and measures were taken in 1987 to address them. It was proposed to reform and restructure (with foreign assistance) the BNDA (the specialized credit for agriculture and rural development), and to liquidate BICT (for public works) and BNEC (for housing). The BIDI and CCI (for industry) were to be merged. In 1989, it was decided to liquidate the BIDI and CCI as well. The program to restructure the BNDA was not effectively implemented, and its future remained in serious doubt.

The government also sought to provide assistance to the commercial banks. In 1988, margins between deposit and lending rates were widened to ease pressures on banking profitability. The problems continued, however, and the government is engaged in a rehabilitation program. Similar difficulties, stemming from the payments arrears problem, have been faced by the insurance sector. In response, the government has introduced measures to restructure the sector, including new regulatory arrangements.

Agricultural policies The weaknesses of Ivorian agriculture came once again to the fore as international prices of coffee and cocoa fell sharply in 1987. Value added in agriculture grew on average 3.8 percent a year during 1965-80 (with the export crop sector growing 6.5 percent a year). But during 1980-87 value added declined by 1.5 percent a year on average (and the export crop sector declined by 0.5 percent a year). So the adjustment policy reform in agriculture had not been sufficient to restore agricultural growth, and further reforms were to be on the policy reform agenda for the remainder of the decade.

The main policy issue facing the government was the continued weakness in world commodity prices, especially coffee and cocoa. To reverse the decline in world cocoa prices, the authorities retained part of the cocoa crop in 1988.[13] This policy caused major disruptions to the agricultural marketing cycle. Exporters were not reimbursed by the CSSPPA, and they were unable to obtain export permits. So, they could not repay crop credit, which in turn aggravated the liquidity problems of the banking system. Nor did the retention policy influence the world price, simply because the markets anticipated that the Ivorian stocks would eventually come into the market. This policy cost Côte d'Ivoire some of its market share, notably to Ghana.

Although the initial policy intention under SAL III was to raise producer prices of coffee and cocoa, the marked fall in world prices prevented implementation of the policy. Reforms therefore concentrated on two main objectives. The first was to increase price incentives for coffee production relative to cocoa. The government had persistently in ignored a world price difference in favor of coffee (25 percent on average during 1987-89). This was corrected by introducing a coffee quality premium of CFAF 33 per kilogram. The second was to reform the marketing arrangements for both crops, restructuring the CSSPPA, whose charter was amended in April 1991 to limit its operations to cocoa and coffee, for which domestic marketing arrangements had been liberalized. The CSSPPA was also to cease direct exports on its own account. A new system of setting producer prices on the basis of the average realized export prices of forward sales was implemented in late 1991. The role of the CSSPPA in quality control, ineffective at encouraging farmers to produce good quality produce, was abolished. These reforms were to reduce the costs (margins) of export crop marketing, and thus create the potential for higher producer prices.

Trade policy Trade policy reform was to achieve a uniform effective protection rate of 40 percent across activities, including a 20 percent subsidy payment for exports. In effect, the reforms were to mimic an exchange rate depreciation. Quantitative import restrictions were to be replaced by temporary import surcharges throughout the manufacturing sector. The new tariff code was to be reviewed. The export subsidy scheme was to be funded in the 1987 budget. A permanent monitoring system was to be created to measure the impact of the reform on subsectors and enterprises together with the reform's tax and budgetary repercussions. To help industry to adjust to the new incentive environment, the World Bank provided a loan of $30 million in 1986.

Most of the basic legislative changes to implement trade reforms were enacted between 1985 and 1988. But this was a subject of difficult negotiations between the Bank and the government – and was very much criticized by the national press and local industrialists. The government increased import duties by 30 percent in 1987, raising the target level of effective protection to 52 percent and partly compensating for the continuing deterioration in the terms of trade and the declining dollar. But growing pressure on the exchequer reduced enthusiasm for the export subsidy scheme, due to be paid at 20 percent of value added by June 1990. Despite its intention the government had not yet taken into account the 30 percent increase in import duties in calculating the export subsidy. This lack of symmetry between import taxation and the rate of export subsidy operated to the disadvantage of exports. The government did streamline the approval process, but government officials and the industrial community were not confident that the export subsidy would continue. So, investments to take advantage of export opportunities were not made. But the export subsidy scheme did raise profits of exporters, enabling them to remain in business despite the overvalued real exchange rate.

The removal of import controls was painful for Ivorian manufacturers, especially in textiles, footwear, electronic equipment, appliances, and vehicles. The press and some officials alleged that the elimination of import controls made it easier to avoid customs inspection or to practice extensive underinvoicing. Government estimates suggest that CFAF 30 billion in tax receipts (or 13 percent of the tax receipt in 1987) may have been lost annually. But import tax collection figures and omissions recorded in the balance of payments, revealed no evidence of fraud. Nevertheless, the government reapplied reference prices and quantitative restrictions to some 300 products in February 1988, including textiles and footwear, in response to fears of fraud. This was a setback. Without a system to value imports effectively and realistically, the problem remained.

The government did not fully appreciate the pain of the import reforms for the industrial sector, especially from 1986 onward as the CFA franc appreciated against the dollar, while competitor countries devalued their currencies as part of their adjustment. Particularly damaging to the industrial sector, removing quantitative restrictions on imports proved politically unsustainable.

Public enterprise reforms During 1987-91 public enterprise reforms changed gear, with greater emphasis gradually being placed on divestiture, not on simple restructuring. But policies have also been framed to strengthen public enterprises, giving them greater financial and management autonomy and requiring greater accountability. Between 1987-89, almost 30 public enterprises were privatized. Divestiture techniques usually involved direct negotiations with potential buyers. Conducted with little transparency, the privatizations were not particularly well managed. In 1990, the new government adopted a more considered and strategic approach to privatization, supported by an IDA-financed Privatization Support project. Under this initiative, the government privatized four enterprises and was bringing another 20 enterprises to the market to complete a first phase of privatizations (during 1991-93). A further phase involving some 30 enterprises, was programmed after 1993. Subject to repeated delays in implementation, the privatization program's progress has been patchy.

Principal economic outcomes

Do economic outcomes confirm the weaknesses of the adjustment programs of the 1980s? We consider the outcomes for four main groups of macroeconomic policy objectives: stabilization, resource allocation, economic growth, and equity and poverty reduction. Table 1.5 summarizes the main economic outcomes of the decade, distinguishing the destabilizing, partial adjustment and fettered adjustment phases.

Stabilization

How successful were the adjustment programs in restoring macroeconomic balance in the face of the serious destabilizing events of the decade? The main macroeconomic aggregates are reviewed in turn.

Fiscal deficit Although the government restrained the primary deficit to 3.6 percent of GDP on average during 1987-91, two fiscal problems remained: an overall deficit of more than 13 percent of GDP and imbalances in the fiscal accounts, which call for major revision (Tables 1.5 and 1.6). The main cause was the strain on the government accounts from interest payments on public debt, which increased from negligible levels in the early 1980s to 12.3 percent of GDP by 1991, mostly on external debt. The debt service problem has been solved by letting arrears accumulate, making interest payments self-financing. The debt problem therefore remained unresolved.

Closing the primary deficit to approximate balance in 1991 should not be interpreted as solving the fiscal problem, because restoring this macro balance introduced imbalances to the structure of the fiscal accounts, with effects as serious as a persisting deficit. Two major imbalances emerged as a result of contractionary fiscal policy in the second half of the 1980s: that between investment and recurrent expenditures, and that between wages and salaries and other recurrent expenditures. During the period of fettered adjustment, investment expenditures constituted only 9.4 percent of total expenditures, down from 50 percent during the boom of 1978-80. Future generations therefore have to bear much of the burden of the current adjustment. To restore growth, and to 'crowd in' private investment, the need is still urgent for a major fiscal adjustment in Côte d'Ivoire – to restore investment expenditures by government.

But this is only one aspect of the fiscal problem. The composition of government recurrent expenditure has become seriously distorted as a consequence of fiscal constraint. The share of wages and salaries in noninterest expenditures increased from 49 percent during 1975 - 80 (the

Table 1.5
Macroeconomic indicators of adjustment, 1975-91

	Destabilizing period			Partial adjustment			Fettered adjustment
	1975-77	1978-80	1975-80	1981-83	1984-86	1981-86	1987-91
Immediate results							
Real effective exchange rate (index)	104.8	128.8	116.8	110.4	106.5	108.5	124.8
Relative inflation rate (index)	99.3	115.4	107.4	110.2	102.3	106.3	95.5
Money supply growth (% pa)	34.2	3.7	18.9	6.0	11.9	9.0	-2.2
Real interest (discount) rate (%)	3.3	6.0	4.6	9.9	10.0	9.9	9.5
Fiscal deficit/GDP ratio (%)	-1.4	-10.6	-5.8	-11.9	-2.7	-7.3	-13.2
BoP current account/GDP ratio (%)	-6.8	-14.6	-10.7	-14.9	-1.6	-8.3	-12.4
Final results		(Percentage)					
Real GDP growth	5.3	5.3	5.3	1.6	2.4	2.0	-1.6
Private investment/GDP ratio	13.5	15.8	14.6	14.1	8.5	11.3	7.1
Domestic investment/GDP ratio	24.3	28.6	26.5	23.2	12.6	17.9	11.5
Domestic savings/GDP ratio	28.2	25.3	26.8	19.3	23.3	21.3	15.4
Exports of GNFS/GDP ratio	40.4	35.1	37.7	36.0	43.6	39.8	35.1
Imports of GNFS/GDP ratio	36.4	38.4	37.4	39.9	32.9	36.4	31.2
Real growth rate of exports	-0.1	6.9	3.4	0.1	7.7	3.9	6.0
Real growth rate of imports	16.3	5.9	11.1	-8.4	6.6	-0.9	-4.5

Source: Table in Annex 1.

Table 1.6
Fiscal deficit, 1976-91

	Destabilizing period		Partial adjustment		Fettered adjustment
	1976-77	1978-80	1981-83	1984-86	1987-91
	(% of GDP)				
A. Total revenue	33.5	31.7	28.0	30.7	24.1
Tax revenue	20.8	20.5	21.4	19.3	19.9
Nontax revenue	12.7	11.1	6.6	11.4	4.2
B. Total expenditure	34.9	42.3	39.9	33.4	37.3
Current expenditure	16.4	21.1	25.7	26.5	33.9
Capital expenditure	18.5	21.1	14.2	6.8	3.5
C. Primary deficit	0.1	-8.0	-4.9	6.0	-3.6
D. Overall fiscal balance	-1.4	-10.6	-11.9	-2.7	-13.2

Source: World Bank data.

destabilizing period) to 54 percent in 1981-86 (the period of partial adjustment), and remained at this level through 1991. The ratio of wages to materials costs rose from 1.8 to 2.9 over the same period. Wage and salary levels in the government sector are significantly higher than in other countries of the region. For example, the average wage rate in the Ivorian public sector in 1985 was twice that of Congo's and 1.8 times that of Cameroon's. It has been estimated that the average civil service wage was nine to ten times the GDP per capita, spotlighting the need for civil service reform and a reduced wage and salary component in public spending.

Arrears Given the monetary discipline imposed on the authorities through WAMU, the government had few options for financing its fiscal deficits. External borrowing has been significantly reduced, in part because of the debt overhang. Significant borrowing from nonbanking domestic sources is limited by the shallowness of the domestic financial sector. This leaves a third source of finance: accumulating arrears, a significant feature of government financial operations, that has affected both its domestic and external transactions.

External arrears increased from negligible amounts over 1975-1985 to a problem of major proportions subsequently. In 1986, the stock of total arrears to external creditors was $37 million, in 1991 they were $2.2 billion. The figures speak for themselves about the effects of the destabilization on Côte d'Ivoire's international creditworthiness. But another major problem from the failure of the government to reduce its fiscal deficit and find a long term solution to its financial crises has been the accumulation of arrears to domestic creditors. By the end of 1989, the Central Government and other public bodies had accumulated arrears of CFAF 556 billion (more than $4 billion, or about 18 percent of GDP). These arrears are due not only on repayments of interest and principal on loans from the private banking system but also on bills due to private suppliers and contractors. Almost every firm supplying the government or receiving refunds or subsidies from the government was affected – even small and medium-size enterprises (Ruenda-Sabater and Stone, 1992). The government and its agencies simply stopped paying their bills.

Money supply growth and inflation Price inflation is one aggregate which was stabilized under Côte d'Ivoire's adjustment program, mainly because of the restoration of monetary discipline during the decade. The expansionary monetary policies of the crisis period (which witnessed average annual growth in money supply (M2) of 19 percent) were corrected during both the partial and fettered adjustment phases – falling to nine percent a year during 1981-86 and to -3.2 percent a year during 1987-90 (Table 1.7).

Table 1.7
Measures of price inflation, 1976-90

	1976-80	1981-86	1987-90
Inflation rate (CPI based; % a year)	16.7	5.8	4.3
GDP deflator (% increase a year)	15.0	7.1	-2.8
CPI/FWPI	120.5	111.3	95.0
GDPD/FWPI	132.2	104.9	76.1
Money supply growth (M2)	20.8	9.0	-3.2

Source: World Bank data.

This restoration of monetary discipline is reflected in recorded rates of price inflation, as measured by the consumer price index, and the implicit GDP deflator. Apart from the period 1981-86, the GDP deflator indicates a lower rate of price increase than the CPI-based inflation index. However, the GDP deflator recorded a much greater decline in inflation over the period (from 15 percent during 1976-80 to -2.8 percent in 1987-90).

The external deficit The investment boom of the late 1970s widened the current account deficit to 14.6 percent of GDP during 1978-80 (Table 1.5). This deficit was reduced to just 1.6 percent of GDP during 1984-86, mainly because of the recovery in commodity prices. But the continued deterioration in prices thereafter, and the growing burden of interest payments on external debt, were responsible for the reemergence of current account deficits of more than 12 percent of GDP during 1987-91 (Table 1.8).

Table 1.8
Balance of payments trends, 1975-91

	Destabilizing period	Partial adjustment		Fettered adjustment
	1975-80	1981-83	1984-86	1987-91
		(Millions US$ current)		
Exports of GNFS	2,668.1	2,719.6	3,271.2	3,431.3
Imports of GNFS	2,773.4	2,949.1	2,478.6	3,161.6
Resource balance	-105.4	-229.6	792.6	269.6
(As % of GDP)	0.3	-3.9	10.7	3.9
Net factor income	-304.2	-511.2	-602.7	-1,019.2
Net current transfers	-428.1	-401.9	-332.5	-470.5
Current account				
Balance before official grants	-837.6	-1,142.6	-142.6	-1,220.1
(As % of GDP)	-10.7	-14.9	-1.60	-12.4
Official capital grants	28.8	23.9	41.7	80.4
Balance after official grants	-808.8	-1,118.7	-100.9	-1,139.8
Long term capital inflows	617.4	784.4	247.1	267.6
Other items	155.1	110.4	-269.1	602.5
Changes in net reserves	16.6	14.7	213.0	-17.3

Source: World Bank data.

As with the fiscal deficit, the 1980s have seen very little change in the current account deficit, which was only marginally lower at the end of the decade (in terms of GDP) than at the beginning. The main difference in the external account is the increase in interest payments on external debt. In 1991, interest payments accounted for over 80 percent of gross factor payments, which rose from just $184 million in 1975 to $1.3 billion in 1991. The current account deficit of $1.1 billion in 1991 can thus be explained almost entirely by interest payments.

Given the negative effect of net factor income and net current transfers on the current account of the balance of payments (including interest payments on external public debt), the resource balance needs to be sufficiently in surplus to keep the current account deficit within acceptable bounds. This was not the case for much of the decade. In some years (1979-83), the resource balance was negative. Apart from 1984-86, during the second commodity price boom, the resource balance has not been sufficient, (generally amounting to just under four percent of GDP).

Export growth was insufficient to achieve the objectives of external balance under the structural adjustment programs, so that the adjustment in the external resource balance was brought about by import compression. For much of the 1980s, export growth was sluggish, averaging only 3.9 percent a year during the period of partial adjustment, and -0.2 percent between 1987 and 1988 (Table 1.9). The recent improvement due to a significant increase in export volumes of cocoa (in 1989) and coffee (in 1990) is encouraging. But import volumes declined for much of the decade (averaging -one percent a year during 1981-86 and -eight percent a year in 1987-88). This contrasts with positive growth of over 13.9 percent during the crisis period (1976-80). Given the declines in real GDP during 1987-91 (see Table 1.5), it is clear that expenditure reduction played a more important part in Ivorian adjustment than expenditure switching.

Table 1.9
Average annual growth rates of real exports, imports
and GDP, 1976-90 (percent)

	Destabilizing period	Partial adjustment	Fettered adjustment	
	1976-80	1981-86	1987-88	1989-90
Exports of goods and nonfactor services	4.9	3.9	-0.2	12.1
Imports of goods and nonfactor services	13.9	-0.9	-8.0	-1.0
GDP growth	4.3	2.0	-1.4	-1.8

Source: World Bank data.

What were the factors underlying the movements in the resource balance? To investigate the underlying real-economy sources of external adjustment in Côte d'Ivoire, the changes in the resource balance have been decomposed on the basis of the underlying identities in the national income and product accounts. During the destabilizing period, the current account deficit increased to about 17 percent of GDP, which was associated with a deterioration in the resource balance (Table 1.10). During 1980-85, roughly the period of partial adjustment, both the current account and the resource balances improved. And during 1985-91, roughly the period of fettered adjustment, the current account deficit increased to 12 percent of GDP and the resource balance declined.[14]

Table 1.10
Trade and resource balances and their related identities, 1975-91

Item	Change 1977 to 1980		Change 1980 to 1985		Change 1985 to 1991	
	CFAF (billions)	(%)*	CFAF (billions)	(%)*	CFAF (billions)	(%)*
Resource balance	-231.5	100.0	548.9	100.0	-285.9	100.0
GDP	682.4	-294.8	916.2	166.9	-447.8	156.6
Total expenditures	913.9	-394.8	367.3	66.9	-161.9	56.6
Public consumption	186.2	-80.4	87.1	15.9	-12.2	4.3
Private consumption	521.7	-225.4	449.4	81.9	26.2	-9.2
Public investment	35.2	-15.2	-83.6	-15.2	-43.0	15.0
Private investment	170.8	-73.8	-85.6	-15.6	-132.9	46.5

* Components as a percentage of changes in the resource balance.

Source: World Bank data.

To what extent were the changes brought about by changes in aggregate supply or aggregate demand? Keep in mind that increases in GDP will reduce the external deficit, other things being equal, while raised expenditures will increase it. Taking the first period (1977-80), the increase in output was insufficient to prevent a deteriorating external situation in the face of the massive increase in aggregate expenditure (Table 1.10). This is not surprising, given of the investment-led boom of the late 1970s. The growth in aggregate absorption dominated during this period. In the partial adjustment phase (1980-85), the improvement in the external balances was associated with an expansion in aggregate supply, rather than an adjustment in absorption. Total expenditure increased, but by significantly less than the growth in output, reducing the external deficit (Table 1.10). So, insofar as adjustment took place during this period, it was through an expansion in supply rather than a contraction in demand.[15] The deterioration in the external deficit in the second half of the decade appears to have been a result of a contraction in aggregate output, rather than changes in aggregate absorption. In fact, absorption declined during the period, which would, have reduced the external deficit. But these absorption cuts were simply insufficient to counteract the output shortfalls that increasingly characterized the Ivorian economy in the late 1980s.

Interestingly, the surge in absorption during the crisis period (1977-80) was not only related to public investment – it came mainly from increases in private and (to a lesser extent) public consumption (Table 1.10). The peak in public investment appeared earlier than the emerging external deficit (it reached 13.3 percent of GDP in 1978, when the current account deficit was 11.1 percent of GDP, far below its peak of 17.5 percent in 1980). While the boom in public investment triggered the destabilization, it was the related boom in private and public consumption that really fueled domestic absorption and led to the deterioration in the external balances. Private investment had no significant role in the destabilization.

During the period of partial adjustment, both consumption components continued to rise – and thus to exert an upward pressure on the external deficit. But the growth in GDP during this period dominated these absorption changes. Note that both investment components of absorption declined during 1980-85, reinforcing (albeit marginally) the beneficial effects on the external deficit. The end of the decade saw cuts in public consumption and (especially) investment and reductions in private investment. But these were not sufficient to prevent a continued increase in the external deficit, due to declining GDP.[16]

Changes in trade distortions

The failure of the adjustment effort to reverse the real exchange rate appreciation that has dominated the decade (especially its second half) has already been identified. But what of trade policy? How have the reforms changed this source of incentive distortion? With the increasing overvaluation of the CFA franc, any significant reduction in the protection granted though trade controls would be unlikely, given the penalty of an overvalued exchange rate to export producers and import-substituting producers alike. As already noted, the major thrust of SALs II and III was to increase protection to import-competing activities and allocate subsidies to exporters to mimic a real exchange rate depreciation.

Given the inevitability of maintaining levels of protection, how can trade policy reforms be assessed from the standpoint of structural adjustment and its objectives? Reforms could have reduced the distortionary effects of trade policy in two respects without doing violence to the objective of mimicking a devaluation. First, some trade liberalization could be achieved by substituting tariffs for quantitative import restrictions. Second, the tariff structure could be designed to minimize the distortion of the incentive structure and resource allocation. Both objectives were part of the adjustment lending operations of the World Bank. The first was an essential part of the tariff-cum-subsidy scheme, since the replacement of quantitative restrictions with tariffs would generate revenue flows to the exchequer and would finance export subsidies. The second objective, which was set during SALs II and III, sought a uniform effective protection rate of 40 percent for all protected activities. Were these more limited trade liberalization measures achieved?

The replacement of quantitative restrictions with tariffs was initiated in 1985, with surcharges to be temporarily applied during the transition. But the continued appreciation of the CFA franc, the persistent decline in commodity prices, the devaluations in Nigeria and Ghana, and the well-based rumors of fraud, smuggling, and underinvoicing led to a progressive reversal of this policy after 1987. About a third of imports continued to be subject to quantitative restrictions at the end of the decade. Consumer goods with mass-market potential – such as textiles, clothing, shoes, refined oil, rubber products, processed food, and electrical appliances – all continued to be subject to licensing. About half the food imports continued to be subject either to prior authorization or to licensing. In short, the limited liberalization objective of replacing quantitative restrictions with tariffs was not met.

Table 1.11
Structure of nominal and effective protection, 1990

	Nominal protection		Effective protection		Net effective protection
	Outputs	Inputs	Actual export subsidies	Full export subsidies	Actual export subsidies
Sector					
Textiles	19.1	18.4	29.7	44.2	-1.6
Agro-industry	0.1	15.0	-39.8	-39.4	-54.8
(Excluding cocoa)	10.4	21.8	-16.9	16.0	-34.3
Wood	6.5	11.8	3.8	10.6	-22.2
Plastics/packaging	30.6	13.7	41.5	41.5	-6.8
Total	0.4	15.1	-38.8	-38.3	-54.1
Excluding cocoa	16.0	19.1	8.8	30.2	-16.4

Source: World Bank data.

Achieving a uniform level of effective protection to minimize the resource allocation distortions of trade policy is not an easy matter. Such rates can change as input use responds to major changes in relative prices, throwing the policy off track. These difficulties, as events proved, confounded trade policy in Côte d'Ivoire (Table 1.11). Recall that trade policy under the SALs involved a combination of tariffs and export subsidies. The subsidies were not consistently paid to exporters, so the protection they received was significantly less that the level they were entitled to. There was a wide dispersion in protection afforded by trade policy at the end of the decade, ranging from -40 percent in agro-industry to more than 40 percent in plastics and packaging.[17] The effect of the export subsidy arrears problem is clear. But even if the export subsidy had been paid in full, it would not have been sufficient to compensate for the exchange rate overvaluation.[18] Most activities, despite some high rates of effective protection, remained taxed as a result of the trade policy regime.

In sum, the limited attempts at trade liberalization were not effectively implemented during the partial and fettered adjustment periods. The role of the real exchange rate appreciation in limiting the government's room for maneuver is evident. Yet even within this constraint, there was little or no advance at removing import restrictions – or making trade policy more evenhanded. That policy seems to have been as much a source of incentive distortion and resource misallocation at the close of the decade as at the beginning.

Economic growth

Côte d'Ivoire's growth record in the 1980s is dismal. For 1983-91, the growth of real GDP has averaged -0.4 percent a year, despite the high growth in 1985 and 1986, when commodity prices were favorable. Growth was negative in six years of the decade. At the same time, population growth increased steadily from 3.4 percent a year during the early 1980s to 3.9 percent in 1991 and 1992. The result: a devastating decline in per capita incomes.

Mean per capita income reached CFAF 333, 959 in 1980 but fell to just CFAF 209, 411 in 1991 (Table 1.12). Even before the boom years, in 1975 per capita GNP was almost CFA 300,000. It grew during the second half of the 1970s at 1.7 percent a year, but then turned downward with only a handful of years of positive growth. Over the 1980s, per capita GNP has declined on average by 2.4 percent a year. The situation is worse for private consumption, which declined by 4.9 percent a year during 1980-91. Compare that with the annual growth in real consumption of four percent toward the end of the 1970s.

39

Table 1.12
Real GNP per capita: levels and growth, 1975-91

	1975	1976	1977	1978	1979	1980
Real GNP per capita (CFAF)	296,016	310,281	308,136	320,978	315,820	333,959
GNP per capita growth	NA	4.8%	-0.7%	4.2%	-1.6%	5.7%
Real private consumption per capita (CFAF)	180,921	198,454	11,467	224,635	219,307	171,717
Real private consumption per capita growth	NA	9.7%	6.6%	6.2%	-2.4%	-21.7%

	1981	1982	1983	1984	1985	1986
Real GNP per capita (CFAF)	331,495	319,173	298,260	283,181	273,353	279,244
GNP per capita growth	-0.7%	-3.7%	-6.6%	-5.1%	-3.5%	2.2%
Real private consumption per capita (CFAF)	197,714	188,688	182,232	190,191	175,556	197,171
Real private consumption per capita growth	15.1%	-4.6%	-3.4%	4.4%	-7.2%	11.7%

	1987	1988	1989	1990	1991	
Real GNP per capita (CFAF)	263,156	253,512	239,706	223,143	209,411	
GNP per capita growth	-5.8%	-3.7%	-5.4%	-6.9%	4.8%	
Real private consumption per capita (CFAF)	177,049	146,214	143,810	118,467	111,615	
Real private consumption per capita growth	-10.2%	-17.4%	-1.6%	-17.6%	-5.8%	

Memorandum items	1976-79	1980-91
GNP per capita growth	1.67	-2.38
Private consumption per capita growth	4.02	-4.86

Source: World Bank data.

Assessment of the adjustment programs

What room for maneuver did the Ivorian Government have in framing its adjustment policies any differently from the historical record? In assessing its attempts at macroeconomic adjustment in Côte d'Ivoire, three areas of policy failure are identified. The first concerns macroeconomic mismanagement in general, and specifically the government's failure to restore fiscal balance. Second, exchange rate management was severely constrained, which led to an undue reliance on expenditure-reducing policies and given the weaknesses in macroeconomic management, expenditure reduction was targeted mainly at investment, with serious implications for long term growth. The third area covers the implications of macroeconomic policy for private investment in Côte d'Ivoire, which declined markedly during the 1980s.

Public sector economic mismanagement

The main issues of economic management during the 1980s relate to the ownership of the adjustment programs by the government, and the persistence of the fiscal deficit.

The weak commitment to adjustment The SAL audits suggest that the government failed to identify closely enough with the programs and that the private sector thus did not consider them credible and sustainable. It was not so much that the policies and programs were ill conceived. It was that their implementation was limited by a lack of government commitment. In framing the adjustment programs, the World Bank and IMF did not pay enough attention to getting the government on board. Moreover, the government did not fully appreciate the seriousness of the macroeconomic situation, and was unresponsive to changes in the country's international situation.

Failure to close the fiscal deficit A concrete manifestation of the lack of real commitment to macroeconomic adjustment is the failure of government to close the fiscal deficit. The fiscal deficit in 1991 was 13 percent of GDP, wider than in 1980 (12 percent). Fiscal undiscipline during the second half of the 1970s dominated subsequent events because expenditures during these boom years were financed mainly through foreign borrowing. The macroeconomic accounts were since dominated by the servicing of this debt. At the end of the 1970s interest payments on public debt amounted to about two percent of GDP, but by 1991 they had risen to 12 percent (about equal to the fiscal deficit in 1991). Uncorrected, this burden will pass to future generations. That the government is not servicing its debt but financing it through an accumulation of arrears means that a large overall deficit is not critical. But

41

such an accumulation cannot continue indefinitely. And there are signs that it is having fundamental repercussions on the economy at large, disrupting the financial sector and discouraging investment.

With hindsight, the problems of the 1980s would have been solved if the fiscal excesses of the 1970s had been avoided. Berthélemy and Bourguignon (1992) suggest that excessive and inefficient spending by government was the main cause of the macroeconomic crises that dominated the 1980s. But they also show that if private sector savings had not fallen so rapidly, the investment program could have been financed without recourse to heavy external borrowing. This is confirmed in the decomposition analysis in this chapter, which reveals that the expansion in private consumption expenditures was also responsible for the growing current account deficit at the end of the 1970s. And the decline in savings is readily explained by the severity of the external shock and the ensuing decline in profits.

Debt service is not the only item in government expenditures that stands out. Expenditure on wages and salaries also increased relative to other items of expenditure and to GDP. In 1985, when the overall fiscal deficit was just 1.5 percent of GDP, wages and salaries amounted to just over eight percent of GDP (or 25 percent of total central government expenditure). By 1991, expenditure on wages and salaries were more than 12 percent of GDP and 35 percent of total expenditure (or 52 percent of primary expenditure and 60 percent of total public consumption spending). In spite of the freeze on public salaries between 1984 and 1986, for the decade as a whole, public sector employment and earnings have been protected from the major burden of adjustment.[19]

With other consumption items cut only somewhat, the main burden of adjustment fell on public investment expenditures, which declined from 18 percent of GDP during 1978-83 to only three percent in 1987-91. The simple fact remains that if public sector employees had borne a burden of adjustment similar to the private sector – leaving public sector wages and salaries constant as a percentage of GDP over 1985-91 – public investment could have been raised to almost seven percent of GDP (roughly what it was in the middle of the decade). The failure of government to control wages and salaries is a tangible symptom of its failure to undertake adjustment in earnest.

The real exchange rate

Given the policy instruments at its disposal, the government has been unable to reverse the major exchange rate appreciation that has dominated the scene since 1985. Although there is some indication that the appreciation was contained toward the end of the decade, the limits imposed by CFA franc zone membership stymied the adjustment effort. An exchange rate appreciation does not in itself prove that the real exchange rate is overvalued, since appreciation may be a result of an undervalued exchange rate in earlier years. Even if it can be shown that the REER has not appreciated since some base year when it was in equilibrium, this does not prove the absence of overvaluation, since the *equilibrium rate* itself may well have changed during the period. In particular, if the terms of trade deteriorate, the equilibrium real exchange rate will depreciate. Under such circumstances, a constant REER would imply growing overvaluation, since the equilibrium REER would have fallen. In Côte d'Ivoire during the 1980s, the degree of overvaluation would be an outcome of these two forces: the increase in the REER and the decline in the equilibrium REER brought about by the declines in the terms of trade and in capital inflows.[20]

The appreciation in the REER must therefore be interpreted with caution. For example, assume that the REER for 1985 represents the equilibrium REER (on the basis that the resource balance was 13 percent of GDP, and the current account was marginally in surplus – 0.6 percent of GDP), up to 1991 the REER appreciated by 43 percent. This does not mean, however, that the Ivorian REER is overvalued by 43 percent, which is the case only if the equilibrium REER had remained unchanged since 1985. The terms of trade declined by 37 percent between 1985 and 1991, which means that the equilibrium REER is certain to have fallen. This means a greater degree of overvaluation than indicated by the REER time series – one reason for some observers to have placed the overvaluation of the CFA franc at modest levels (Boughton, 1991 and 1992; Stolberg and Vagenas, 1992). The estimate of a 43 percent overvaluation in 1991 might therefore be considered a lower bound to the true degree of overvaluation.

A key issue in assessing adjustment in Côte d'Ivoire is why the government was unable to prevent this serious macroeconomic distortion. The first and obvious reason is Côte d'Ivoire's membership of the CFA franc zone. The tying of the CFA franc to the French franc made exchange rate policy inflexible, and macroeconomic policy a hostage to fortune. In particular, the nominal appreciation of the French franc during the second half of the 1980s had serious repercussions for Côte d'Ivoire, since much of the country's trade was outside the franc zone, leading to a strong upward movement in the nominal effective exchange rate (also a result of devaluations among Côte d'Ivoire's competitors). This overvaluation has since been corrected by the CFA franc devaluation in January 1994. However, macro policy in Côte d'Ivoire remains subject to this external constraint. Further deteriorations in the terms of trade, or nominal appreciations in the French franc could create similar problems in the future.

There can be little debate over this explanation of nominal inflexibility underpinning the Ivorian case – and over the limits that apply to relying on internal adjustments to restore the equilibrium REER. So the government tried an alternative to a nominal depreciation: a combination of export subsidies and import tariffs. In a two-commodity world, this policy which raises the domestic price of the tradable commodity) is an exact equivalent of a nominal depreciation. This theoretical equivalence was the foundation for the policy strategy selected in SAL II and (especially) SAL III. The policy did not succeed, however, and was abandoned. Understanding why the policy failed is critical.

The tariff-cum-subsidy scheme, had both technical and implementation problems. The implementation of the policy left much to be desired. Its financing over time was left indeterminate, which led to doubts in the private sector about its sustainability and permanence. Ivorian officials never believed that the export subsidy would gain primary access to the budgetary resources – despite the creation of a Special Fund in the Treasury, which at one point included CFAF 16 billion. In theory, the additional revenue needed for export subsidy payments was to come from the application of import duties. But as already observed, there was too much avoidance of such duties for the scheme to imply a serious fiscal commitment to it. And with the government under pressure to reduce the fiscal deficit, the policy lacked credibility from the start. Payment of the export subsidy was patchy, the distortions in incentives remained, and the system had no impact on investment.

The collapse of private investment

The third key issue is the devastating effect of the 1980s on private investment, which fell from almost 16 percent of GDP in 1978-80 to only seven percent in 1987-91 (Table 1.1). The direction and order of magnitude of the change in investment is probably correct even though these estimates usually underrecord informal sector investment. The reasons for this disturbing outcome:

- *Limited credit* A survey of private enterprises reported that they listed lack of access to finance as the single most important obstacle to the growth of the enterprise (Ruenda-Sabater and Stone, 1992). It seems that each of the mechanisms used by the government to finance its deficits and service its debt crowded out private investment.

- *Labor market effects* Another sense in which the public sector crowded out the private was in bidding away the most educated members of the labor force. Graduates are guaranteed civil service employment at highly favorable rates of remuneration. It is difficult for the private sector to compete with these salaries. At the same time, however, higher public sector pay has an effect on wages and salaries in the private sector, making it difficult to maintain competitiveness and create productive investment opportunities. Employers in the private sector also faced numerous labor market interventions.

- *Inappropriate macroeconomic policies* The overvaluation of the CFA franc especially discouraged private investors. Such overvaluation, combined with rigidities in the labor market, reduced the returns to investment in tradeable activities. At the same time, the reliance on expenditure-reducing policies significantly reduced the size of the domestic market, eroding investment opportunities.

- *Private sector arrears* The ubiquitous nature of this problem undermined productive investment in the private sector. It is now generally accepted that the financing of the public sector deficit through the accumulation of arrears hurt the liquidity position of enterprises and seriously undermined the confidence of private investors (Ruenda-Sabater and Stone, 1992). The arrears problem is compounded by the profit tax imposed on firms for entitlements to an export subsidy rather than for receipts of the subsidy. Even if the subsidy is paid, it may create liquidity problems for firms. But if the subsidy is seriously delayed, or not paid at all, the government in effect taxes firms for income they do not receive (Ruenda-Sabater and Stone, 1992).

Concluding observations

Côte d'Ivoire has been subjected to three types of destabilizing shocks. First were the unsustainable expenditures in the late 1970s brought about in part by the commodity price boom and access to low-cost external finance. Second were the terms of trade and real exchange rate shocks, that occurred mainly during the second half of the 1980s. Third were the policy-induced distortions and public sector influences, affecting production, trade, and exchange. The policy responses to these destabilizing features of Ivorian economic history were simply inadequate, relying almost entirely on an internal adjustment strategy that emphasized expenditure cuts rather than fundamental structural adjustments.

If the only source of destabilization had been the unsustainably high public investment during the late 1970s, the policy response would have been appropriate and perhaps even sufficient to restore balance. An indication of this is the measure of success achieved before to 1987. Thereafter, the deterioration in the barter terms of trade – and the appreciation in the real exchange rate – made this policy response inadequate. But even without further shocks in the latter half of the decade, the policy response taken probably would not have been sufficient to regain a path of sustainable growth. The domestic economy had become so distorted by trade and price interventions and by direct government involvement in productive activities that the reliance on internal adjustment was critically flawed. An internal, expenditure-reducing adjustment strategy can be truly effective only if there is enough flexibility and responsiveness in the economic system. For example, internal adjustment can be effective only if there is enough price and wage flexibility in the domestic economy. At the very least, the initial destabilizing events required that the rigidities and distortions in the domestic economy be first corrected. Otherwise, the internal adjustment effort would be frustrated by an insufficient response of the domestic economy.

In the second half of the decade, the Ivorian economy suffered external shocks that made internal adjustment inappropriate. Later attempts to improve the functioning of the domestic economy were too late to rescue the internal adjustment strategy. The terms of trade shock and the appreciation in the real exchange rate called for a different adjustment approach, one in which an equilibrating movement in the real exchange rate is brought about within a reasonable time frame. It is only after a delay of some considerable time that this was achieved, the depreciation in the CFA franc occurring not until January 1994.

What lessons can be drawn from this catalogue of fettered adjustment?

- The real exchange rate is a critical relative price to get right in an adjustment program. Failure to correct for a disequilibrium in real exchange rate can undo the major part of the adjustment effort. In Côte d'Ivoire, the overvaluation of the real exchange rate has not only seriously fettered trade policy. It obliged the authorities to rely heavily on internal adjustment, increasing the cost of adjustment significantly. It has also made it difficult to achieve other objectives of adjustment with such a serious underlying relative price distortion. Trade liberalization and export diversification are difficult, if not impossible, when real exchange rates are misaligned.

- On the phasing of policy reforms, internal adjustment required that the distortions and inflexibilities in the domestic economy be addressed prior to (or at least concurrently with) the internal macroeconomic adjustment. In Côte d'Ivoire, these measures were undertaken after almost a decade of internal adjustment.

- The 1980s have shown how difficult it can be for countries to extricate themselves from the longer term effects of unsustainable investment programs. The debt overhang that emerged from a relatively short period of Ivorian history (basically just five years of easy spending) has dominated macroeconomic policy since 1980. But there are more fundamental lessons from the debt experience. Given the constraints that it faced, the Ivorian government had little choice but to allow arrears to accumulate. Although a short term solution of a sort, it has deep-seated effects that pervade the economy, but especially the financial system and private investment activities. There are also concerns about what the nonpayment of debt might mean for the underlying fabric of trade and exchange. If economic agents consistently default on payments, the economic system might be weakened in a more fundamental sense.

Notes

1   This chapter is a revised version of 'Côte d'Ivoire: Fettered Adjustment' by Lionel Demery, which appeared originally as Chapter 3 in I. Husain and R. Faruquee (eds.), *Adjustment in Africa - Lessons from Country Case Studies,* World Bank Regional and Sectoral Studies, Washington, D.C., 1994. The material is used with permission of the World Bank.

2   For further details of the history and structure of the CFA zone and its monetary unions, see Boughton (1991 and 1992).

3   As part of a reform package, direct controls were replaced with indirect monetary controls in October 1989, and the system of sectoral credits has been abolished.

4   The relationship between the BCEAO and the French Treasury is complicated by a similar arrangement with the Banque des Etats de l'Afrique Centrale (BEAC). While the BCEAO has acquired a sizable overdraft on its Operations Account, the BEAC has generally maintained large surpluses. It has been suggested that the French Treasury take the overall balance of *both* unions into account in considering the urgency of correcting an Operations Account imbalance.

5   The effects of the terms of trade expressed in GDP terms is given by,

47

$$\Delta P_x \bullet \frac{X}{GDP} \ - \ \Delta P_m \bullet \frac{M}{GDP}$$

where P_x and P_m are the export and import prices (respectively), Δ is a difference operator, and X and M are respectively exports and imports of goods and nonfactor services.

6   Although temporary, the shock would raise permanent incomes.

7   Chamley and Ghanem (1991) conclude from a multivariate analysis of the real exchange rate that both aggregate demand shocks and public expenditure appeared to be positively correlated with REER. However, they were not confident about the robustness of the latter relationship.

8   The results they report for Côte d'Ivoire were based on an unpublished study by Achi Atsain and Allechi M'Bet (Centre for Economic and Social Research, Université Nationale de Côte d'Ivoire, Abidjan).

9   Recall that the unsustainably high investment expenditure led to the destabilization and financial crisis in the first place.

10   The 'big four' commercial banks – Société Générale de Banques en Côte d'Ivoire (SGBI), Banque Internationale pour le Commerce et l'Industrie de la Côte d'Ivoire (BICICI), Société Ivoirienne de Banque (SIB), and Banque Internationale pour l'Afrique Occidentale/Côte d'Ivoire (BIAO/CI) – dominate the Ivorian banking scene. They account for 80% of net domestic credit.

11   Taxes on petroleum and tobacco, coffee and cocoa exports, and rice imports were raised, and VAT was extended to the distribution sector.

12   These were either directly or indirectly due to public sector arrears. Producers not paid by the government (such as exporters suffering from the CSSPPA arrears) defaulted on their credit repayments.

13   Recall that Côte d'Ivoire has a large share of world cocoa sales.

14   These periods differ slightly from the periods of crisis, partial adjustment and fettered adjustment because the trade balance began to widen after 1985 (rather than 1986).

15   The supply response, need not have been the result of adjustment policies, but simply the improvement in commodity prices.

16   Private consumption continued to increase and thus to fuel the external imbalance, but this was not of great quantitative significance.

17   These averages are themselves subject to wide within-group dispersion.

18   These calculations are similar to (but not identical with) those reported earlier from Schiff and Valdés (1992). The exchange rate is assumed to be overvalued by 33 percent in the calculations in Table 1.11.

19   The evidence of the Côte d'Ivoire Living Standards Study discussed in following chapters suggests that poverty among public employees rose steeply in 1987-88. This may well be a result of the salary freeze, as well as the fact that cuts in public employment have been directed mainly at the lower paid, something also suggested by the CILSS data.

20   Edwards (1989) demonstrates that the equilibrium real exchange rate will change as a result of changes in tariffs, government consumption expenditure, and long term capital transfers from the rest of the world. The net effect of these changes on the equilibrium real exchange rate is certain to be complex and to depend on whether the changes are (and are perceived to be) permanent or transitory. Edwards concludes that 'Generally speaking, it is not possible to know how the effect of import tariffs and terms of trade shocks on the equilibrium real exchange rate will be distributed through time' (p. 51).

Annex 1
Annual macroeconomic data for Côte d'Ivoire

	1975	1976	1977	1978	1979	1980	1981
A. GDP and sector growth			(% annual change)				
GDP at market prices	10.2	5.8	-0.2	13.9	2.9	-0.8	4.3
Agriculture	9.4	6.0	-4.4	9.5	0.4	12.9	2.1
Industry	14.5	15.5	10.0	19.1	8.0	8.8	10.0
Services, etc.	18.9	-22.5	-25.6	54.3	8.9	-22.0	9.8
Gross domestic investment	2.8	26.3	43.8	16.4	-7.0	18.5	-21.3
Gross domestic income	4.6	15.0	12.6	8.2	-1.2	-4.5	-0.4
Total consumption	13.3	5.6	1.3	16.3	4.1	-9.1	10.3
Exports (GNFS)	-4.0	11.7	-7.9	5.7	2.3	12.7	6.9
Imports (GNFS)	-2.7	25.7	26.0	14.7	-3.2	6.2	-5.0
B. Prices							
Consumer price index							
(1985 = 100)	35.3	39.5	50.4	56.9	66.4	76.1	82.8
Relative prices							
(1985 = 100)	114.8	112.5	96.6	91.0	87.6	85.6	87.4
Relative inflation							
(1985=100)	94.9	95.2	107.9	110.8	116.9	118.4	113.0
Real interest rate	2.8	3.2	4.0	4.6	5.3	8.0	8.7
C. Terms of trade and							
exchange rate							
Terms of trade							
(1985 = 100)	77.9	100.5	140.2	126.4	112.7	98.1	85.4
Real eff. exchange rate							
(1985 = 100)	101.2	100.0	113.2	121.5	131.0	133.9	119.7
Nominal exchange rate	224.3	248.5	235.3	209.0	201.0	225.8	287.4
D. External accounts			(as % of GDP)				
Current A/C balance							
(Excluding official							
grants)	-10.8	-6.0	-3.5	-11.1	-15.2	-17.5	-16.9
Exports of GNFS	36.7	41.7	42.6	36.5	34.6	34.0	35.2
Imports of GNFS	36.6	36.2	36.3	37.4	37.7	40.1	42.3
Resource balance	0.1	5.5	6.3	-0.9	-3.1	-6.1	-7.1
E. Public finance			(as % of GDP)				
Total expenditure	-	32.6	37.2	42.7	44.0	40.1	38.9
Total revenue	-	28.9	38.1	34.0	33.2	27.8	27.5
Fiscal deficit (-)/Surplus (+)	-	-3.7	0.9	-8.8	-10.8	-12.2	-11.3
F. Investment and savings			(as % of GDP)				
Gross domestic investment	22.4	23.0	27.3	29.8	28.0	28.2	25.9
Public investment	9.2	9.5	10.8	13.3	13.3	9.0	8.8
Private investment	12.8	12.7	15.1	16.3	13.8	17.1	15.5
Gross domestic saving	22.6	28.5	33.6	28.8	24.9	22.2	18.8
Gross national saving	14.5	18.9	25.0	19.2	14.5	10.0	6.8

(Annex 1, cont.)

Annex 1
Annual macroeconomic data for Côte d'Ivoire

1982	1983	1984	1985	1986	1987	1988	1989	1990	1991
(% annual change)									
1.6	-1.2	-1.1	5.2	3.0	-1.2	-1.6	-1.0	-2.6	-1.8
-1.4	-11.0	4.7	-23.0	4.8	1.1	10.1	7.4	2.3	0.1
-15.0	3.1	4.7	-18.3	8.7	14.1	-3.8	-4.5	-7.7	-9.2
22.9	12.0	-13.7	55.9	-0.7	9.0	-2.5	-24.8	18.4	5.5
-13.7	-8.0	-52.1	40.0	-3.3	-11.8	23.6	-38.4	-11.6	0.0
0.8	-0.7	3.6	6.0	4.5	-8.1	-4.4	-5.3	-7.5	0.4
0.7	0.3	5.0	0.5	9.5	-4.1	-6.7	0.7	-8.8	0.0
1.4	-8.0	10.3	-0.4	13.2	1.3	-1.7	12.1	12.1	0.0
-11.0	-9.3	-9.3	-2.4	31.5	-10.1	-5.8	0.5	-2.5	0.0
88.9	94.2	98.2	100.0	106.6	112.2	120.7	122.5	120.6	0.0
88.6	91.7	97.1	100.0	93.0	94.6	93.7	98.8	102.3	102.4
110.9	106.6	103.2	100.0	103.8	99.9	101.4	96.7	91.0	88.3
11.1	9.9	10.3	10.5	9.1	9.5	11.5	13.5	13.3	0.0
83.4	84.9	97.0	100.0	102.8	83.9	77.1	69.0	62.4	63.0
110.4	101.2	100.3	100.0	119.1	125.4	126.2	120.4	125.8	126.3
336.3	417.4	479.6	378.1	322.8	267.0	302.9	289.4	256.4	278.6
(as % of GDP)									
-13.8	-14.1	-1.5	0.6	-3.9	-10.7	-12.6	-13.5	-13.2	-11.9
36.4	36.5	45.8	45.8	39.3	35.4	32.0	34.9	36.7	36.7
39.3	38.2	34.3	32.6	31.8	31.0	29.2	31.8	32.2	31.9
-2.9	-1.7	11.5	13.2	7.5	4.4	2.8	3.0	4.4	4.8
(as % of GDP)									
40.3	40.6	35.5	32.7	31.9	33.7	40.3	40.6	36.2	35.8
27.0	29.6	31.9	31.2	29.0	25.5	25.7	23.1	23.6	22.7
-13.3	-11.0	-3.6	-1.5	-2.9	-8.2	-14.6	-17.6	-12.6	-13.1
(as % of GDP)									
23,2	20.6	10.9	14.6	12.2	11.7	15.1	10.3	9.8	10.5
6.8	6.3	4.6	3.7	4.7	3.9	4.7	3.2	2.8	2.8
14.9	11.9	7.7	9.7	8.3	6.7	7.2	6.8	7.0	7.7
20.3	18.9	22.4	27.8	19.7	16.1	18.0	13.4	14.2	15.2
8.4	6.7	10.8	14.3	7.7	2.6	4.6	-1.6	-3.0	4.0

Source: World Bank and IMF data.

Relative prices index is the domestic consumer price index (CPI) divided by the trade-weighted foreign wholesale price index (FWPI). The relative inflation index is the home country CPI divided by the trade-weighted foreign CPI. The real interest rate is the discount rate adjusted for inflation based on CPI (1985 = 100). The real effective exchange rate index is the nominal effective exchange rate multiplied by the ratio of CPI and divided by weighted foreign wholesale price index. The nominal effective exchange rate is measured as a trade weighted average for Côte d'Ivoire's 20 most important trading partners. An increase in the REER means an appreciation in the exchange rate. External account GDP ratios are based on current CFA francs. IMF data, Report No. SM/91/184, EBS/85/291, EBS/85/113, EBS/84/81, and EBS/81.

2 Data source and methodological issues

In charting the evolution of household welfare and poverty in Côte d'Ivoire between 1985 and 1988 and understanding their regional and socioeconomic patterns, we relied on a range of data, methodological constructs, and weighting indexes. Some have been applied previously in empirical analysis of poverty in Côte d'Ivoire, but many have been newly developed for the analysis in this book. The purpose is not just to generate a precise profile of poverty in Côte d'Ivoire, but also to provide a more useful analysis for guiding policy formulation in the future.

The primary data source: The Côte d'Ivoire Living Standards Survey (CILSS)

Here, we briefly describe the large, rich database on which our analysis is founded. Later in this chapter, we show how we used the panel nature of this survey to support our analysis of the change in poverty as Côte d'Ivoire increasingly experienced economic decline throughout the period of analysis.

The CILSS was conducted from 1985 to 1988 by the Direction de la Statistique, with financial and technical support from the World Bank during the first two years. The sample size each year was 1,600 households and the sample design was a rotating panel – that is, 50 percent of the households were revisited the following year, and the other half was replaced with new households. The survey thus yielded a sequence of four cross-sectional data sets (each of which is representative of the country as a whole), as well as three overlapping panels of approximately 800 households each (1985-86, 1986-87, and 1987-88). The survey collected detailed information on employment, income, expenditures, assets, basic needs, and other socioeconomic characteristics of the households. Over the four years, coverage and methodology of the data collection were held constant so that

53

results are comparable over time (Grootaert, 1986, provides further discussion on the content and methodology of the CILSS). The usefulness of the CILSS data for analysis and policy design has been amply demonstrated by the studies that were carried out with the 1985 data (Deaton and Benjamin, 1988; Glewwe, 1987; Grootaert, 1987; Kanbur, 1990; van der Gaag and Vijverberg, 1989; and many others).

The fact that data were collected for four consecutive years is important to our analysis. The 1985-88 period represents a particularly critical phase in Côte d'Ivoire's process of structural change. Adjustment efforts in Côte d'Ivoire started in 1981, and were sustained for six years. After showing signs of improvement in 1985-86, the economy nosedived in 1987-88, and the government abandoned the structural adjustment program (it was resumed in late 1989). The initial years of CILSS data (1985-86) are thus able to pick up the effects of sustained adjustment, while the latter years (1987-88) reflect the abandonment of the effort and rapid economic decline – in effect, a period of destabilization. This feature is particularly important, because it provides a 'natural' way to disentangle adjustment from recession effects.[1]

The survey results reported in this book suggest large changes in welfare and poverty which occurred in a short period of time. This raises the question about the quality and reliability of the survey data. While the quality of survey data can never be proved in an absolute way, two investigations are possible to provide an assessment of data quality. First, one can review sampling and field procedures that affect sampling and measurement error in the data. As discussed in Annex 1, we reviewed these in detail and made the necessary corrections to compensate for certain sampling deficiencies. Quality control during CILSS data collection and data entry was extraordinary in comparison with usual survey practice (see Ainsworth and Munoz, 1986; Grootaert, 1986; Daho, 1992). The many analyses undertaken with the data have shown that the data have a high degree of internal consistency. This brings us to the second course of investigation: consistency with other data sources – census, other surveys, and national accounts. Such comparisons must be treated with caution, because it is not always clear that the quality of the 'reference data' are better than the quality of the survey results. As we report in Annex 1, household size in the 1988 CILSS closely matched that reported in the 1988 Population Census. Selected demographic variables from the survey have been compared with the Côte d'Ivoire Fertility Survey and were found to be consistent (Ainsworth, 1989). Farming information in the CILSS was evaluated against other sources and found to be quite good (Deaton and Benjamin, 1988). Most important to our analysis is that the pattern of household expenditures observed for Côte d'Ivoire as a whole is entirely consistent with the pattern of evolution at the macroeconomic level recorded in the national accounts and in other macroeconomic data. Both the upturn in

54

1986 and the decline in 1987-88 are picked up by the CILSS data. In summary, we feel confident that the CILSS data are valid data source for exploring the evolution of welfare and poverty, and that its main shortcoming – sampling deficiencies – has been corrected adequately in this research, as explained in Annex 1.

Measuring welfare and poverty: indexes to support the analysis

The welfare index

Household welfare or level of living[2] is a multidimensional concept that captures all aspects of both the direct consumption of goods and services and nonconsumption activities and services (see Grootaert, 1983; Sen, 1987). Direct consumption activities comprise items that are either purchased directly from the market or produced by the household itself. Nonconsumption activities comprise services often provided by the state such as health, education, and access to clean water, that contribute directly and indirectly to a household's level of living. Because the value of these 'basic services' cannot easily be quantified, our analysis in Chapter 3 discusses the direct consumption components of household welfare separately from the household's so-called basic needs (which are the subject of Chapter 4).[3]

Thus, the complete pattern of direct consumption must be quantified into a single indicator of welfare. Of course, the standard economic solution is to convert consumed quantities into a total value as measured by their prices – market prices for actual purchases, and imputed prices for in-home production or in-kind transfer income. The CILSS facilitates the task of imputing prices for all nonpurchased items because it asks households to provide an estimate for their equivalent market value.[4]

The measure of household welfare used in our analysis is thus household expenditures.[5] This measure is preferred over household income for conceptual and pragmatic reasons. Conceptually, household expenditures are a proxy for permanent income or consumption – the ideal measure because it incorporates decisions made by the household over time (for example, using savings to substitute current for future consumption). But estimating this measure requires longitudinal data on household consumption over several years. The two-year panels of the CILSS go some way towards supporting this estimation and this feature of the data is explored in Chapter 5. In developing countries current expenditures are likely to represent permanent income better than does current income, because they tend to be less subject to short-term fluctuations. Moreover, experience with data collection has strongly indicated that expenditures tend to be recorded more accurately than is income. This is especially true in settings where nonmarket income is important.

Using household expenditures as a measure of household welfare requires accounting for the size and composition of the household, because consumption needs vary according to the number of household members and their age and gender. Household size can be accounted for by expressing household expenditures on a per capita basis. Accounting for household composition requires using an adult-equivalent scale. Constructing this scale endogenously – from the data themselves – is a complex exercise fraught with conceptual and practical difficulties, and the literature has not reached consensus about the best procedures (see, for example, Deaton and Muellbauer, 1980). We have not attempted to calculate such a scale for this study. Some analysts have used an exogenously derived scale from another country. For instance, Glewwe (1987) used an adult-equivalent scale based on data from Sri Lanka and Indonesia in his analysis of CILSS data. But we believe that the validity of using equivalent scales across countries has not been proved and is intrinsically very questionable, and thus that using these scales would not necessarily improve upon simple per capita measures.[6]

Prices for consumption items

In any one country, different households may face different prices because they function in different markets. To the extent practical, such differences should be accounted for when household expenditures are used as a welfare measure; the typical procedure for doing so is to deflate household expenditures with a cost of living index. Previous research with the CILSS data has largely been unsuccessful at constructing a comprehensive index. The most complete index was developed by Glewwe (1987), which other researchers have also used (Kanbur, 1990). But Glewwe's index includes only one nonfood item – a can of tomato paste. This item, which constitutes about one percent of an average Ivorian household's nonfood budget, can hardly represent the entire nonfood basket.

We have thus drawn on a richer database to construct a cost of living index – the prices collected in Côte d'Ivoire in 1985 under the auspices of the International Comparisons Project (ICP). Researchers have used these prices to calculate exchange-rate differentials among countries based on purchasing power parity (see Kravis et al., 1982; Eurostat, 1989). However, our application of the ICP data to drawing welfare comparisons *within* a country is a novel approach. In Chapter 6, we provide a detailed investigation of the relevant procedures. Here we briefly summarize that discussion.

We calculated a Paasche regional cost of living index (basis = Abidjan) by matching the prices of 260 product categories from ICP data with expenditure shares for 27 food categories and 25 nonfood categories from the CILSS. The index shows that Abidjan is the highest-cost region in Côte d'Ivoire (Table 2.1). The cost of living in other urban areas is about 8 percent lower, and in rural areas 13 to 25 percent lower. A comparison of our index with Glewwe's index reveals that the latter underestimates cost of living differences in rural areas, but overestimates price differences between Abidjan and other cities.

Table 2.1
Regional cost of living index, 1985-88

Region	1985	1986	1987	1988
Abidjan	100.00	100.00	100.00	100.00
Other cities	92.84	93.62	91.49	92.57
East Forest	87.01	87.01	88.12	86.58
West Forest	78.25	74.66	75.64	72.42
Savannah	75.97	80.12	81.86	81.88

Since ICP price data are available only for 1985, we had to assume that regional differences in prices remained steady for the other years. We did, however, update the expenditure shares for each year and recalculated the cost of living index accordingly. The resulting index is quite stable, except for West Forest and Savannah. The cost of living differential for West Forest increased from about 22 to 28 percent, while for Savannah it fell from 24 to 18 percent. As a result, in 1988, West Forest showed the greatest cost of living difference in relation to Abidjan, consistent with the fact that the erosion of welfare in this region was the most severe: between 1985 and 1988, real household expenditures per capita fell by 41 percent. This decline is likely to have depressed prices. In the Savannah, real household expenditures also declined, but by less than the national average.

Since our analysis involves welfare comparisons over time, it is also necessary to incorporate general price increases over time. To do so, we applied the consumer price index (Table 2.2) uniformly to the regional cost of living index. In other words, we assumed (again) that regional cost of living differences remained constant during the four-year period.

Table 2.2
Consumer price index, 1985-88

	1985	1986	1987	1988
CPI	100.00	107.30	107.75	115.31

Source: IMF, *International Financial Statistics.*

57

After the welfare index and a suitable cost of living deflator are constructed, it is necessary to set a poverty line that distinguishes the poor from the nonpoor. This paper is not the place to review the large body of literature on this topic (see, for example, Sen, 1987; Kanbur, 1987; Ravallion, 1992), but suffice it to say that it constitutes a controversial area in poverty analysis. The two main alternative strategies entail calculating a relative poverty line and an absolute poverty line. An absolute poverty line is frequently based on minimum nutritional intake requirements, which are 'translated' into minimally necessary food expenses to which a nonfood basket deemed to constitute an essential minimum is added. Beyond the issues raised in the literature about the feasibility of both establishing nutritional minimums and converting them into food expenses (see Srinivasan, 1981; Sen, 1987), setting the nonfood minimum is fundamentally arbitrary. The process is clearly influenced by social, cultural, political, and other norms. We make this point not so much to criticize the approach, but to emphasize that an absolute poverty line does contain an arbitrary and relative element.

A relative poverty line is determined entirely by the expenditure data to which it is to be applied. The strategy entails setting a poverty line that cuts off an arbitrarily preselected percentage of the population on the expenditure distribution. An alternative procedure is to set the poverty line at an equally arbitrarily preselected proportion of mean expenditure (Boateng et al., n.d., use this method in a poverty study on Ghana).

Regardless of the strategy chosen, it is important to recognize that the poverty line is a largely arbitrary divider between the poor and the nonpoor. Thus, a sensitivity analysis must be undertaken to ensure that the incidence and patterns of poverty are not unduly altered by small shifts in the line. In practice, policymakers must accept and support the chosen line to ensure that the poverty analysis is policy-relevant.

For this study we have opted to define two poverty lines, based on the relative strategy. The first poverty line – 128,600 CFAF annually – was chosen to cut off the bottom 30 percent of individuals ranked by household expenditure per capita in 1985. The second line – 75,000 CFAF annually – was chosen to identify people in extreme poverty, since it cuts off the bottom 10 percent of the distribution.[7] These thresholds correspond to about one-half and one-third of mean per capita household expenditures, respectively. Our analysis includes a sensitivity analysis of those lines, as well as dominance tests. To analyze the evolution of poverty over time we held the two poverty lines constant *in real terms*. Thus, although the lines were initially selected in a relative way, the analysis over time follows an absolute approach (under a purely relative approach, the incidence of poverty, by definition, does not change over time.

The results of the sensitivity analyses and dominance tests are discussed in greater depth in Chapter 3. Briefly, sensitivity analysis examines whether observed cross-sectional and over-time patterns are robust to changes in the poverty line. We thus recalculated the regional and national poverty measures for alternative poverty lines set at 10 percent below and above the original ones, and found that our analysis and findings are not sensitive to the exact position of the poverty line.

Sensitivity analysis is useful primarily for checking whether the observed general pattern of poverty is robust to relatively small changes in the location of the poverty line. It is useful to expand the inquiry to cover a wider range of poverty lines and also to include changes in poverty measures. This is achieved by dominance analysis – plotting the entire distribution curves for the regions, socioeconomic groups, or years to be compared.

The most stringent test – first-order dominance – plots the cumulative expenditure distribution, showing the cumulative percentage of people at successive levels of expenditures per capita. If this curve for, say, year one lies entirely to the right and below that for year two, then poverty has unambiguously increased between years one and two, regardless of where one draws the poverty line and regardless of the poverty measure used (at least as long as the measure has certain basic desirable properties). If the two distribution curves intersect, the conclusions about changes in poverty will depend upon where one sets the poverty line and may also vary for different poverty measures. In that case, it is possible to restrict the comparison to a narrower class of poverty measures, such as those which reflect the depth of poverty. If one then plots a 'poverty deficit curve' (defined by the area under the cumulative distribution), one can test for second-order dominance. Higher-order dominance tests also exist.[8]

Constructing the poverty index

Our final analytical measure – a poverty index – must summarize information about the incidence and depth of poverty. In line with other recent work (Boateng et al., n.d.; Kakwani, 1990; Kanbur, 1990; Ravallion, 1992) and with the strategy suggested in Grootaert and Kanbur (1990), we have selected the so-called P-alpha class of poverty measures developed by Foster, Greer, and Thorbecke (1984).[9] The general formula is:

$$P_\alpha = \frac{1}{n} \sum_{i=1}^{q} \left(\frac{z - y_i}{z} \right)^\alpha$$

where n = the number of people
      q = the number of poor people
      z = the poverty line
      y_i = the per capita expenditures of individual i
      α = a poverty aversion parameter

The poverty aversion parameter can assume any positive value or zero. The higher the value, the more the index 'weighs' the situation of the extreme poor – that is, the people farthest below the poverty line. Of specific interest are the cases where α = o and α = 1.

If α = o, the index becomes:

$$P_o = \frac{q}{n},$$

which is the simple headcount ratio of poverty – the number of poor people as a percentage of the total population. While this is a useful first indicator, it fails to capture the severity or the depth of poverty. To do so, we must also examine the extent to which the expenditures of poor people fall below the poverty line. This measure is customarily expressed as the 'income gap ratio,' which expresses the average shortfall as a fraction of the poverty line itself:

$$\frac{z - \bar{y}_i}{z},$$

where $\bar{y}_i$ is the average income or expenditure of the poor.

A useful index is obtained when the headcount ratio of poverty is multiplied with the income gap ratio:

$$P_1 = \frac{q}{n}\left(\frac{z - \bar{y}_i}{z}\right),$$

which reflects both the incidence and depth of poverty. This measure has a particularly useful interpretation because it indicates the fraction of the poverty line that each individual would have to contribute in order to eradicate poverty through income transfers, under the assumption of perfect targeting. Since this assumption is not likely to apply in practice, this measure can be considered the minimum amount of resources necessary to eradicate poverty. In the tables in Chapter 3, we show P_0, P_1, and P_2. Since P_2 is more sensitive to the situation of the poorest, a comparison with P_1 can show whether the distribution *among* the poor has deteriorated or improved.

The P-alpha poverty measure is also advantageous because it can be decomposed. For example, the measure at the national level can be expressed as the sum of regional measures weighted by the share of the population of each region:

$$P_\alpha = \sum_{j=1}^{m} k_j P_{\alpha j},$$

where $j = 1,..., m$ regions
$k_j =$ the share of the population of region j

This formulation makes it possible to calculate the 'contribution' c_j of each region to national poverty:

$$c_j = \frac{k_j \ P_{\alpha j}}{P_\alpha}.$$

This feature helps make poverty analysis directly relevant to policymaking. Decompositions along such policy-relevant dimensions as region and socioeconomic group can indicate how macroeconomic events have changed poverty in the country by affecting specific regions or groups. Knowing the share of each region or group in total poverty is essential for targeting interventions. Therefore, in conjunction with presenting the P_α measure for a = 0,1 and 2, the tables in Chapter 3 will also show the decomposition of the measure.

Constructing panel data sets from the CILSS

While the analysis in Chapters 3 and 4 utilizes the four-year cross-sectional data from the CILSS, in Chapter 5 the panel data are utilized. Each year half of the households in the survey were replaced and half of the households were kept in the sample. Thus, of the 1,600 households sampled in 1985, 800 were replaced, but 800 were surveyed again in 1986. The *new* households brought in during 1986 were surveyed again in 1987, and so on. Thus, in principle, we should have three panels of about 800 households each – for 1985-86, 1986-87, and 1987-88. In practice, the construction of the panels is not quite so straightforward and each panel ultimately contained about 700 households.

The main problem stems from the fact that not all households surveyed in the CILSS have a unique identification number. In particular, when during the second survey (one year after the first), enumerators could not locate the same household in the same dwelling, they were instructed to interview the new household living in that dwelling and to keep the same identification number. This less-than-ideal procedure has made it impossible to identify panel households simply by matching identification numbers across survey years. This shortcoming would indeed generate a large number of 'type 2' errors – that is, having the panel capture households that in reality are not the same in the two years. Fortunately, as of 1986, the CILSS contained a supplementary section that, for households originally designated to be resurveyed, reprinted the original household roster and listed membership at the time of the resurvey. Household members present in both rosters were flagged. We retained households in the panel if at least one household member was the same in both years. This 'minimalist' requirement reflects our concern to keep the number of panel households as large as possible and yielded three panels containing respectively 714, 693, and 701 households. Had we increased the requirement to two common members the panels would have contained respectively five percent, eight percent, and 11 percent fewer households. These are significant reductions from panels which are not very large to begin with. More importantly, dropping these households would surely introduce a bias in our results by excluding from analysis the most volatile households – an exclusion which is not likely to be random from the point of view of poverty dynamics. Moreover, volatility in household size and composition is a social reality in Côte d'Ivoire, and it should be retained in the data set as much as possible.

The procedure described so far eliminates 'type 2' error, but it still leaves open the possibility of 'type 1' errors – having panels exclude households that are the same in both years and are thus true panel households. This error would occur if the supplementary section were not filled out for each panel household. The only way to ensure that this error does not occur is by checking the names of household members across both years. Since the data at our disposal contained actual names only for 1987 and 1988, we could check names only for the third panel. Ultimately, we had nine cases of 'type 1' error – about one percent. Thus, we are confident that relying on the supplementary section to identify panel households does not introduce significant error.[10]

We should note two implications of this procedure for constructing panels. First, the requirement that only one household member be the same across the two years means that meaningful statistics for the panels can be computed only at the household level. We indeed have panels of households, but clearly not of individuals. Second, the fact that the retained panels contained 10 to 15 percent fewer households than the originally intended 800 households calls into question whether this attrition biases the representativeness of the panels. The answer is unfortunately affirmative: our comparison of the 'rejected' households with retained households indicates that the per capita expenditure levels of rejected households are systematically higher. Thus, panel results may not accurately represent country averages, and, in terms of poverty analysis, panel results will somewhat overestimate the incidence of poverty. However, the extent of attrition is certainly not such that it invalidates the analysis of the panel data. In fact, in the African context, characterized by high mobility and difficult conditions for survey field work, retaining 85 to 90 percent of households for a panel survey can be considered quite a success. Moreover, since the bias is concentrated at the upper end of the distribution, it will probably have little effect on our analysis of the dynamics of poverty.

In this context, we must also point out that the sample rotation in the CILSS that created the panels – the replacement of 50 percent of the households each year – was accomplished by replacing all households in 50 percent of the survey clusters (as opposed to replacing 50 percent of households in all clusters). This procedure was undertaken because it was simpler to manage in the field, but it does somewhat compromise the precision of estimates from the panels. Together with the attrition problem, this shortcoming implies that, paradoxically, over-time analysis with the CILSS data is best undertaken with four-year comparisons of cross-sectional results. The unique value of the panels is not so much that they provide correct averages of welfare and poverty variables, but that they reveal internal dynamics from one year to the next – and it is this feature that we shall exploit in Chapter 5.

Notes

1   Obviously, this a simplification. Even after the adjustment program was abandoned, some effects continued to bc felt. Likewise, the subsequent economic decline will also take time before it shows up in poverty and basic needs measure.

2   We use the terms 'welfare' and 'level of living' interchangeably. Notwithstanding the name of the Côte d'Ivoire Living Standards Survey, we prefer not to use the term 'standard of living' because it is sometimes applied normatively.

3   Many basic needs are components of both direct and indirect household consumption. For example, even if the state provides health services, the household will usually also augment these services with

its own outlays on health care, either because services are not entirely provided for free by the state, or because they are purchased from a private provider. Only in rare cases will total direct outlays correspond to the total consumption of the household of health services – hence the necessity of reviewing the satisfaction of basic needs beyond the fraction that is captured by the measure of direct consumption.

4   We recognize that this procedure may introduce an element of subjectivity. Yet households may well be in a better position to assess what something is worth in the market that is part of their daily living environment, than is an outside analyst who is trying to impute prices 'objectively' from an estimated model of that market.

5   Johnson et al. (1990) describe how total household expenditures were constructed from the CILSS data.

6   However, in order to check the robustness of our results, we have also calculated the poverty estimates reported in Chapter 3 using an adult equivalent scale (first adult = 1; other adults = 0.7; children = 0.5). This led of course to different levels of poverty, but the regional and socioeconomic patterns of poverty, as well as the overtime trends remained the same. After normalizing the results to obtain the same national poverty incidence in 1985 as with the per capita measure, the regional per equivalent adult indices differed at most by about two percentage points and the socioeconomic indices by about four percentage points. E.g. in 1988 poverty incidence in Savannah was estimated at 67.6 percent instead of 65.2 percent; for export crop farmers the estimate became 51.6 percent instead of 54.8 percent. Over time, poverty was estimated to rise from 30 percent in 1985 to 45 percent in 1988 instead of to 46 percent. These differences are slight enough to confirm the robustness of our results based on per capita measures.

7   The minimum wage is sometimes suggested as the threshold for the poverty line. But using this threshold for Côte d'Ivoire is unsuitable because the guaranteed hourly industrial wage (SMIG) was set at 191.40 CFAF during the 1985-88 period, which adds up to an individual income of 306,240 CFAF annually (on the basis of 1,600 work hours). This figure is almost 50 percent *above* mean expenditures per capita in 1985.

8   Atkinson (1987), Foster and Shorrocks (1988), and Ravallion (1992) provide a further discussion on dominance.

9   Foster (1984) and Atkinson (1987) review poverty measures.

10 For a further discussion of the technical and computational aspects of how the panels were constructed from the CILSS data, see Oh and Venkataraman (1992).

Annex 1
Corrective weights for the CILSS

As part of the research underlying this book, we undertook a detailed review of the sampling procedures and properties of the CILSS. Although the survey sample had been designed to be self-weighting, we found that various errors occurred in practice during the construction of the sample, that require applying expost weights to the data. These errors were brought to light when several anomalies in the survey results were uncovered.

First, household expenditures appeared to be overestimated in Abidjan in 1985 and 1986. This could be traced to an incorrect selection of primary sampling units (PSUs), which generated an overrepresentation of rich areas. To the extent possible, expost weights for Abidjan were constructed to correct the overestimates. The majority of the studies that have used data from the early CILSS years have applied these weights (see earlier citations).

Second, average household size as calculated from the survey declined from about eight to six persons between 1985 and 1988. Demery and Grootaert (1994) have investigated this phenomenon in detail and concluded that it did not correspond to a demographic reality. The culprit was found to be a flawed field procedure for listing the households from which the 1985 and 1986 samples were drawn. There was a bias towards listing larger dwellings, and thus larger households. This bias in the listing was of course reflected in the final sample of the survey. The listing procedures were revised in 1987, and a comparison with 1988 Population Census results indicated that household size derived from the 1987-88 CILSS closely matches census figures. Consequently, the distribution of household size for the 1985 and 1986 samples (and the 1987 panel component derived from the early sample list) was reweighted to eliminate this sampling bias. As Demery and Grootaert have shown, the sampling bias in the 1985-86 data corresponds to an overestimation of poverty in the order of 10 to 15 percent at the national level, and as much as 20 to 30 percent for some regions and socioeconomic groups. The proper correction is thus not trivial, but has serious implications for policy. Unlike the first set of weights (for Abidjan), this correction for household size has not been applied by other researchers. Given the magnitude of the correction, several of the results reported in earlier work may prove not to be robust to this correction for sampling bias.

Third, the share of rural households in the CILSS dropped suddenly between 1986 and 1987, from 57 to 50 percent. Results from the 1988 Population Census indicated that this drop did not correspond to reality. It stemmed from an update of the sampling frame that occurred in 1987 and was based on results from an electoral census (Daho, 1992). The latter proved to have incorrect coverage of households, so that an excessive number of urban PSUs were selected for the sample. With the benefit of hindsight – that is, with the 1988 Population Census results – it became clear that the updated set of PSUs was actually further from reality than was the 1985-86 set. Consequently, we reweighted the 1987 and 1988 regional distribution of households so that it would match census figures. (This reweighting affected only the distribution of the sample *across* strata – that is, regions. In contrast, the revision of the listing procedures in 1987 – which were a great improvement over the early procedures – affected only the second stage of the sampling (that is the listing and selection of households *within* PSUs and strata). This explains why the estimates of household size within each region were correct in 1987-88.)

This reweighting is particularly important for longitudinal comparisons of welfare and poverty, in view of the wide urban-rural welfare differential in Côte d'Ivoire. If one were not to apply these weights, the sudden drop in the percentage of rural households in the sample in 1987 would produce a false drop in the estimated incidence of poverty (given that poverty was much higher in rural than in urban areas).

The three corrective factors discussed herein were combined in one series of household weights to be applied to the data in order to eliminate the three identified sources of sampling bias. The series was normalized to keep degrees of freedom in the data constant (see Oh and Venkataraman, 1992 for details). All tables in this book are based on survey results to which the series of corrective sampling weights have been applied.

66

3 Household expenditure and the incidence of poverty[1]

This chapter presents the main empirical results of our analysis of poverty in Côte d'Ivoire, 1985-88. In view of the country's macroeconomic evolution, as discussed in Chapter 1, the results focus on three themes. First, since our main objective is to interpret observed patterns of welfare and poverty in a macroeconomic context, we compare findings for the 1985-86 period with those for the 1987-88 period. Indeed, totally different macroeconomic scenarios characterize the two periods. In the first period, GDP increased, and the government was actively managing the economy's adjustment program. In 1987-88, this effort was abandoned, and the dominating macroeconomic event was a sharp fall in GDP and aggregate consumption. (In describing these macroeconomic scenarios, we do not imply causality between the adjustment program and the macroeconomic conditions.)

Second, since the main redistributive feature of the adjustment process was a shift in the rural-urban terms of trade toward rural areas, we attempt to determine its effects by disaggregating the results by urban-rural area and region. However, for policy purposes, it is important that we also identify where the poverty and welfare effects were concentrated – that is, who the losers and gainers were. Thus, we disaggregate our results by socioeconomic group.

Third, we attempt to link our results with specific policy measures, particularly those related to the consumer or producer prices of specific commodities (coffee, cocoa, cotton, and rice) or groups of commodities (export crops and food crops). We do so by examining income and expenditure patterns in detail.

The evolution of household expenditures

Table 3.1 shows nominal and real household expenditures per capita for Côte d'Ivoire and for each of the five regions. We first deflated the nominal figures with the regional price index, in order to make expenditure figures comparable *within* each year. We then expressed all expenditures in constant 1985 CFAF by applying the CPI (see Chapter 2).

Table 3.1.A shows average household expenditures per capita calculated from their distribution across all households; Table 3.1.B shows the average calculated from their distribution across individuals. In the household distribution, expenditures per capita are viewed as the welfare level attributable to the household as a unit. This reflects the fact that many decisions pertaining to income/expenditures are made by the household as a unit or are influenced largely by the behavior and the decisions of the head of household. Conversely, one must recognize that conceptually welfare and poverty are individual attributes and are ultimately experienced by individuals. From that point of view, the individual becomes the unit of analysis, and the assumption is then made that household welfare – expressed by expenditures per capita – is distributed evenly across all household members. The literature has not reached consensus about the empirical validity of this assumption, but work by Haddad and Kanbur (1989) suggests that consideration of intrahousehold distribution of consumption does not necessarily invalidate patterns of poverty derived from measures of household expenditures per capita. As shown in Table 3.1, switching from the household to the individual as the unit of analysis lowers average welfare levels, because the size of poor households is above average, and the individual distribution is skewed more to the left than the household distribution.

For purposes of this book, the overriding consideration is the conceptual one – that poverty and welfare are individual attributes – and all remaining calculations are with the individual as the unit of analysis (except where noted).

For the country as a whole, real household expenditures per capita declined by about 30 percent during 1985-88 (Table 3.2). About two-thirds of the decline occurred in 1988, consistent with the real negative growth in GDP in both 1987 and 1988 and with national account figures on aggregate consumption (see Chapter 1). The regional disparity stayed roughly the same during the period: the Abidjan average remained about 2.4 times higher than that of the poorest region – the Savannah. But the relative position of the other regions changed: among urban areas, the welfare decline in Abidjan was less than the country's average, while in other cities the decline exceeded the average. Among rural areas, the largest decline in welfare was recorded in West Forest, which became a poorer region than East Forest. The Savannah

Table 3.1
Nominal and real household expenditures per capita
(CFAF per year; 1985 = 100)

A. Household distribution

	1985	1986	1987	1988
Côte d'ivoire				
Nominal	263,610	260,792	259,043	208,369
Regionally deflated	292,236	289,659	284,806	233,293
Real	292,236	269,953	264,321	202,300
Abidjan				
Nominal	457,812	394,489	477,894	390,778
Regionally deflated	457,812	394,489	477,894	390,778
Real	457,812	367,650	443,521	338,864
Other cities				
Nominal	318,352	340,139	309,319	224,485
Regionally deflated	342,919	363,334	338,080	242,508
Real	342,919	338,615	313,763	210,292
East Forest				
Nominal	166,884	190,907	184,469	173,352
Regionally deflated	191,803	219,423	209,338	200,217
Real	191,803	204,495	194,281	173,618
West Forest				
Nominal	213,423	186,985	160,868	134,149
Regionally deflated	272,748	250,463	212,662	185,225
Real	272,748	233,423	197,366	160,618
Savannah				
Nominal	142,457	163,342	146,291	135,077
Regionally deflated	187,517	203,879	178,699	164,966
Real	187,517	190,009	165,846	143,050

(Table 3.1, cont.)

Table 3.1
Nominal and real household expenditures per capita
(CFAF per year; 1985 = 100)

B. Individual distribution

	1985	1986	1987	1988
Côte d'Ivoire				
Nominal	213,634	216,173	212,191	178,051
Regionally deflated	237,853	240,250	233,780	199,587
Real	237,853	223,905	216,965	173,072
Abidjan				
Nominal	376,108	335,698	401,220	332,938
Regionally deflated	376,108	335,698	401,220	332,938
Real	376,108	312,859	372,361	288,708
Other cities				
Nominal	252,387	271,758	246,469	190,190
Regionally deflated	271,864	290,290	269,385	205,460
Real	271,864	270,540	250,010	178,165
East Forest				
Nominal	143,104	160,890	159,491	152,267
Regionally deflated	164,472	184,922	180,993	175,864
Real	164,472	172,341	167,974	152,501
West Forest				
Nominal	187,120	163,782	138,380	120,225
Regionally deflated	239,134	219,383	182,934	165,999
Real	239,134	204,457	169,776	143,947
Savannah				
Nominal	115,910	132,968	120,017	113,957
Regionally deflated	152,573	165,967	146,605	139,172
Real	152,573	154,676	136,061	120,684

Note: The basis for regional deflation is Abidjan.

70

Table 3.2
Pattern of real household expenditures per capita, by region
(index; Côte d'Ivoire, 1985 = 100)

Region	1985	1986	1987	1988	1988/85
A. Household distribution					
Abidjan	156.7	125.8	151.8	116.0	0.74
Other cities	117.3	115.9	107.4	72.0	0.61
East Forest	65.6	70.0	66.5	59.4	0.91
West Forest	93.3	79.9	67.5	55.0	0.59
Savannah	64.2	65.0	56.8	49.0	0.76
Côte d'Ivoire	100.0	92.4	90.4	69.2	0.69
B. Individual distribution					
Abidjan	158.1	131.5	156.6	121.4	0.77
Other cities	114.3	113.7	105.1	74.9	0.66
East Forest	69.1	72.5	70.6	64.1	0.93
West Forest	100.5	86.0	71.4	60.5	0.60
Savannah	64.1	65.0	57.2	50.7	0.79
Côte d'Ivoire	100.0	94.1	91.2	72.8	0.73

remained Côte d'Ivoire's poorest region during 1985-88, but its average expenditure level declined by less than the national average.

The evolution of poverty

The 30 percent decline in household expenditures per capita during 1985-88 has significantly increased poverty and extreme poverty in Côte d'Ivoire (Tables 3.3 and 3.4). The proportion of the population that was poor rose from 30 percent to 45.9 percent, and the proportion that was extreme poor rose from 10 percent to 14.1 percent. Thus, in Côte d'Ivoire about 2.8 million people were poor in 1986, and 4.8 million people were poor in 1988 – an increase of 71 percent. In 1985, about 940,000 people were living in extreme poverty; in 1988, this figure had risen to 1.5 million – an increase of 57 percent.

The key observation is that the pattern of change in poverty and extreme poverty for 1985-86 differs from the pattern for 1987-88. As discussed in Chapter 1, 1985-86 were the final two years of the adjustment effort that began in 1981, and were also marked by a brief economic upturn. In contrast, when the upturn ended in 1987, the government abandoned the adjustment program, and a severe economic decline had set in by 1988.[2] Between 1985 and 1986, the incidence of poverty did not change, while the incidence of extreme poverty fell by more than a third. In 1987, the incidence of both poverty and extreme poverty rose and the increase accelerated sharply in 1988. In 1988 alone, the incidence of poverty rose by 32 percent, and the incidence of extreme poverty by 55 percent. Obviously, the juxtaposition of these results does not prove causality between the adjustment effort and the sustained or lower level of poverty, but it does indicate two things. First, the incidence of poverty in a country can change dramatically from one year to another. This suggests that mobility into poverty and also possibly out of it can be great, and that poverty must be monitored on a regular basis – at least annually. As we explained in Chapter 2, the CILSS contains panel data that are more suitable than the cross-sectional approach herein for investigating mobility into and out of poverty. Work on this panel component (see Chapter 6) confirms the existence of a 'hard-core' type of poor, but also indicates that a large proportion of the poor change from year to year. Second, the large increase in poverty in 1988 indicates that the 'trickle down' from economic recession and destabilization can be rapid, severely affecting the welfare of households and individuals.[3]

The increase in the incidence of poverty noted for Côte d'Ivoire as a whole did not occur to the same degree in each region. The regional pattern of poverty displayed in Tables 3.3 and 3.4 and the regional decomposition of the poverty index provide a first clue about the extent to which the observed changes in poverty can be related to the macroeconomic evolution. The main observation is that in Abidjan and other cities poverty rose more rapidly than did the national average. However, the base from which this increase occurred was quite small, since the incidence of poverty in cities, especially Abidjan, was quite low in 1985. The decomposition of P_0 reported in Table 3.3.B shows that the share of urban poverty in total poverty in the country rose from 19.1 percent in 1985 to 24.5 percent in 1988. This is consistent with the wage-freeze policy of the adjustment program and with its overall tendency to shift the terms of trade in favor of rural areas. Among the latter, however, a major shift occurred: in West Forest, the incidence of poverty more than tripled, making it the second poorest region in 1988 (in 1985, it had the second lowest incidence of poverty among all regions). The reason for this sharp decline pertains to the socioeconomic composition of this region – it is the prime cocoa and coffee growing area, four-fifths of households are farmers, and farm income fell very sharply during the period (see below).

Table 3.3

Incidence of poverty in Côte d'Ivoire, by region: 1985-88
(poverty line = 128,600 CFAF per year)

Region	1985			1986			1987			1988		
	P_0	P_1	P_2	P_0	P_1	P_2	P_0	P_1	P_2	P_0	P_1	P_2
A. P-alpha measures												
Abidjan	0.034	0.009	0.004	0.166	0.035	0.012	0.074	0.019	0.009	0.139	0.023	0.006
Other cities	0.236	0.075	0.037	0.223	0.062	0.024	0.224	0.053	0.019	0.410	0.106	0.040
East Forest	0.479	0.155	0.069	0.395	0.115	0.045	0.435	0.111	0.041	0.494	0.145	0.062
West Forest	0.178	0.036	0.013	0.200	0.042	0.013	0.376	0.102	0.043	0.553	0.154	0.064
Savannah	0.502	0.183	0.088	0.481	0.142	0.058	0.578	0.197	0.093	0.652	0.258	0.131
Côte d'Ivoire	0.300	0.098	0.045	0.299	0.082	0.032	0.348	0.101	0.043	0.459	0.142	0.063
B. Decomposition (percent)												
Abidjan	2.3	1.8	1.6	11.0	8.4	7.8	3.9	3.6	3.8	5.2	2.8	1.5
Other cities	16.8	16.3	17.6	17.1	17.4	17.3	14.6	12.0	10.0	19.3	16.1	13.7
East Forest	37.1	36.8	35.3	31.8	33.7	34.5	29.3	25.8	22.4	25.5	24.1	23.3
West Forest	8.3	5.1	4.1	9.2	7.1	5.5	11.8	11.1	11.0	18.6	16.8	15.6
Savannah	35.6	39.9	41.4	30.9	33.3	34.9	40.3	47.5	52.9	31.4	40.2	45.9
Total	100.0	100.0	100.0	100.0	100.0	100.0	100.0	100.0	100.0	100.0	100.0	100.0

Note: Calculations for the P-alpha measures are discussed in Chapter 2.

73

Table 3.4
Incidence of extreme poverty in Côte d'Ivoire, by region: 1985-1988
(poverty line = 75,000 CFAF per year)

Region	1985			1986			1987			1988		
	P_0	P_1	P_2	P_0	P_1	P_2	P_0	P_1	P_2	P_0	P_1	P_2
						A. P-alpha measures						
Abidjan	0.007	0.002	0.001	0.014	0.005	0.002	0.017	0.006	0.003	0.000	0.000	0.000
Other cities	0.080	0.025	0.014	0.055	0.009	0.002	0.047	0.007	0.001	0.073	0.016	0.005
East Forest	0.132	0.038	0.016	0.095	0.019	0.007	0.086	0.015	0.004	0.139	0.033	0.011
West Forest	0.016	0.005	0.003	0.019	0.002	0.000	0.093	0.024	0.009	0.161	0.031	0.010
Savannah	0.226	0.053	0.019	0.121	0.025	0.008	0.194	0.057	0.022	0.305	0.088	0.034
Côte d'Ivoire	0.100	0.027	0.011	0.064	0.013	0.004	0.091	0.023	0.008	0.141	0.035	0.013
						B. Decomposition (percent)						
Abidjan	1.4	1.4	1.1	4.3	8.0	10.5	3.4	4.7	5.8	0.0	0.0	0.0
Other cities	17.1	20.4	26.8	19.6	15.9	12.6	11.8	6.7	4.1	11.1	9.6	8.6
East Forest	31.0	32.9	32.3	35.7	36.5	37.8	22.1	15.9	11.8	23.3	22.2	20.5
West Forest	2.2	2.8	3.9	4.2	2.0	1.3	11.1	11.5	11.6	17.6	13.5	11.8
Savannah	48.3	42.5	35.9	36.2	37.7	37.8	51.7	61.3	66.7	47.9	54.7	59.2
Total	100.0	100.0	100.0	100.0	100.0	100.0	100.0	100.0	100.0	100.0	100.0	100.0

Note: Calculations for the P-alpha measures are discussed in Chapter 2.

Although the increase in poverty in the Savannah was well below the national average, it remained Côte d'Ivoire's poorest region in 1988; with a 65.2 percent incidence of poverty, it accounted for almost one third of all poor.

Although the countrywide evolution of extreme poverty between 1985 and 1988 paralleled the evolution of poverty, the regional pattern was not the same. In particular, the incidence of extreme poverty did not increase in urban areas. The main increase occurred in West Forest, where the incidence of extreme poverty rose tenfold, from 1.6 to 16.1 percent. Equally important was the 22.6 to 30.5 percent increase in the Savannah, implying that Savannah accounted for almost half of all extreme poor in Côte d'Ivoire in 1988. In fact, one of every two poor persons in the Savannah was in extreme poverty. Obviously, this region remains a prime target for poverty-oriented policy interventions.

Depth of poverty

We examine the depth of poverty on the basis of P_1 and P_2 in Tables 3.3 and 3.4. Over time, these two measures display the same pattern as does P_0, but less pronounced. For example, P_2 for overall poverty rose from .045 to .063 between 1985 and 1988 – a 40 percent increase, as opposed to a 53 percent rise in P_0. Thus, conditions among the people at the very bottom of the distribution deteriorated relatively less than for the poor as whole. In one region, East Forest, P_2 was actually lower in 1988 than in 1985.

In order to distinguish the evolution of the depth of poverty more clearly from the incidence of poverty, we examine the mean expenditure level of each poverty group and the expenditure gap ratio – the mean proportionate shortfall of expenditures from the poverty line (see Chapter 2). As shown in Table 3.5, mean expenditures per capita for both the poor and the extreme poor increased between 1985 and 1986 but fell thereafter (although the 1988 mean was still two percent above the 1985 mean). In contrast, the mean expenditures of the nonpoor fell by 19 percent during the period.[4]

Similarly, the expenditure gap ratio for the poor and extreme poor declined between 1985 and 1986; that is, the distance of the average poor person's expenditures from the poverty line diminished. In 1987 and 1988, the ratio increased, indicating that the poor became poorer during that period (in addition to the fact that the number of poor people increased).

Both the difference in the evolution of mean expenditures per capita between the poor and the nonpoor and the difference in the trends between 1985-86 and 1987-88 indicate that one intent of the adjustment program – to shift the burden of adjustment to the better-off – may have in fact been realized. They also show that the rich have not been shielded from the recession in 1987-88.

The figures in Tables 3.3 to 3.5 provide some useful guidance for designing and targeting policy interventions to alleviate poverty. First and foremost, the results show that efforts to alleviate poverty have become much more necessary in view of the sharp rise in poverty. Second, the main target zones are West Forest, where poverty has risen most rapidly, and Savannah, where extreme poverty affects one third of the rural population. Together, the two zones account for half of all poor in Côte d'Ivoire. Third, urban poverty is rising in Côte d'Ivoire and will require greater attention. Fourth, the rapid evolution and shifting pattern of poverty indicate that the phenomenon must be monitored regularly at the subnational level.

Table 3.5
Mean household expenditures per capita and
expenditure gap ratio, by poverty status

Poverty status	1985	1986	1987	1988	Change: 1985-88
	Household expenditures per capita (CFAF a year)				
Extreme poor	55,008	60,087	56,447	56,222	+2.2%
Poor	86,781	93,280	91,395	88,752	+2.3%
Nonpoor	302,767	279,731	284,095	244,547	-19.2%
Côte d'Ivoire	237,853	223,905	216,965	173,072	-27.2%
	Expenditure gap ratio				
Extreme poor	0.272	0.203	0.253	0.248	-8.8%
Poor	0.326	0.274	0.290	0.309	-5.2%

How much resources are necessary to eradicate poverty?

The poverty indices (especially P_1) are useful to estimate the size of resources needed to eradicate poverty. If it was possible to perfectly target resources to the poor, then, in 1985 a total amount of 118.5 billion CFAF (P_1 x poverty line x population) would have been needed to bring the expenditure of all poor up to the level of the poverty line. This represented 3.8 percent of GDP in that year. One particularly troublesome aspect of a rise in poverty in combination with economic decline is that the share of GDP needed to potentially eliminate poverty increases faster than poverty itself. Between 1985 and 1988, the incidence of poverty rose by about 50 percent, but the minimum share of GDP needed to raise the expenditure of the poor to the poverty line almost doubled to 7.2 percent. This also implies that the minimum economic growth rate needed to achieve significant poverty reductions increases. Assuming a 'steady state' without structural shifts and assuming that the poor benefit from increases in aggregate consumption in proportion to their share in aggregate consumption, a three percent per capita real growth from 1985 on would have had to be sustained for six years in order to bring the expenditure of the current poor to the poverty line. In 1988, the same growth rate would take almost 12 years to achieve the same effect. To put this in historical perspective, given that population growth exceeds three per cent per annum, no less than a repeat of Côte d'Ivoire's pre-1980 'miracle' growth performance would be needed to make such poverty reduction possible. To the extent that such performance is unlikely, targeted poverty alleviation policies may well be needed. Our results suggest that the main target zones would have to be West Forest, where poverty has risen fastest, and Savannah, where extreme poverty affects one-third of the rural population. The rising trend in urban poverty will also require increasing policy attention and resources.

The socioeconomic pattern of poverty

In order to understand how changes in welfare and poverty pertain to macroeconomic events, we use the decomposition property of the P_α measures to estimate how poverty changed among socioeconomic groups in Côte d'Ivoire and what contribution it made to total poverty. For this purpose, we define socioeconomic groups according to the household's main source of income and/or the main economic activity of the head of household. Since many of the adjustment measures were geared towards certain types of income earners (for example, government and parastatal employees, and export crop farmers), this classification of households provides a direct link with the macroeconomy.

We defined eight mutually exclusive socioeconomic groups. First, we distinguished between farming and nonfarming households. A farming household had cultivated fields during the survey's reference year, and derived more than 50 percent of its earned income from agricultural activities. Second, in view of the importance of policy measures related to export crops, we divided farmers into export crop and food crop farmers. Export crop farmers derived more than 50 percent of farm revenue from the sale of export crops. Third, we subdivided nonfarming households according to main sectors of employment and the work status of the head of household. We distinguished inactive, unemployed, self-employed, and employed (wage-earner) heads of household, based on standard ILO definitions of these concepts. We divided wage earners further into sectors. The public sector consisted of government and parastatal enterprises. The private sector consisted of formal or informal employment, depending whether employees received any form of legal or social protection associated with the formal sector. The CILSS recorded several attributes useful for this purpose, such as whether the employee had a written contract, whether there was a union at the workplace, whether minimum wages applied, and whether the employee received social security benefits (pension, paid leave, paid sick leave, and so forth). In view of the fact that benefits are provided only infrequently, an employee was considered to be in the formal sector if he/she was the beneficiary of at least one of these benefits (Grootaert, 1987 and 1992, provides more in-depth discussion and analysis of the distinction between formal and informal employment).

Tables 3.6 and 3.7 show that the incidence and depth of poverty varied a great deal across different socioeconomic groups as did the over-time patterns. On a relative basis, poverty increased the most for households of public sector employees, no doubt as a result of the salary freeze and subsequent low increases. Of course, they started from a very low basis, and in 1988, they still made up only 6.2 percent of the poor (but this represents about 20 percent of all urban poor). Their depth of poverty rose markedly and the expenditure gap ratio almost doubled from 0.14 to 0.23. The pronounced increase in P_2 suggests that this affected predominantly lower-skilled civil servants at the bottom of the earnings scale who were unable to compensate for the real decline in their incomes. Bonuses and in-kind benefits for civil servants increased substantially during this period, as a way to circumvent the salary caps, but these were typically given to civil servants at the middle and upper management levels. From a policy point of view, this suggests that special protective measures for government employees on the lower part of the civil salaries scale would have been in order (possibly even exempting them from the caps).

In the modern private sector, average wages continued to rise through most of the eighties, and adjustment to the crisis was done through employment reductions. While there can be little question that wage rigidity is a hallmark of the Ivorian labor market, part of the increase in average wages is explained by changes in the skill mix over the period. Indeed, the employment reduction mostly occurred among unskilled workers. For those who remained employed, the real purchasing power of their wages fell more for those with lower levels of qualification (Levy and Newman, 1989). As a result, the inequality in the distribution of wage income increased and poverty rose among formal sector employees.

Table 3.6
Incidence of poverty in Côte d'Ivoire, by socioeconomic group: 1985-88
(poverty line = 128,600 CFAF per year)

Socioeconomic group	1985			1986			1987			1988		
	P_0	P_1	P_2	P_0	P_1	P_2	P_0	P_1	P_2	P_0	P_1	P_2
A. P-alpha measures												
Export crop farmer	0.366	0.094	0.038	0.354	0.099	0.037	0.477	0.150	0.063	0.548	0.179	0.087
Food crop farmer	0.434	0.144	0.065	0.411	0.121	0.048	0.473	0.132	0.055	0.590	0.196	0.087
Publ. sector employee	0.049	0.007	0.001	0.056	0.006	0.001	0.072	0.016	0.006	0.213	0.050	0.018
Private formal sector employee	0.071	0.014	0.005	0.096	0.009	0.001	0.061	0.012	0.004	0.151	0.025	0.007
Inform. sec. employee	0.262	0.075	0.028	0.401	0.097	0.028	0.364	0.090	0.040	0.542	0.183	0.093
Self-employed	0.262	0.104	0.058	0.287	0.077	0.030	0.333	0.084	0.033	0.462	0.127	0.052
Inactive	0.183	0.075	0.043	0.211	0.047	0.015	0.327	0.141	0.080	0.319	0.080	0.031
Unemployed	0.041	0.005	0.001	0.346	0.119	0.067	0.312	0.049	0.009	0.383	0.151	0.076
Côte d'Ivoire	0.300	0.098	0.045	0.299	0.082	0.032	0.349	0.101	0.043	0.459	0.142	0.063
B. Decomposition (percent)												
Export crop farmer	14.5	11.5	10.0	21.8	22.2	21.6	25.9	28.0	27.9	17.7	18.7	20.6
Food crop farmer	63.6	65.2	63.8	51.2	54.9	56.4	48.8	47.2	46.4	52.4	56.2	56.9
Publ. sector employee	1.7	0.8	0.3	2.4	1.0	0.4	3.0	2.4	1.9	6.2	4.8	3.8
Private formal sector employee	2.4	1.4	1.1	2.3	0.7	0.3	1.5	1.0	0.8	3.0	1.6	1.0
Inform. sec. employee	1.5	1.3	1.0	1.8	1.6	1.2	1.8	1.5	1.6	1.6	1.7	2.0
Self-employed	12.8	15.6	18.7	14.1	13.8	14.0	12.9	11.3	10.3	14.8	13.2	12.2
Inactive	3.3	4.2	5.1	4.9	4.0	3.4	5.6	8.3	11.1	3.5	2.8	2.4
Employed	0.2	0.1	0.0	1.5	1.8	2.7	0.6	0.3	0.1	0.9	1.1	1.3
Total	100.0	100.0	100.0	100.0	100.0	100.0	100.0	100.0	100.0	100.0	100.0	100.0

Table 3.7
Incidence of extreme poverty in Côte d'Ivoire, by socioeconomic group: 1985-88
(poverty line = 75,000 CFAF per year)

Socioeconomic group	1985			1986			1987			1988		
	P_0	P_1	P_2	P_0	P_1	P_2	P_0	P_1	P_2	P_0	P_1	P_2
A. P-alpha measures												
Export crop farmer	0.086	0.020	0.006	0.081	0.013	0.004	0.148	0.031	0.009	0.210	0.058	0.022
Food crop farmer	0.150	0.036	0.013	0.101	0.020	0.006	0.111	0.029	0.010	0.197	0.047	0.016
Publ. sector employee	0.003	0.000	0.000	0.000	0.000	0.000	0.009	0.002	0.001	0.039	0.005	0.001
Private formal sector employee	0.008	0.002	0.001	0.000	0.000	0.000	0.013	0.001	0.000	0.007	0.002	0.001
Inform. sec. employee	0.099	0.004	0.001	0.000	0.000	0.000	0.067	0.028	0.016	0.220	0.071	0.026
Self-employed	0.115	0.043	0.025	0.052	0.012	0.005	0.070	0.015	0.004	0.107	0.027	0.009
Inactive	0.063	0.032	0.021	0.028	0.005	0.001	0.176	0.065	0.032	0.072	0.013	0.006
Unemployed	0.000	0.000	0.000	0.137	0.061	0.027	0.000	0.000	0.000	0.088	0.049	0.028
Côte d'Ivoire	0.100	0.027	0.011	0.064	0.013	0.004	0.092	0.023	0.008	0.140	0.035	0.012
B. Decomposition (percent)												
Export crop farmer	10.4	8.8	5.7	23.2	19.2	17.0	30.7	25.7	20.8	22.2	24.7	26.3
Food crop farmer	66.5	60.2	51.5	59.1	58.1	55.1	43.8	45.1	43.6	57.3	55.2	53.7
Publ. sec. employee	0.3	0.0	0.0	0.0	0.0	0.0	1.4	1.3	1.4	3.7	2.0	1.4
Private formal sector employee	0.8	0.8	0.5	0.0	0.0	0.0	1.2	0.2	0.0	0.4	0.6	0.5
Inform. sec. employee	1.7	0.3	0.1	11.9	14.1	17.7	1.3	2.1	3.5	2.1	2.7	2.8
Self-employed	16.9	23.5	32.2	3.1	2.5	2.2	10.2	8.6	7.1	11.1	11.4	10.8
Inactive	3.4	6.5	10.0	2.7	6.1	8.0	11.4	16.9	23.6	2.5	1.9	2.3
Employed	0.0	0.0	0.0				0.0	0.0	0.0	0.7	1.5	2.3
Total	100.0	100.0	100.0	100.0	100.0	100.0	100.0	100.0	100.0	100.0	100.0	100.0

Many of the workers laid off from the formal sector had to find new jobs in the informal sector. As a result, during the 1980s the employment pattern in Côte d'Ivoire changed dramatically. As Table 3.8 shows, modern sector employment fell by 14 percent, employment in the informal sector more than doubled, and unemployment tripled. In 1980, the informal sector was smaller than the modern sector, but in 12 years time it has become almost three times the size of the modern sector and now accounts for three quarters of urban employment. This appears to be an impressive growth rate in the midst of a protracted economic crisis, but there is a little doubt that the informal sector hides a lot of underemployment and low productivity work. In 1985, average annual earnings in the informal sector were around 360,000 CFAF, which is only one-fifth of those in the formal sector (Grootaert, 1987). It is no surprise, therefore, that poverty incidence among informal sector workers (employees as well as self-employed) was the highest (26 percent) of any urban group. Between 1985 and 1988, poverty incidence in this group doubled to about 50 percent.

Table 3.8
Employment in Côte d'Ivoire, 1980-1992 ('000 persons)

	1980	1985	1990	1992	Change 1980-1992
Agriculture	2,284	2,547	2,964	3,150	+ 38%
Modern sector	440	405	385	380	- 14%
Informal sector	430	678	964	1,090	+ 153%
Unemployment	110	182	280	330	+ 200%
Total	3,264	3,812	4,593	4,950	+ 52%
Share modern sector	13.5%	10.6%	8.4%	7.7%	-
Share informal sector	13.2%	17.8%	21.0%	22.0%	-
Unemployment rate	3.4%	4.7%	6.1%	6.7%	-

Source: Côte d'Ivoire, Annuaire Statisque du Travail, 1992.

However, increases in P_1 and P_2 were much more pronounced for informal sector employees suggesting a substantial deterioration for those employees at the bottom of the earnings scale. The figures also reveal an important dichotomy within the informal sector. Poverty incidence rose less for self-employed workers than for employees. While for the latter the expenditure gap ratio (the ratio of P_1 over P_0) worsened from 0.29 to 0.34, for the self employed it fell from 0.40 to 0.27. While P_2 for informal sector employees more than tripled, it declined for the self-employed. Similarly, extreme poverty declined between 1985 and 1988 for the self-employed but doubled for the employees. This suggests that the ownership of a small enterprise can serve as a buffer against economic decline, and that in time of hardship employees in small enterprises will be the first to suffer.

This dichotomy in the informal sector has been observed before and was found to be linked to the human capital of various types of workers. Own account workers have more formal education and longer work experience (Grootaert, 1992). Although they are not a large group, accounting from only 1.6 percent of the poor, informal sector employees have the highest incidence of poverty (54 percent) and of extreme poverty (22 percent) of any urban socioeconomic group. They should be a prime target group for urban poverty alleviation efforts.

The situation of the informal sector has an important gender dimension, since the informal sector is almost the sole source of employment for urban women. Less than one in ten employed women in Ivorian cities finds a job in the modern sector. The poverty and vulnerability in the informal sector thus hits women disproportionately (Table 3.9).

Table 3.9
Labor force distribution, by gender, 1992

	Male	Female
Agriculture	60.6%	66.9%
Modern sector	12.9%	2.0%
Informal sector	15.6%	29.0%
Unemployment	10.9%	2.1%
Total	100.0%	100.0%

From a policy perspective, it has to be recognized that the continued rapid population growth in Côte d'Ivoire implies high and growing annual influxes of new labor market entrants. The informal sector will have to absorb an increasing share of them. A policy to promote this sector will thus not only have to be a cornerstone of growth policy, but will play an equally vital role in antipoverty policy.

Among farmers, the incidence of poverty was highest among food crop farmers, but poverty rose more rapidly among export crop farmers. In fact, the representation of food crop farmers among all poor fell significantly during the four years, from 63.6 to 52.4 percent. The depth of poverty and the incidence of extreme poverty also became a more severe problem among export crop farmers. This confirms the regional shifts observed earlier and points at an important failure of the adjustment program's objective to protect incomes of export crop farmers.

A more in-depth understanding of these trends would come from the simultaneous consideration of regional and socioeconomic patterns, since socioeconomic groups are not distributed equally across regions. Unfortunately, the CILSS sample size is too small to permit this; a cross-tabulation of region by socioeconomic group yields a table that contains 40 cells, but almost half of the cells contain less than 30 observations. However, a meaningful cross-tabulation can be made for farmers and rural regions (Table 3.10). The cross-tabulation shows that the distribution of types of farmers across the regions remains fairly stable over time. The main change is an increase in the number of export crop farmers in the Savannah (due to an increase in production of cotton in that region).

Table 3.10
Distribution of farmers across rural regions

Rural region	Export crop farmers			Food crop farmers		
	1985	1988	Change: 1985-88	1985	1988	Change: 1985-88
	Distribution of individuals (percent)					
E. Forest	51.4	45.8	-10.9	32.3	29.9	-7.4
W. Forest	30.7	31.4	+2.3	19.0	21.8	+14.7
Savannah	9.4	16.9	+79.8	41.0	41.1	+0.2
Total*	91.5	94.1	+2.8	92.3	92.8	+0.5
	Average household expenditures per capita (CFAF a year)					
E. Forest	181,031	146,344	-19.2%	147,667	157,312	+6.5%
W. Forest	239,000	158,550	-33.7%	250,298	132,519	-47.1%
Savannah	116,605	87,406	-25.0%	152,800	118,332	-22.6%
	Farm income (CFAF a year)					
E.Forest	1,268,456	1,123,182	-11.4%	587,029	611,293	+4.1%
W. Forest	1,115,022	798,630	-28.4%	971,953	507,687	-47.8%
Savannah	847,434	529,456	-37.5%	642,770	564,564	-12.2%

* The totals do not equal 100 percent because some farmers are located in areas designated as urban in the CILSS.

More important, the cross-tabulation shows that welfare levels within each farmer category differed a great deal across regions and changed differently over time. The average household expenditures of export crop farmers in West Forest were more than twice those of their colleagues in the Savannah in 1985, but they declined much more rapidly. The household expenditures of food crop farmers in West Forest also fell sharply: a 47 percent drop between 1985 and 1988. The increased incidence of extreme poverty among export crop farmers is concentrated in West Forest and the Savannah; in the latter region, the average household expenditures of these farmers was barely above the extreme poverty line. The relative improvement among food crop farmers was due largely to the figures for East Forest, where the welfare level showed an absolute increase. As shown in Table 3.10 the reasons for the change in welfare are due to the evolution of farm income. The farm income of export crop farmers in West Forest fell by almost half during the four-year period; as such, the large rise in poverty is not surprising.

The CILSS results show that farmers received the official unit price for their crops, but that their revenue from the sale of coffee and cocoa fell sharply, due to a reduction in the quantity sold (Table 3.11). In turn, the reduction in quantity reflected the diminished cropping area devoted to these two crops, but the reduction was also much less than the fall in output sold, suggesting declining yields. Although this pattern occurred for both cocoa and coffee, it was much more pronounced for coffee. It was also much more pronounced in West Forest than in East Forest. One lesson from these findings is that price-support measures for export crops are not sufficient for ensuring sustained production and income for farmers. It would be desirable to accompany price measures with a comprehensive support system, including extension services, the provision of farm inputs, and so forth.

Table 3.11
Average area under production and sales of cocoa and
coffee per farmer in East and West Forest, 1985 and 1988

Crop	East Forest			West Forest		
	1985	1988	Change: 1985-88	1985	1988	Change: 1985-88
			Area under production (hectares)			
Cocoa	4.37	4.25	-2.7%	3.08	3.36	+9.1%
Coffee	3.69	3.12	-15.5%	3.98	3.00	-24.6%
			Quantity sold (kilograms)			
Cocoa	2,067	1,870	-10.5%	2,121	1,043	-50.8%
Coffee	1,858	1,252	-32.6%	2,773	978	-64.7%

The findings on the patterns of poverty among socioeconomic groups lead to two policy considerations. First, in general, poverty has become more widespread across the socioeconomic spectrum in Côte d'Ivoire – meaning that targeting the poor effectively will become more necessary, but also more difficult. Second, the results show no evidence that one of the objectives of the structural adjustment program – the promotion of export crops through price supports – has led to reduced poverty among these farmers. However, given that coffee and cocoa are both tree crops, the price incentives are likely to have had mainly long term effects, which may not have been picked up in the four-year period of CILSS data. If one views the longer period 1975-1985, domestic coffee and cocoa prices more than doubled and production as well as farm incomes rose. After four years of price stability, official producer prices of coffee and cocoa were cut in half in 1989. This measure may well have led to higher poverty among export crop farmers. However, the main lesson is that in the short run price measures are not a dominant determinant of poverty incidence among farmers.

How robust are the findings?

Sensitivity analysis

As we explained in Chapter 2, the two poverty lines on which this analysis is based were selected so as to cut off in the initial year 30 percent and 10 percent of individuals ranked by household expenditures per capita. The selection of these cutoff points was of course arbitrary – we argued that the key issue was to keep the poverty lines constant over time in real terms to support a consistent assessment of the evolution of poverty. However, a sensitivity analysis is essential for examining whether observed cross-sectional and longitudinal patterns are robust to changes in the poverty line. We thus recalculated the regional and national P_α measures for alternative poverty lines set at 10 percent below and above the original ones. The results are that levels of poverty decreased or increased accordingly, but by more than 10 percent (Tables 3.12 and 3.13). This result is normal, and will be obtained as long as the poverty line is below the median, given that the expenditure distribution is skewed to the left.

More important is that Tables 3.12 and 3.13 show that the same cross-sectional patterns and longitudinal trends are observed as with the original lines. This pattern confirms that the analysis and findings presented thus far are not sensitive to the exact position of the poverty line.

Dominance test

Sensitivity analysis is useful primarily for examining whether the observed general pattern of poverty is robust to relatively small changes in the location of the poverty line. It is possible to expand the inquiry to cover a wider range

Table 3.12
Incidence of poverty in Côte d'Ivoire, results of the sensitivity analysis

Region	1985 P_0	1985 P_1	1985 P_2	1986 P_0	1986 P_1	1986 P_2	1987 P_0	1987 P_1	1987 P_2	1988 P_0	1988 P_1	1988 P_2
A. Poverty line increased by 10 percent (that is, to 141,460 CFAF per year)												
Abidjan	0.054	0.012	0.003	0.193	0.048	0.017	0.132	0.028	0.011	0.186	0.035	0.010
Other cities	0.274	0.091	0.045	0.278	0.079	0.032	0.276	0.071	0.026	0.476	0.137	0.054
East Forest	0.536	0.187	0.087	0.493	0.145	0.060	0.483	0.142	0.056	0.547	0.180	0.080
West Forest	0.237	0.052	0.018	0.283	0.061	0.019	0.501	0.134	0.056	0.588	0.192	0.083
Savannah	0.579	0.214	0.107	0.550	0.176	0.075	0.633	0.234	0.114	0.725	0.298	0.157
Côte d'Ivoire	0.350	0.118	0.056	0.366	0.105	0.042	0.409	0.126	0.055	0.515	0.174	0.080
B. Poverty line decreased by 10 percent (that is, to 115,740 CFAF per year)												
Abidjan	0.029	0.006	0.003	0.109	0.023	0.009	0.048	0.015	0.007	0.091	0.013	0.003
Other cities	0.185	0.060	0.030	0.185	0.047	0.017	0.172	0.038	0.013	0.316	0.077	0.028
East Forest	0.418	0.122	0.052	0.339	0.087	0.032	0.337	0.080	0.028	0.400	0.113	0.046
West Forest	0.113	0.024	0.009	0.152	0.027	0.008	0.272	0.076	0.032	0.437	0.117	0.047
Savannah	0.421	0.151	0.069	0.410	0.109	0.041	0.506	0.159	0.073	0.582	0.219	0.106
Total	0.248	0.078	0.035	0.246	0.061	0.022	0.280	0.077	0.032	0.375	0.112	0.048

Table 3.13
Incidence of extreme poverty in Côte d'Ivoire, results of the sensitivity analysis

Region	1985 P_0	1985 P_1	1985 P_2	1986 P_0	1986 P_1	1986 P_2	1987 P_0	1987 P_1	1987 P_2	1988 P_0	1988 P_1	1988 P_2
A. Extreme poverty line increased by 10 percent (that is, to 82,500 CFAF per year)												
Abidjan	0.010	0.002	0.001	0.039	0.006	0.003	0.022	0.007	0.003	0.009	0.000	0.000
Other cities	0.087	0.031	0.017	0.076	0.014	0.004	0.054	0.011	0.003	0.119	0.023	0.008
East Forest	0.192	0.049	0.021	0.125	0.027	0.010	0.115	0.023	0.007	0.182	0.044	0.016
West Forest	0.034	0.007	0.004	0.037	0.004	0.001	0.119	0.031	0.012	0.193	0.044	0.015
Savannah	0.270	0.071	0.027	0.178	0.036	0.012	0.267	0.073	0.029	0.375	0.110	0.045
Côte d'Ivoire	0.127	0.034	0.015	0.095	0.019	0.006	0.121	0.030	0.011	0.183	0.047	0.018
B. Extreme poverty line decreased by 10 percent (that is, to 67,500 CFAF per year)												
Abidjan	0.007	0.001	0.000	0.011	0.004	0.002	0.017	0.004	0.002	0.000	0.000	0.000
Other cities	0.049	0.021	0.012	0.031	0.005	0.001	0.026	0.003	0.001	0.050	0.010	0.003
East Forest	0.112	0.028	0.012	0.060	0.013	0.005	0.054	0.009	0.002	0.113	0.023	0.007
West Forest	0.011	0.004	0.003	0.004	0.001	0.000	0.080	0.017	0.006	0.118	0.020	0.006
Savannah	0.169	0.039	0.013	0.075	0.017	0.006	0.170	0.043	0.015	0.238	0.066	0.024
Total	0.075	0.020	0.009	0.039	0.009	0.003	0.072	0.016	0.005	0.108	0.025	0.009

of poverty lines and also to include changes in poverty measures. We do so with a dominance analysis, which requires plotting the entire distribution curves for the regions, socioeconomic groups, or years to be compared. In principle, the complete distributions must be plotted, but in practice this can be restricted to the highest possible location of the poverty line.

Our main concern is to test the robustness of two of the main findings – the overall increase in the incidence of poverty between 1985 and 1988, and the increase in poverty in urban areas. Figure 3.1 compares the cumulative distribution of per capita expenditures, first on an annual basis and then for the entire period (the distribution is shown only up to about the seventieth percentile – surely a reasonable upper limit for the poverty line). Between 1985 and 1986, the curves intersect repeatedly between the twentieth and thirtieth percentile, showing that the conclusions about the incidence of poverty are sensitive to where in that range the poverty line is set. Only a poverty line below the twentieth percentile will yield an unambiguous reduction in poverty. In contrast, Figure 3.1.B shows that the 1987 distribution is entirely to the left and above the 1986 distribution, indicating an unambiguous increase in poverty. Figures 3.1.C and 1.D also show this configuration for 1987-88 and for the entire 1985-88 period.

Figure 3.2 breaks the 1985-88 comparison down by region. In Abidjan, first-order dominance is very clear, except at the very bottom (about one percent of individuals). Obviously, the conclusion that poverty increased in Abidjan during the period is not affected. For other cities, the case is a bit less clear. There are several intersections below the 10 percent mark, indicating that conclusions about extreme poverty are not likely to be robust. However, the rest of the 1988 distribution is dominated very clearly by the 1985 distribution, indicating an unambiguous increase in poverty. Finally, for rural areas, first-order dominance is met completely.

In summary, some caution is required when the change in the incidence of countrywide poverty between 1985 and 1986 and the change in the incidence of extreme poverty in cities other than Abidjan are assessed, since the conclusions may be affected by the location of the poverty line and possibly also by the type of poverty measure used. However, all other findings are clearly robust, particularly the two main findings that overall poverty increased in Côte d'Ivoire between 1985 and 1988, and that it did so in each region. This conclusion holds regardless of where the poverty line is placed and what poverty measure is used.

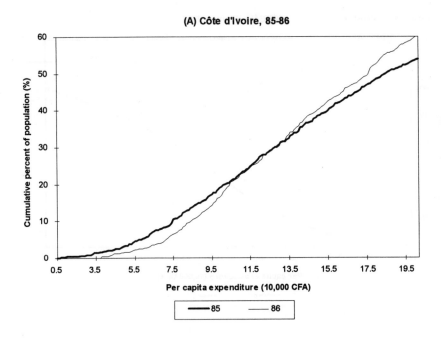

(A) Côte d'Ivoire, 85-86

Per capita expenditure (10,000 CFA)

— 85   — 86

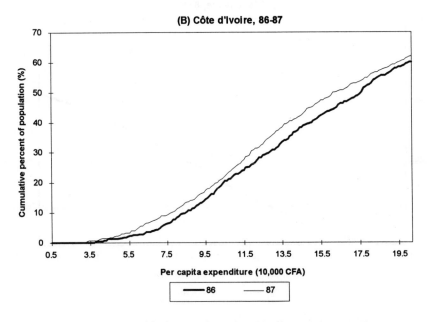

(B) Côte d'Ivoire, 86-87

Per capita expenditure (10,000 CFA)

— 86   — 87

Figure 3.1   Cumulative distribution of household expenditures per capita, Côte d'Ivoire: 1985-88

(Figure 3.1, cont.)

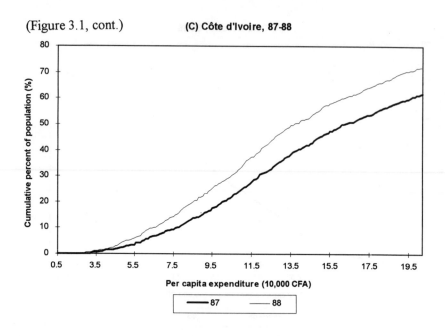

(C) Côte d'Ivoire, 87-88

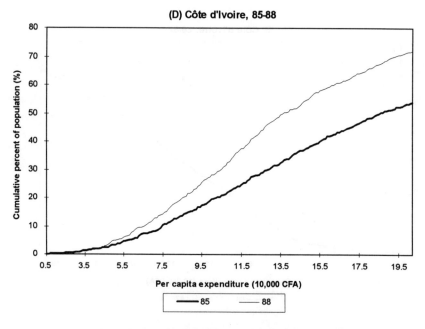

(D) Côte d'Ivoire, 85-88

Figure 3.1   Cumulative distribution of household expenditures per capita, Côte d'Ivoire: 1985-88

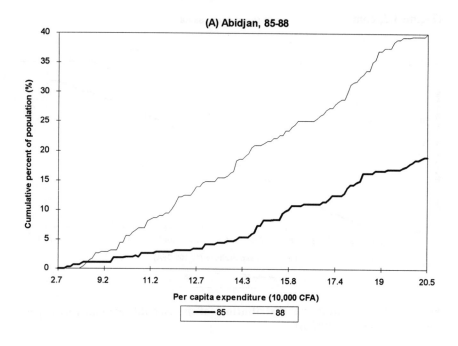

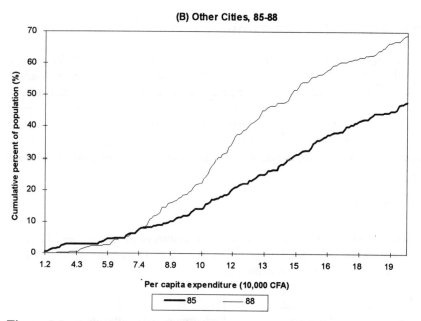

Figure 3.2   Cumulative distribution of household expenditures per capita, by region: 1985-88

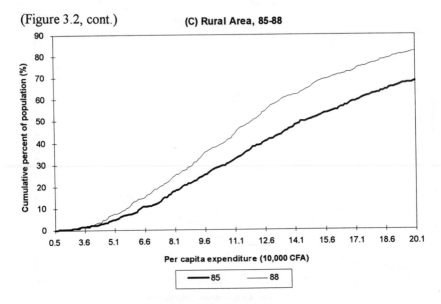

(Figure 3.2, cont.) **(C) Rural Area, 85-88**

Figure 3.2 legend: —— 85   —— 88

Y-axis: Cumulative percent of population (%)
X-axis: Per capita expenditure (10,000 CFA)

Figure 3.2   Cumulative distribution of household expenditures per capita, by region: 1985-88

Decomposition of changes in poverty

The changes in poverty that occurred in Côte d'Ivoire between 1985 and 1988 are the net result of two effects: a decline in the mean level of household expenditures per capita and a change in their distribution. It may be useful to separate out the two effects, so as to assess the policies of the period properly and to determine where future policy must be focused.

Following Ravallion and Datt (1991), we can write the change in P_α as the sum of a growth component, a redistributional components, and a residual. Let:

$$P_{\alpha,t} = P_\alpha (z/M_t, D_t),$$

where z is the poverty line, M_t is mean expenditures per capita, and D_t is the distribution of expenditures per capita in year t. The change in P_α between 1985 and 1988 can then be written as:

$$P_{\alpha,88} - P_{\alpha,85} = G (85, 88; r) + D (85, 88; r) + R (85, 88; r),$$

$$\underset{\substack{\text{Growth} \\ \text{component}}}{} \quad \underset{\substack{\text{Redistributional} \\ \text{component}}}{} \quad \underset{\text{Residual}}{}$$

92

where r refers to the reference point. If we select the initial year as the (logical) reference point, the components are defined as follows:

$$G (85, 88; 85) \equiv P_\alpha (z/M_{88}, D_{85}) - P_\alpha (z/M_{85}, D_{85})$$

$$D (85, 88; 85) \equiv P_\alpha (z/M_{85}, D_{88}) - P_\alpha (z/M_{85}, D_{85}).$$

The growth component thus captures the effect of the change in the level of mean expenditures between 1985 and 1988 without a change in 1985 distribution. The redistributional component shows the effect of a change in the distribution between 1985 and 1988 without a change in mean expenditures from their 1985 value. The residual reflects the interaction between changes in the mean and the distribution.[5]

Table 3.14
Decomposition of the annual change in poverty into growth and redistributional components

Annual change	Growth component	Redistributional component	Residual	Total change
		P_0		
1985-86	0.029	-0.035	0.005	-0.001
1986-87	0.017	0.024	0.008	0.049
1987-88	0.151	-0.061	0.021	0.111
1985-88	0.169	-0.060	0.050	0.159
		P_1		
1985-86	0.012	-0.028	0.000	-0.016
1986-87	0.007	0.011	0.001	0.019
1987-88	0.065	-0.017	-0.007	0.041
1985-88	0.079	-0.032	-0.003	0.044
		P_2		
1985-86	0.007	-0.019	-0.001	-0.013
1986-87	0.003	0.007	0.001	0.011
1987-88	0.033	-0.009	-0.004	0.020
1985-88	0.044	-0.019	-0.007	0.018

Table 3.15
Decomposition of the annual change in extreme poverty into growth and redistributional components

Annual change	Growth component	Redistributional component	Residual	Total change
P_0				
1985-86	0.020	-0.053	-0.003	-0.036
1986-87	0.006	0.025	-0.004	0.027
1987-88	0.077	-0.013	-0.014	0.050
1985-88	0.102	-0.043	-0.018	0.041
P_1				
1985-86	0.004	-0.017	-0.001	-0.014
1986-87	0.001	0.007	0.002	0.010
1987-88	0.021	-0.007	-0.002	0.012
1985-88	0.033	-0.015	-0.011	0.007
P_2				
1985-86	0.002	-0.008	-0.001	-0.007
1986-87	0.001	0.003	0.000	0.004
1987-88	0.009	-0.003	-0.001	0.005
1985-88	0.016	-0.007	-0.007	0.002

Table 3.14 shows the breakdown of P_0, P_1, and P_2 between 1985 and 1988, on an annual basis and for the period as a whole.[6] The most important finding is that the redistributional component is negative, meaning that changes in the distribution that occurred in Côte d'Ivoire between 1985 and 1988 helped *reduce* poverty. The finding also implies that the observed increase in poverty during the period is due entirely to the negative growth in expenditures. Had mean household expenditures in Côte d'Ivoire remained the same between 1985 and 1988, the incidence of poverty would have declined by six percentage points – that is, by 20 percent (not considering the interaction effect). Moreover, the absolute value of the redistributional component becomes larger relative to the total change as one moves from P_0 to P_2, meaning that the poverty reduction effect stemming from the changes in distribution benefited the poorest to the greatest extent. The same conclusion applies to extreme poverty (Table 3.15), except that the relative importance of the redistributional effect is twice as large: had mean expenditures not

94

changed, the change in redistribution would have reduced extreme poverty by more than 40 percent. This finding strongly underscores the role that the absence of economic growth played in generating poverty. What was necessary to fight poverty in Côte d'Ivoire in 1988 was not redistributive policies, but policies that could have halted and then reversed the decline in household expenditures.

The year-by-year decomposition shows that the poverty reduction effect of the redistributional component occurred throughout the period, except in 1986-87. We speculate that this anomaly may be related to the onset of the recession after the end of the upturn of 1985-86. This finding would suggest that the poor and possibly the 'middle class' whose expenditure levels were just above the poverty line were the first to be hit by the recession, so that the expenditure distribution became more unequal.

Table 3.16
Decomposition of the change in poverty (P_0, 1985-88)
into growth and redistributional components,
by region and socioeconomic group

Region and socioeconomic group	Growth component	Redistri- butional component	Residual	Total change
Abidjan	0.076	-0.002	0.031	0.105
Other cities	0.213	-0.111	0.072	0.174
East Forest	0.046	-0.061	0.030	0.015
West Forest	0.355	-0.005	0.025	0.375
Savannah	0.146	0.022	-0.018	0.150
Export crop farmer	0.213	-0.090	0.059	0.182
Food crop farmer	0.162	-0.037	0.031	0.156
Public sector employee	0.208	-0.001	-0.043	0.164
Private formal sector employee	0.102	-0.040	0.018	0.080
Informal sector employee	0.306	-0.042	0.016	0.280
Self-employed	0.123	-0.045	0.122	0.200
Inactive	0.126	-0.068	0.078	0.136
Unemployed	0.114	0.047	0.181	0.342
Côte d'Ivoire	0.169	-0.060	0.049	0.158

It is instructive also to perform the decomposition by region and socioeconomic group. Tables 3.16 and 3.17 show the results for P_0 during the entire 1985-88 period. For poverty overall, the redistributional component is negative for all regions except the Savannah, and for all socioeconomic groups except households with an unemployed head (a very small category). But the

95

relative magnitudes differ a great deal. In West Forest (the region with the largest increase in P_0), virtually the entire effect is due to a decline in mean expenditures – again emphasizing the importance of (the absence of) growth to poverty. In contrast, in 'other cities,' half of the increase in poverty due to declining mean expenditures was offset by the equalizing effect of the distributional change. The positive redistributional component in Savannah for poverty, combined with the negative component for extreme poverty, suggests an increased skewness in the distribution, except at the bottom tail.

The strongest redistributional effect on poverty occurred among export crop farmers – a group whose poverty, and especially extreme poverty, increased significantly during the period. This finding might indicate that the larger and richer farmers were relatively more affected by the negative evolution in export crops, generating an equalizing effect. But, again, the decline in mean expenditures far outweighs this effect, generating a net increase in poverty. At the same time, very poor farmers were also severely affected, since both declining mean expenditures and a changing distribution contributed to an increase in extreme poverty.

Table 3.17
Decomposition of the change in extreme poverty (P_0, 1985-88)
into growth and redistributional components,
by region and socioeconomic group

Region and socioeconomic group	Growth component	Redistri- butional component	Residual	Total change
Abidjan	0.003	-0.007	-0.003	-0.007
Other cities	0.101	-0.062	-0.046	-0.007
East Forest	0.047	-0.011	-0.029	0.007
West Forest	0.127	0.003	0.015	0.145
Savannah	0.108	-0.034	0.005	0.079
Export crop farmer	0.090	0.006	0.028	0.124
Food crop farmer	0.125	-0.062	-0.016	0.047
Public sector employee	0.046	-0.003	-0.007	0.036
Private formal sector employee	0.008	-0.001	-0.008	-0.001
Informal sector employee	0.126	0.013	-0.018	0.121
Self-employed	0.079	-0.072	-0.015	-0.008
Inactive	0.076	-0.041	-0.026	0.009
Unemployed	0.041	0.088	-0.041	0.088
Côte d'Ivoire	0.102	-0.043	-0.018	0.041

Income and expenditure patterns

The analysis thus far has focused on total household expenditures, as the measure of welfare. As discussed in Chapter 1, several of the adjustment measures pertained to specific items of expenditures or sources of income. For example, some measures pertained to coffee, cocoa, cotton, rice, and maize, and others to food crops as a whole. Households can be affected by those measures as consumers and/or as producers. Thus, it is useful to determine the importance of these items both to the expenditures of households and to their income, and to determine whether this differs according to poverty status.

As we have done thus far, we want to distinguish the extreme poor from the poor and the nonpoor. However, in order to show more effectively how expenditure and income patterns change with rising welfare levels, the tables in this section contain a different poverty category – the 'mid-poor.' We thus have three mutually exclusive poverty categories: the 'extreme poor' are (as before) those whose expenditures per capita are below the extreme poverty line; the 'mid-poor' are those who are between the two poverty lines; and the 'nonpoor' are those above the regular poverty line.

We present expenditure patterns in the following tables in two ways. Part A of each table shows the shares of the different categories of total expenditures within each poverty group. These shares sum vertically to 100 percent. This presentation is useful for showing how important an item or a category of expenditure is for each poverty group, and indicates the extent to which each group may be affected by changes in the price of the item when, for example, subsidies are cut. Part B of the tables shows how much of aggregate expenditures for a given category is accounted for by each poverty group. These shares sum horizontally to 100 percent. This presentation is useful for evaluating the leakage on general subsidies or taxes, or the effect of any general policy related to an item or source of revenue that is not targeted specifically at the poor. This dual presentation of expenditure and income information is maintained throughout this section.

The mid-poor and the extreme poor devoted more than 50 percent of their expenditures to food (Table 3.18). For the nonpoor, this figure is only slightly lower – about 47 percent – suggesting that the Engel curve in Côte d'Ivoire is quite flat. This has been observed for other African countries as well (Boateng and others, n.d.) In 1985, the Engel curve appears to have an inverted U-shape, since the food share for the extreme poor is lower than that of the mid-poor. This phenomenon might indicate that at very low levels of living such nonfood necessities as shelter and clothing, which must be met but cannot easily be divided into small quantities, force households to cut back on the food purchases that can be divided more easily. In 1988, the U-pattern

Table 3.18
Composition of household expenditures, by poverty status (percent)

Expenditure item	Extreme poor		Mid-poor		Nonpoor	
	1985	1988	1985	1988	1985	1988
(A)						
Food purchases	21.9	21.7	28.6	29.4	34.4	33.2
Consumption of home-produced food	30.5	38.0	27.5	27.9	13.1	13.9
(All food)	(52.4)	(59.7)	(56.1)	(57.3)	(47.5)	(47.1)
Nonfood purchases	46.5	39.5	41.3	40.7	49.0	49.2
Consumption of home-produced nonfood	0.6	0.2	1.4	0.4	0.6	0.9
(All nonfood)	(47.1)	(39.7)	(42.7)	(41.1)	(49.6)	(50.1)
Remittances	0.5	0.7	1.2	1.5	2.8	2.9
Total	100.0	100.0	100.0	100.0	100.0	100.0
(B)*						
Food purchases	1.6	2.8	8.4	16.9	89.9	80.3
Consumption of home-produced food	5.0	9.1	18.2	29.3	76.9	61.6
Nonfood purchases	2.4	3.5	8.5	15.8	89.2	80.7
Consumption of home-produced nonfood	2.2	1.2	19.3	10.8	78.4	88.0
Remittances	0.5	1.1	4.8	11.0	94.7	87.9
All expenditures	2.5	4.2	9.9	18.3	87.6	77.5

* Percentages sum horizontally.

98

seems to have disappeared, but this could be due to the fact that the larger number of people in extreme poverty hides the pattern.

The food share increased between 1985 and 1988, which of course reflects the declining level of total expenditures during the period. Within the food category, the consumption of home-produced food is much more important for the poor, especially the extreme poor, and its share also rose between 1985 and 1988. Clearly, as economic conditions deteriorated, the extreme poor had to rely increasingly on their own fields to provide them with food.

The last row of Table 3.18B gives an idea of the inequality of the distribution of welfare in Côte d'Ivoire: in 1985, the poorest 10 percent of people accounted only for 2.5 percent of all expenditures, and the poorest 30 percent for 12.4 percent. In 1988, the share of the poor (that is, extreme poor and mid-poor) almost doubled to 22.5 percent. The distribution had thus become more equal, since the increase in the share exceeds the increase in the number of poor. (This finding is of course consistent with the decomposition analysis earlier in this chapter, which showed a poverty-reducing change in distribution).

Table 3.19 examines the composition of food expenditures in more detail and is more useful for assessing the potential impact of the item-specific measures of the adjustment program. The two most important items to the diet of the extreme poor and mid-poor are fish and rice, together accounting for about one third of expenditures. There is a clear substitution of meat and poultry for fish as welfare increases. The 'luxury' nature of meat is also shown clearly by the decline in its share – for each group – in 1988.

Maize and millet appear to be the two most explicit 'inferior' foods, at least in 1985. In 1988, the consumption of these items among the extreme poor had fallen, but among the mid-poor it had increased sharply – these two groups accounted for 40 percent of all maize and millet consumption. The 'temporary' subsidization of rice production that began in 1982 had increased rice production, contributing to a shift in consumption towards rice, especially among the extreme poor. As shown in Table 3.19B, none of the foods appears to be so heavily consumed by the poor that they could be subsidized without significant leakage. Sugar, salt, and bouillon cubes are the only other items for which the budgetary share among the poor is distinctly higher than among the nonpoor, and for which the share of total consumption among the poor is well above average.

G'ven our earlier observation that the consumption of home-produced food is more important to the poor than to the nonpoor, a detailed examination of its composition is insightful (Table 3.20). In 1985, rice, maize, and yams comprised 71 percent of home-produced consumption among the extreme poor. In 1988, the share of rice had more than doubled, while the share of yams was more than halved. The government's support for food production under the structural adjustment program and the subsidization of rice thus benefited the poor as producers (an in-kind benefit for home-produced consumption). Although it is an item that is relatively unimportant to the total diet, millet is the item that the poor produce most heavily for home consumption. In 1985, the poor accounted for 44 percent of all home-produced consumption of millet; in 1988, the figure was 70 percent.

The results thus far clearly show that the economic hardship of 1987-88 has induced major consumption shifts – in both purchased in and home-produced items, and among both the poor and the nonpoor – towards less desired foods. The nonpoor consumed more fish and less meat and poultry. The poor consumed more maize and millet. The subsidy for rice has undoubtedly contributed to a major shift in purchased and home-produced consumption towards rice. (This shift shows the risk of this type of subsidy, since the increased production and consumption increase the cost of the subsidy to the government and exerts greater pressure to maintain it, since the number of beneficiaries increases.)

Table 3.19
Composition of household food expenditures,
by poverty status (percent)

Food expenditure item	Extreme poor		Mid-poor		Nonpoor	
	1985	1988	1985	1988	1985	1988
(A)						
Rice	11.7	19.3	12.2	16.1	10.8	11.8
Maize and millet	6.4	1.9	2.5	3.1	1.5	1.1
Cassava	3.5	3.2	3.2	4.2	3.8	4.4
Other grains	4.4	3.6	3.5	4.5	3.9	3.6
Bread	4.0	4.6	5.4	4.8	4.6	4.8
Yams and taro	3.0	2.6	3.1	3.4	3.3	3.4
Fruit	2.0	2.8	4.3	3.5	4.9	5.4
Fish	23.8	22.9	22.7	18.8	14.2	15.9
Meat and poultry	8.8	5.4	10.5	8.5	16.3	14.2
Oils	5.0	4.6	5.3	4.6	4.1	3.7
Butter and margarine	0.0	0.0	0.1	0.0	0.7	0.4
Sugar	4.5	2.6	3.0	2.1	1.8	1.5
Salt	3.8	2.7	1.8	1.3	0.7	0.6
Alcoholic beverages	3.4	3.4	5.3	4.3	4.8	3.4
Nonalcoholic beverages	0.8	0.3	1.3	0.4	1.8	1.1
Bouillon cubes	4.8	5.0	3.3	3.5	1.7	2.0
Tomato paste	1.4	1.2	0.8	1.1	1.1	1.1
Vegetables	1.7	4.5	2.6	4.5	4.3	4.4
Food outside home	4.7	5.6	5.8	6.9	11.8	13.0
Other food	2.1	3.8	3.3	4.4	3.7	4.2
Total	100.0	100.0	100.0	100.0	100.0	100.0

Table 3.19
Composition of household food expenditures,
by poverty status (percent)

Food expenditure item	Extreme poor		Mid-poor		Nonpoor	
	1985	1988	1985	1988	1985	1988
(B)*						
Rice	1.6	4.2	9.3	21.5	89.0	74.3
Maize and millet	5.6	3.5	12.4	36.0	81.9	60.5
Cassava	1.4	2.0	7.1	16.5	91.5	81.4
Other grains	1.7	2.6	7.7	20.5	90.6	76.9
Bread	1.3	2.6	9.8	17.1	88.9	80.3
Yams and taro	1.3	2.1	7.9	17.1	90.8	80.7
Fruit	0.6	1.5	7.6	11.8	91.8	86.6
Fish	2.4	3.8	12.6	19.4	85.0	76.9
Meat and poultry	0.8	1.1	5.6	11.1	93.6	87.7
Oils	1.8	3.2	10.5	19.9	87.7	76.9
Butter and margarine	0.0	0.0	1.0	1.1	99.0	98.9
Sugar	3.5	4.3	12.9	21.9	83.5	73.9
Salt	6.7	9.7	17.6	28.8	75.8	61.6
Alcoholic beverages	1.1	2.7	9.3	20.6	89.6	76.8
Nonalcoholic beverages	0.7	0.8	6.0	7.2	93.3	92.0
Bouillon cubes	3.8	5.6	14.6	25.8	81.7	68.4
Tomato paste	1.9	2.9	6.4	17.1	91.7	80.1
Vegetables	0.6	2.8	5.4	17.3	93.9	79.9
Food outside home	0.6	1.3	4.4	10.0	95.0	88.7
Other food	0.8	2.4	7.7	17.9	91.4	79.7
All food	1.5	2.7	8.4	17.0	90.1	80.2

* Percentages sum horizontally.

The final category for examination is nonfood items (Table 3.21). The budgetary share for most of these items rises with total expenditures, but the exceptions are the interesting items. One exception is public transport, the share of which is roughly the same across the three poverty groups – the expectation is usually that it is lower among the nonpoor. Moreover, the share of each poverty group in total public transport expenditures is the same as its share in all nonfood expenditures. Public transport in Côte d'Ivoire, as in almost all developing countries, is subsidized heavily. Clearly, this subsidy does not benefit the poor primarily. However, we would like to use this example to illustrate a general point. The observation that a subsidy is not

Table 3.20
Composition of the consumption of home-produced food,
by poverty status (percent)

Consumption item	Extreme poor		Mid-poor		Nonpoor	
	1985	1988	1985	1988	1985	1988
(A)						
Rice	12.6	32.9	15.3	24.9	24.5	18.1
Maize	19.5	19.9	16.2	8.5	11.3	6.0
Millet	4.3	4.0	3.2	1.4	1.3	0.5
Cassava	7.5	10.1	12.8	11.7	15.9	10.5
Yams	39.4	16.5	30.4	37.9	26.0	47.0
Bananas	3.7	5.0	13.2	9.3	12.0	11.7
Taro	3.6	1.6	3.3	1.6	4.5	2.4
Other grains	9.5	9.9	5.6	4.6	5.0	3.8
Total	100.0	100.0	100.0	100.0	100.0	100.0
(B)*						
Rice	2.7	13.1	12.5	34.3	84.7	52.6
Maize	7.5	21.5	23.5	31.6	68.9	46.9
Millet	11.7	32.1	32.5	38.2	55.8	29.7
Cassava	2.4	7.9	15.6	32.0	81.9	60.1
Yams	7.0	3.4	20.2	26.8	72.8	69.9
Bananas	1.5	4.1	20.4	26.4	78.1	69.5
Taro	4.0	6.6	14.3	23.0	81.7	70.4
Other grains	9.2	18.6	20.4	29.8	70.4	51.6
All home-produced food	4.9	8.5	18.2	29.4	76.9	62.0

* Percentages sum horizontally.

progressive does not imply that abolishing it would not hurt the poor to a relatively greater extent. Average propensities (such as those reported in Table 3.21) may well differ significantly from marginal effects. The rich may have alternatives to public transport which the poor do not, implying that the price elasticity of public transport fares may be very low among the poor. If so, higher fares might significantly increase the budgetary share that the poor must devote to transport, forcing them to cut back on more price-elastic items, such as health care and education. A study of cross-price elasticities is outside the scope of this work, but it should be undertaken before changes in subsidies and indirect taxes are recommended.

Table 3.21
Composition of nonfood expenditures,
by poverty status (percent)

Nonfood item	Extreme poor		Mid-poor		Nonpoor	
	1985	1988	1985	1988	1985	1988
(A)						
Clothing	14.8	14.4	30.5	25.0	27.9	19.2
Personal care	13.0	14.9	8.2	10.3	6.1	9.5
Home products and furniture	2.4	1.8	4.0	2.9	9.4	5.0
Charcoal	0.6	0.4	0.7	2.7	2.3	3.8
Wood	0.8	1.0	1.2	2.3	1.3	1.0
Fuel (kitchen)	11.3	14.5	6.4	7.2	3.3	4.3
Fuel (car)	7.6	3.6	3.8	1.6	8.2	9.6
Car repair	5.9	3.5	2.8	2.2	3.1	2.5
Education	19.2	14.1	12.5	14.4	9.6	11.7
Health	5.9	6.2	10.2	9.8	8.8	9.9
Cigarettes	7.3	8.1	5.8	5.4	3.0	3.4
Public transport	9.8	15.9	12.1	13.9	11.6	14.1
Communications	0.0	0.0	0.1	0.0	0.7	0.6
Other	1.2	1.4	1.5	2.3	4.7	5.3
Total	100.0	100.0	100.0	100.0	100.0	100.0
(B)*						
Clothing	0.7	2.0	8.1	20.3	91.2	77.7
Personal care	2.7	4.1	9.5	17.0	87.8	78.9
Home products and furniture	0.4	1.1	3.3	10.4	96.3	88.5
Charcoal	0.4	0.3	2.3	12.4	97.3	87.3
Wood	0.8	2.2	7.2	29.6	91.9	68.2
Fuel (kitchen)	4.1	7.8	12.9	23.1	82.9	69.0
Fuel (car)	1.3	1.2	3.6	3.2	95.1	95.5
Car repair	2.6	3.9	6.7	14.7	90.7	81.4
Education	2.6	3.1	9.3	19.1	88.1	77.7
Health	0.9	1.7	8.5	16.2	90.6	82.1
Cigarettes	3.0	5.7	13.1	22.5	83.8	71.7
Public transport	1.1	3.1	7.7	15.9	91.2	81.0
Communications	0.0	0.0	1.7	0.0	98.3	100.0
Other	0.4	0.8	2.5	7.9	97.1	91.3
All nonfood	1.3	2.7	7.4	16.2	91.2	81.1

* Percentage sum horizontally.

The budgetary share for three categories of nonfood items declines sharply with rising welfare: personal care, kitchen fuel, and education. The decrease for the first two reflects their low elasticity of demand typical for a necessity. The high share of education for the extreme poor (18 percent in 1986, and 14 percent in 1988) is remarkable, and suggests that extreme poor households do 'tighten the belt' in order to send their children to school. The shares of these three categories are much lower among the mid-poor, while a matching increase in the share of clothing occurs – indicating just where the extreme poor tighten the belt (at least within the nonfood items). It is a sad note, however, that the extreme poor spend more on cigarettes than on health. Of course, the fact that only one percent of all health expenditures come from the extreme poor does not provide a case for eliminating the subsidies for health care, but rather for targeting them.

One general thrust of adjustment programs is to change the allocation of resources in the economy between tradeable and nontradeable goods and services, toward promoting exportables and import substitutes (World Bank 1990). Countries do so usually by devaluing the exchange rate. Since Côte d'Ivoire is a member of the CFAF zone, this tool was unavailable in 1980s, and the structural adjustment program included a series of substitute measures (primarily import tariffs and export subsidies) that sought to achieve the same effects (see Chapter 1). In order to estimate the impact on household expenditures, we categorized all expenditure items into tradeable and nontradeable categories. All services, foods consumed away from the home, and some obviously local items, such as wood and charcoal, were considered nontradeables. Food was also considered nontradeable, except rice, maize, millet, macaroni, meat, refined oil, butter, margarine, salt, alcoholic beverages, and the 'other foods' category in the survey.

In 1985, slightly more than 40 percent of expenditures by the mid-poor and nonpoor were tradeables (Table 3.22). Two-thirds of this amount was accounted for by nonfood items. In 1988, the share of tradeables had fallen to 35 percent, primarily through cuts in imported nonfood items, suggesting that the import tariffs may have had an effect. Among the extreme poor, the tradeable component was initially lower at 35.6 percent, but it rose to 38.8 percent in 1988. Here, the increase was due primarily to food items – that is, import substitutes, especially rice. We expected that there might be strong regional effects, and repeated the tradeable/nontradeable breakdown in expenditures by region (Table 3.23). The declining share of tradeable items affected the rural areas most heavily. The nonfood component declines to the greatest extent in East and West Forest. The rise in the food component among the extreme poor was concentrated in West Forest (where the increase in extreme poverty was strongest). The absence of an effect in the Savannah, which also contains many extreme poor people, is due to a lower availability (and the absence of the production) of rice.

In short, although the overall share of tradeable items among total expenditures does not differ much across poverty categories, the adjustment measures that sought to mimic devaluation did affect the extreme poor differently than they did the other groups. Distinct regional effects occurred as well.

Table 3.22
Composition of household expenditures according to poverty status and the tradeability of items (percent)

Item	Extreme poor		Mid-poor		Nonpoor	
	1985	1988	1985	1988	1985	1988
(A)						
Tradeables	35.6	38.8	42.6	35.4	41.1	35.0
Food	16.5	25.5	14.3	18.5	13.8	13.7
Nonfood	19.1	13.3	28.3	16.9	27.3	21.3
Nontradeables	64.4	61.2	57.4	64.6	58.9	65.0
Food	34.5	35.9	31.6	37.7	26.2	32.5
Nonfood	29.9	25.3	25.8	26.9	32.7	32.5
Total	100.0	100.0	100.0	100.0	100.0	100.0
(B)*						
Tradeables						
Food	2.4	6.6	10.5	22.8	87.1	70.6
Nonfood	1.4	2.6	10.5	15.4	88.1	82.0
Nontradeables						
Food	2.6	4.2	11.9	20.7	85.5	75.1
Nonfood	1.9	3.2	8.2	15.9	89.9	80.9
All	2.1	3.9	10.1	18.4	87.8	77.6

* Percentages sum horizontally.

Adjustment measures affect households and individuals not only through expenditures, but also – and perhaps primarily – through income. Although the welfare analysis in this book is based on expenditures, we now briefly examine the composition of income among the different poverty groups.[7]

Table 3.23
Composition of household expenditures according to region and the tradeability of items (percent)

Item	Abidjan		Other cities		East Forest		West Forest		Savannah	
	1985	1988	1985	1988	1985	1988	1985	1988	1985	1988
(A)										
Tradeables	36.6	32.8	40.7	39.1	42.4	29.5	48.2	42.6	41.3	33.5
Food	11.9	11.8	11.8	14.2	10.9	12.3	18.1	27.1	22.5	17.2
Nonfood	24.7	21.0	28.9	24.9	31.5	17.2	30.1	15.5	18.8	16.3
Nontradeables	63.6	67.2	59.3	60.9	57.6	70.5	51.8	57.3	58.8	66.5
Food	22.3	24.2	21.5	28.2	32.6	48.5	28.4	32.7	39.2	45.5
Nonfood	41.0	43.0	37.8	32.7	25.0	22.0	23.4	24.6	19.6	21.0
Total	100.0	100.0	100.0	100.0	100.0	100.0	100.0	100.0	100.0	100.0
(B)*										
Tradeables										
Food	25.4	21.8	20.3	27.8	14.6	14.8	22.0	20.1	17.7	15.4
Nonfood	26.8	29.0	25.5	36.2	21.5	15.3	18.7	8.5	7.5	10.9
Nontradeables										
Food	24.6	20.2	19.1	24.7	22.6	26.0	17.8	10.8	15.9	18.3
Nonfood	38.0	38.5	28.4	30.9	14.6	12.7	12.4	8.8	6.7	9.1
All	29.6	27.9	24.0	29.4	18.6	18.0	16.9	11.1	10.9	13.5

* Percentages sum horizontally.

Several adjustment measures did indeed operate on the income side: the freeze of public sector wages, and the increase in export crop prices, which increase farmers' income directly. By the same token, the 1987-88 recession affected not only household expenditures, but also income. The question is, which groups were affected the most? Table 3.24 shows that the extreme poor derive the bulk of their income from farming: 56 percent in 1985 and 62 percent in 1988. Nonfarming income was only 16.6 percent in 1985 and fell slightly thereafter. This pattern differs from the pattern among the mid-poor, whose farm income declined and nonfarm income rose significantly. This difference no doubt reflects the characteristics of the people who became newly poor between 1985 and 1988, many of whom were not farmers (see earlier). In contrast, wage income is clearly the main source of income among the nonpoor: in 1985, 97 percent of all wage income went to the nonpoor. Any form of wage policy will thus not affect the poor initially, although, as we have seen with public sector employees, it can push people into poverty. Also noteworthy is that remittance income became more important for all groups between 1985 and 1988. This finding reflects the existence of a strong system of informal mutual support among extended family members and people from the same village (see Mahieu, 1990).

Given the importance of farming income to the poor, Table 3.25 examines the composition of farm revenue from crop sales (the CILSS data do not permit calculating net income on a crop-specific basis). Among the three main export crops, cotton clearly provides the greatest revenue to the poorest farmers – increasingly so between 1985 and 1988. The simultaneous increase in the price of cotton and cotton fertilizer under the structural adjustment program and the stimulation program for cotton production in Savannah thus yielded a net gain for extreme poor farmers. Benefits from the support of coffee and cocoa prices, however, went primarily to nonpoor farmers, since revenue from these two crops constituted about three-fourths of their crop revenue. The figures also show that there was a shift away from coffee production toward cocoa production between 1985 and 1988, in response to international market conditions. Among food crops, rice is a relatively more important source of revenue among poor farmers than for nonpoor, and its importance has been increasing. The rice price support measures have thus helped poor farmers (although, again, with much leakage, given that 72 percent of all rice sale revenues went to nonpoor farmers in 1985).

A final point about the income figures in Tables 3.24 and 3.25 is a word of caution. As we pointed out in Chapter 2, there are good reasons for preferring to base welfare and poverty analysis on expenditure data rather than on income data – not the least of which is the reliability in reporting. The bottom row of Table 3.24 shows the distribution of total household income. According to this measure, extremely poor households in 1985 received 6.8

Table 3.24
Composition of household income,
by poverty status (percent)

Income source	Extreme poor		Mid-poor		Nonpoor	
	1985	1988	1985	1988	1985	1988
(A)						
Wages	3.6	3.1	7.1	11.3	36.7	40.6
Farm income	56.3	61.8	59.4	43.5	32.5	25.5
Nonfarm income	16.6	15.2	18.9	31.3	16.0	24.7
Rental income	21.2	16.0	11.3	11.1	9.7	7.3
Scholarships	0.4	0.1	0.6	0.2	0.6	0.2
Remittances	1.4	3.7	0.9	2.4	1.0	1.4
Other income	0.5	0.1	1.8	0.2	3.5	0.3
Total	100.0	100.0	100.0	100.0	100.0	100.0
(B)*						
Wages	0.4	0.5	2.6	7.3	97.1	92.2
Farm income	5.0	9.6	18.9	29.5	76.0	60.8
Nonfarm income	3.3	2.9	13.4	25.7	83.3	71.4
Rental income	6.8	9.1	12.8	27.5	80.5	63.4
Scholarships	2.3	1.9	11.4	25.1	86.4	73.1
Remittances	4.6	10.4	10.7	29.4	84.7	60.3
Other income	0.5	2.1	6.5	15.1	92.9	82.8
All income	6.8	9.1	12.8	27.5	80.5	63.4

* Percentages sum horizontally.

percent of all income, and the mid-poor received 12.8 percent. The poorest 30 percent of households thus received 19.4 percent of all incomes – as opposed to only 12.4 percent of expenditures (see Table 3.18). This finding would imply a remarkably equal distribution of income against a rather unequal distribution of expenditures. A further examination of the absolute income figures also reveals that they are well below expenditure figures on average, yielding average negative savings. This finding is not unusual in surveys that collect both income and expenditure data, and it is generally believed that the phenomenon is due to income underreporting, especially by those earning high incomes. This does indeed seem to be the case in the CILSS, since the negative savings rate increases with the level of total income. We are thus inclined to have more confidence in expenditure figures than in income figures. Among the latter, we trust the income composition figures for the extreme poor and mid-poor more than we do those for the nonpoor, since the income and expenditure figures for the former are more consistent.

Table 3.25
Composition of revenue from crop sales,
by poverty status (percent)

Crop	Extreme poor		Mid-poor		Nonpoor	
	1985	1988	1985	1988	1985	1988
(A)						
Cocoa	23.6	31.9	42.6	47.7	43.2	52.8
Coffee	24.7	17.6	24.3	20.8	31.8	22.0
Cotton	25.0	33.1	10.9	12.2	3.3	8.2
Rubber and palm	0.0	0.1	1.7	1.0	2.3	1.7
Other export crops	11.5	5.7	5.5	3.9	5.5	3.2
Rice	5.1	5.4	3.3	4.5	3.0	3.2
Millet	0.1	0.8	0.2	0.2	0.1	0.3
Maize	1.4	3.1	2.7	1.8	2.0	1.4
Banana and fruit trees	2.9	0.1	1.7	0.6	2.7	0.3
Root crops	5.1	1.9	5.9	6.4	4.7	5.5
Vegetables	0.5	0.4	1.1	0.9	1.2	1.3
Total	100.0	100.0	100.0	100.0	100.0	100.0
(B)*						
Cocoa	2.8	6.9	19.1	26.9	78.0	66.2
Coffee	4.2	8.8	15.3	27.1	80.5	64.0
Cotton	21.5	29.3	35.2	28.1	43.3	42.5
Rubber and palm	0.1	0.5	15.8	21.7	84.0	77.8
Other export crops	10.1	16.3	18.0	29.7	71.9	54.0
Rice	8.1	15.1	19.7	32.9	72.3	52.0
Millet	4.0	25.0	23.0	17.2	72.9	57.8
Maize	3.4	19.4	23.6	28.8	73.0	51.9
Banana and fruit trees	5.7	2.3	13.0	40.9	81.2	56.8
Root crops	5.2	3.7	22.4	33.2	72.5	63.1
Vegetables	2.0	4.2	17.6	22.8	80.4	73.0
All crops	5.0	10.6	18.9	27.7	76.1	61.7

* Percentages sum horizontally.

Conclusion

This chapter used static and dynamic decomposition of a poverty index to relate the macroeconomic evolution in Côte d'Ivoire over the period 1985-88 to changes in poverty. This period is a brief but critical period in the longer process of structural change which Côte d'Ivoire has undergone since the late seventies. In particular, the period 1985-88 covers both a managed structural adjustment phase and a phase of destabilization. The results indicate that during the adjustment phase, the overall incidence of poverty did not change and the incidence of extreme poverty was reduced. During the destabilization phase, poverty rose sharply, and in 1988, the incidence of poverty was 50 percent higher than in 1985.

The regional and socioeconomic decomposition of the poverty index allows to relate these changes to some of the key measures in the adjustment program. The social goal of the adjustment program was to move the domestic terms of trade in favor of rural areas, by increasing and then protecting the domestic producer prices of the country's main export crops, cocoa and coffee, and by putting a freeze on salaries in the public and para-public sectors. The decomposition results show that urban poverty rose faster than rural poverty and that poverty among civil servants increased substantially. The distribution-sensitive version of the poverty index for civil servants deteriorated the most, suggesting that the lowest paid among them were affected most. Poverty also increased in the private sector, and especially employees in the informal sector were hard hit. In rural areas, poverty rose rapidly among export crop farmers. This was traced to falling crop yields, suggesting that price protection for producers is not a sufficient condition to ensure poverty protection.

The dynamic decomposition of the poverty index indicates the relative importance of growth and redistribution effects in explaining the change in poverty over time. In the case of Côte d'Ivoire, the entire increase in poverty can be attributed to negative economic growth. Redistribution effects contributed to reducing poverty and especially extreme poverty. Our calculations show that a return to pre-1980 'miracle' growth rates would be needed to successfully reduce poverty through economic growth alone. To the extent that this is not likely to happen, an argument may exist for targeted poverty alleviation policies. Our results indicate which regions and socioeconomic groups should be priority targets.

The analysis of the composition of household income and expenditure suggested that there are no goods which are predominantly produced or consumed by the poor. This implies that commodity-specific price supports or subsidies are not an effective way to help the poor in Côte d'Ivoire. We found that the overall share of tradeable items in the consumption basket is not very

110

different between the poor and nonpoor. However, for the poor the tradeables consist mainly of food, especially import substitutes such as rice, while for the nonpoor, two-thirds of consumed tradeables were imported nonfood items.

Côte d'Ivoire's experience, as documented in this chapter, provides several lessons which may apply to other countries as well. First, one of the most striking findings is the speed with which the destabilization in Côte d'Ivoire in 1987-88 'trickled down' to households, and the magnitude of the effect. There is no reason to assume that such effect could not occur in other countries as well. The explanation probably includes the standard argument that reductions in aggregate demand 'bite' much faster than supply incentives and price realignments. The contrast with the adjustment years provides dramatic evidence of the costs in terms of increased poverty that can stem from even one or two years of unchecked economic decline and destabilization. The important lesson is that it is much more feasible to protect the poor with a managed adjustment program than under conditions of destabilization.

Second, the macroeconomic decline experienced by Côte d'Ivoire during the 1985-88 period is not unique in Africa, and the possibility thus exists that similar increases in poverty occurred elsewhere. They are not likely to be documented though, by virtue of the lack of household surveys. Our results thus imply a strong call for regular – at least annual – monitoring of poverty at the household level.

Third, the results in this chapter illustrate that relatively simple techniques such as the decomposition of a poverty index can be useful in providing policy advice for poverty alleviation strategies. While a formal economy-wide model, capable of simulating counterfactual strategies, is in principle a superior analytic tool, the realities of policy making are such that in most countries they are not available.

Notes

1   This chapter is a revised and expanded version of 'Structural Change and Poverty in Africa: A Decomposition Analysis for Côte d'Ivoire,' by Christiaan Grootaert, which appeared originally in *Journal of Development Economics*, Vol. 47, 1995, pp. 375-401. The material is used with permission of Elsevier Science-NL, Sara Burgerhartstraat 25, 1055 KV Amsterdam, The Netherlands.

2   Again, we do *not* imply that the adjustment program *caused* the economic upturn, nor that the abandonment of the adjustment effort caused the economic decline.

3   When survey results suggest changes in welfare and poverty that are of the magnitude of those reported in Tables 3.3 and 3.4, questions are inevitably raised about the quality and reliability of the survey data. Chapter 2 discusses the investigations we performed to asses the quality of the CILSS data.

4   Note that the countrywide change in Table 3.5 is not an average of the change in each category, because the number of people in each category during the four years does not remain the same. In particular, the number of poor and extreme poor increased considerably.

5   The residual exists because the decomposition is sensitive to the selection of the reference year. Assuming that an initial or a terminal year is one of the two possible choices for reference, the residual will vanish if either the mean or the distribution does not change between the two years, since in that (unlikely) case the reference does not matter. This can be seen from:

$$R\ (85,\ 88;\ 85) = G\ (85,\ 88;\ 88) - G\ (85,\ 88;\ 85)$$
$$= D\ (85,\ 88;\ 88) - D\ (85,\ 88;\ 85)$$

This formulation also shows that switching between the initial and terminal year as the point of reference will reverse the sign but not change the value of the residual.

6   The year-by-year components do not add up to the all-period components because of the moving reference year.

7   Johnson et al. (1990) describe how total household income was derived from the CILSS data.

4 Basic needs and the incidence of poverty[1]

Since welfare and poverty are multidimensional (see Chapter 2), we now examine those aspects that have not been captured in household expenditures per capita – the welfare measures used in the previous chapter. The discussion herein is limited to three key 'basic needs': education, health, and housing. Only the latter has been affected directly by the structural adjustment program in Côte d'Ivoire, as the government has withdrawn from providing housing. We explore whether this decision has affected the poor. The fulfillment of other basic needs has of course been affected indirectly, both by the restraint in overall government expenditures imposed by the adjustment program and by the shortfall of government receipts during the subsequent recessionary years (although in 1988 government expenditures were allowed to rise rapidly despite the lower receipts).

In general, the government of Côte d'Ivoire has protected public expenditures for education and health from the macroeconomic evolution during the second half of the eighties (Table 4.1). Expenditure on education kept rising in real terms until 1987, but have fallen since then. The decline, however, was less than overall expenditure, or than GDP, so that the share of education in total expenditure and in GDP was higher in 1990 than in 1985. Throughout the period, the share of education expenses in the government's budget exceeded 40 percent, which is one of the highest shares in the world. For health, expenditure rose in real terms over the entire period 1985-90, and the share of health expenditure in GDP rose significantly from 0.9 percent to 1.4 percent. Due to Côte d'Ivoire's rapid population growth, exceeding three percent per year, real expenditure per capita, both in education and health, fell slightly between 1985 and 1990. This protection of social expenditure both during adjustment and during economic recession is not unusual in African countries. In reviewing the available data on African countries during the 1980s, Ferroni and Kanbur (1990) found no evidence of a decline in real government resources devoted to the social sectors.

113

However, sectorwide figures on public expenditures are only a weak guide for judging whether such expenditures have benefited the poor. Much depends on the intrasectoral and functional allocation, the efficiency and targeting of service delivery, and other features. Such a detailed review of public expenditures is outside the scope of this book, but Table 4.1 does show the breakdown of education expenditures according to types of education. The usual presumption is that primary education benefits the poor to the greatest extent, while tertiary education benefits the rich. The share going to primary education was just more than 40 percent in 1985 and did not change much until 1987. A slight rise appears to have set in as of 1988, offset by a slight reduction in the share going to secondary education. Tertiary education held steady during the period at about 17 percent but in 1990 it fell to 14 percent. Considering that tertiary enrollment comprises a minute fraction of primary enrollment, it is clear that the amount of government spending per tertiary student is a high multiple of spending per primary student. There is thus clearly room for further reallocation within the education sector.

The functional allocation of education expenditure changed significantly during the eighties. The main trend was the rising share of salaries relative to other inputs. In 1990, the ratio of personnel costs to nonpersonnel costs stood at 10:1, a sharp increase from the 2:1 ratio of 10 years earlier. The situation was most extreme at the primary level, where salaries accounted for 95 percent of recurrent expenditure, and materials such as textbooks less than one percent (Sahn and Bernier, 1993). While in principle the protection of teacher salaries can have a positive impact on the quality of education (by maintaining teacher morale), such effect did not occur in Côte d'Ivoire – in fact the opposite occurred because real expenditure on education fell after 1987 (see Table 4.1) and so did real teacher salaries. The extreme imbalance between teacher and other education inputs, as was the case in primary education, constituted a major internal inefficiency in the delivery of education services in Côte d'Ivoire.

In the health sector, the key distinction is between curative and preventive care. The former often displays an urban and pro-rich bias. Sahn and Bernier (1993) estimate that primary health care received only 35 percent of recurrent expenditure and 22 percent of investment spending in 1990. In contrast, the tertiary level – largely curative hospital-based care – received 54 percent of recurrent spending and 61 percent of capital spending. The share of health spending for the tertiary level rose through most of the eighties, mainly because of near doubling of expenditures at university hospitals. Several inefficiencies result from this situation, most notably a channeling of a too large number of patients to the tertiary level for health problems which should have been addressed at a lower level of care.

Table 4.1
Government expenditures on education and health (billions of CFAF)

Expenditure item	1985	1986	1987	1988	1989	1990
Education	177.0	200.6	211.0	220.4	221.1	208.4
% of GDP	5.6	6.2	6.8	7.2	7.5	7.7
% of current expenditures	20.6	22.7	22.7	20.2	20.0	23.0
% of government budget	42.3	43.7	43.9	44.7	45.8	41.8
CFAF per person	18,830	20,680	20,891	20,990	20,472	18,607
Primary	72.2	82.3	86.0	92.3	93.4	95.8
% of educational expenditures	40.8	41.0	40.8	41.9	42.2	46.0
Secondary	61.3	62.9	66.0	69.2	68.3	60.0
% of educational expenditures	34.6	31.3	31.3	31.4	30.9	28.8
Tertiary	30.8	36.0	37.0	38.1	38.5	28.6
% of educational expenditures	17.4	17.9	17.6	17.3	17.4	13.7
Technical/vocational	12.9	19.5	22.0	20.8	20.9	24.0
% of educational expenditures	7.3	9.7	10.4	9.4	9.5	11.5
Health	29.1	31.5	33.7	36.2	38.5	38.9
% of GDP	0.9	1.0	1.1	1.2	1.3	1.4
% of current expenditures	3.4	3.6	3.6	3.3	3.5	4.3
% of government budget	7.0	6.9	7.0	7.3	8.0	7.8
CFAF per person	3,096	3,247	3,336	3,448	3,565	3,473

Source: World Bank data.

The functional allocation of health care expenditure was somewhat less skewed towards wages than in the case of education expenditure, but personnel costs still represented 77 percent of recurrent health expenditure in 1990. Nonsalary expenditure per capita fell by almost 50 percent during the eighties, to less than seven percent of recurrent expenditure. The situation was aggravated by inappropriate staff ratios and competency profiles: the structure was top heavy, with low and deteriorating nurse-to-doctor ratios, and a competency profile biased towards curative care (Serageldin et al., 1993).

With the information on public expenditures as background, we now examine how the nonmonetary aspects of welfare evolved during 1985-88 (keeping in mind of course that this evolution is due to many factors beyond public expenditures).

Education

As can be expected, the literacy level did not change much between 1985 and 1988, and is still quite low for a country that spends such a high share of its budget on education (Table 4.2.A). Nevertheless, slight improvements in literacy did occur among the nonpoor and the mid-poor, while a distinct deterioration occurred among the extreme poor (perhaps surprisingly, only among men). Under the assumption that it is not possible to 'lose' literacy after it has been acquired, this pattern of literacy must reflect shifts across poverty categories over time, whereby the least literate and educated have become poorer. The regional figures highlight the sharp differences in literacy between urban and rural areas. The literacy rate in the Savannah – Côte d'Ivoire's poorest region, in which 30 percent of the people live in extreme poverty – is a paltry 10 percent.

Literacy is of course due to previous educational efforts. Current efforts are best captured by enrollment rates. Perhaps the most sensitive among them is the net primary school enrollment rate – the number of primary-school-age children (6 to 11 years) enrolled in primary school as a percentage of all children aged 6 to 11. This ratio is sensitive to economic conditions because it reflects parents' withdrawal of children from school in order to work in household enterprises or farms. This withdrawal can be permanent – that is, drop-out – or temporary during part of the school year, which is likely to increase the repetition of grades. The net enrollment rate captures both effects (with a decline in the rate). In contrast, the more frequently reported gross enrollment rate – the number of children of all ages enrolled in primary school as a percentage of all children aged 6 to 11 – will decline only in the presence of drop-outs. It will actually rise when repetition of grades increases, because this increases total primary school enrollment, which is the rate's numerator.

The gross enrollment rate could thus mask an important element of deteriorating educational conditions.

However, for the sake of completeness, we examine both net and gross enrollment rates for both primary and secondary schools (Table 4.2). For Côte d'Ivoire as a whole net primary school enrollment rose slightly to 58.4 percent until 1987, and then fell by four percentage points in 1988, which brought it back to its 1985 level (Table 4.2.B). However, this end result was not the same for all socioeconomic groups and regions in the country. The enrollment of children from nonpoor households was actually higher in 1988 than in 1985. In contrast, a significant drop occurred among girls from extremely poor households, whose enrollment fell to 16.7 percent – one-third of the national figure – and in the Savannah, where enrollment stood at 22.6 percent in 1988. Clearly, the substantial resources which the Ivorian government devotes to education are not distributed equitably. It is hard to see how the fate of the extreme poor in Côte d'Ivoire can be improved as long as their access to schooling remains so dismal. On the positive side, the situation in West Forest deserves special mention: net primary enrollment rose during the period, from 50.6 percent to 58.8 percent. This increase illustrates the importance of examining basic needs indicators separately, since they do not always follow the same time path (or, for that matter, have the same cross-sectional distribution) as monetary indicators. Indeed, as mentioned in Chapter 3, West Forest is the region that experienced the greatest decline in average expenditures and commensurately the greatest rise in poverty.

The gross primary school enrollment rate rose slightly between 1985 and 1988, which probably reflects simply an increase in repetition of primary grades. This problem is evident from Côte d'Ivoire's official school records, but the CILSS data do not permit calculating repetition rates. However, repetition can be examined indirectly by checking the incidence of age-grade mismatches. As shown in Table 4.2.D, almost one-third of primary school pupils in 1985 were at least one grade behind the one normally associated with their age. While in 1985 the percentage of mismatches was about the same among the poor and nonpoor, the percentage among the poor exceeded the percentage among the nonpoor by a substantial margin by 1988. For children from extremely poor households, the incidence of age-grade mismatches almost doubled between 1985 and 1988, to a level of 64 percent among boys and 53 percent among girls. This trend is alarming, indicating a slowdown in educational progress among extremely poor children.

Secondary school enrollment also declined between 1985 and 1988 (Tables 4.2.E and 4.2.F). The decline occurred entirely among poor households, especially among the extreme poor. Secondary enrollment among boys from extremely poor households dropped by two-thirds, to a mere 3.5 percent, and enrollment among girls from these households dropped by almost 80 percent,

Table 4.2
Education indicators, by poverty status and region (percent)

Poverty status/region	1985	1986	1987	1988
	A. Literacy rate			
Extreme poor				
- Male	22.8	19.9	18.2	16.8
- Female	8.0	7.3	7.4	8.3
Mid-poor				
- Male	26.7	31.3	26.3	32.9
- Female	12.9	15.5	10.9	17.1
Nonpoor				
- Male	45.1	45.1	49.8	49.7
- Female	28.0	27.7	31.2	31.8
Abidjan	55.0	53.1	59.5	57.6
Other cities	45.7	45.5	45.1	45.2
East Forest	21.3	24.2	24.4	23.4
West Forest	20.1	20.6	21.1	28.1
Savannah	9.9	10.7	12.0	9.8
Côte d'Ivoire	30.9	31.9	32.4	31.9
	B. Net primary school enrollment rate			
Extreme poor				
- Male	31.7	35.6	34.1	31.0
- Female	22.4	22.9	16.7	16.7
Mid-poor				
- Male	51.1	49.3	48.2	54.3
- Female	41.0	37.6	36.7	41.9
Nonpoor				
- Male	66.3	64.2	78.0	74.1
- Female	54.0	57.5	63.9	57.7
Abidjan	69.4	71.4	77.7	72.0
Other cities	67.7	62.4	71.2	67.4
East Forest	54.3	56.8	60.2	53.6
West Forest	50.6	48.9	58.1	58.8
Savannah	27.8	26.1	30.3	22.6
Côte d'Ivoire	53.6	54.1	58.4	54.0

118

(Table 4.2, cont.)

Table 4.2
Education indicators, by poverty status and region (percent)

Poverty status/region	1985	1986	1987	1988
C. Gross primary school enrollment rate				
Extreme poor				
- Male	50.5	50.7	41.8	48.0
- Female	30.2	28.8	26.1	22.1
Mid-poor				
- Male	69.2	69.4	65.8	76.0
- Female	53.8	47.4	46.4	57.7
Nonpoor				
- Male	87.0	88.3	107.8	100.4
- Female	73.8	78.8	84.5	80.1
All	72.2	73.9	78.7	74.7
D. Age-grade mismatches in primary school (percentage of total enrollment)				
Extreme poor				
- Male	38.0	34.1	37.6	63.9
- Female	27.8	55.3	58.6	52.9
Mid-poor				
- Male	30.1	42.1	41.7	48.7
- Female	27.4	40.4	38.1	47.9
Nonpoor				
- Male	28.5	34.9	31.1	37.3
- Female	33.3	35.3	30.0	37.7
All	30.6	36.7	33.2	42.4
E. Net secondary school enrollment rate				
Extreme poor				
- Male	9.7	3.0	2.8	3.5
- Female	5.3	2.0	4.5	1.2
Mid-poor				
- Male	20.0	16.3	11.5	14.8
- Female	9.8	5.2	4.1	9.0
Nonpoor				
- Male	36.8	37.6	36.8	33.6
- Female	18.8	25.6	22.9	21.1
All	22.9	25.2	22.3	19.1

(Table 4.2, cont.)

Table 4.2
Education indicators, by poverty status and region (percent)

Poverty status/region	1985	1986	1987	1988
F. Gross secondary school enrollment rate				
Extreme poor				
- Male	14.4	3.0	4.9	3.5
- Female	5.3	2.0	4.5	1.2
Mid-poor				
- Male	25.0	20.8	13.3	21.1
- Female	11.0	8.4	4.9	9.4
Nonpoor				
- Male	51.0	53.4	50.2	47.7
- Female	26.2	33.0	30.4	27.2
All	31.2	34.3	29.7	25.7

to 1.2 percent. The remark we made earlier about the abysmal prospects for the extreme poor to escape from poverty through education is obviously applicable here. Moreover, the decline in access to schooling for the poor, especially for girls, could well have deleterious implications for the possibility of realizing a decline from the current high levels of fertility in Côte d'Ivoire, thus adding to the difficulties of increasing per capita incomes in the longer run.

In Table 4.3 we examine household expenditures for education, which fell drastically between 1985 and 1988, by 38 percent. This decline is greater than the decline in total expenditures, indicating that households have cut back proportionately more on educational expenses. This trend is most pronounced among the extreme poor. And the reduction in household spending on education contrasts sharply with increased government spending on the education sector. However, since per capita government spending stayed about the same in real terms, total resources for education suffered a net loss.

Table 4.3 also shows the share of household expenditures for education, which can be interpreted as a household's willingness to pay for education.[2] It is remarkable that in 1985 the willingness of extremely poor households to pay for education was twice as high as the willingness of nonpoor households. Unfortunately, this willingness declined sharply over time so that in 1988 it had fallen to below that of the nonpoor.[3] This decline, in combination with falling enrollment rates and rising age-grade mismatch among children of extreme poor households paints an alarming picture, and presents a strong call for targeted education interventions to promote enrollment and to reduce monetary and opportunity cost of primary school attendance. Measures may well have to include selective subsidization of certain education expenses for the extreme poor, such as the provision of free school meals and books. Given the level of government resources devoted to education in Côte d'Ivoire, such reallocation of resources in a budget-neutral fashion would seem perfectly feasible.

The general conclusion about education is that enrollment rates continued to rise slowly during the adjustment phase, but dropped during the recession. During the 1985-88 period as a whole, the gap between the extreme poor and others widened, further bleakening the prospects of the extreme poor to rely on human capital formation to escape poverty. This trend is not related to the evolution of government expenditures devoted to education, but parallels a reduced willingness to pay for education services by households. This reduction was stronger than the overall fall in levels of living as a result of the economic recession, and could well reflect the recognition by households of the inefficiency of education service delivery in the country, as well as the reduced chances of formal sector employment (which fell throughout the eighties) for which formal education is a prerequisite.

Table 4.3

Household expenditures on education, by poverty status and region

Poverty status/region	Real per capita expenditures (1985 CFAF per year)			Share of household expenditures (percent)	
	1985	1988	Change: 1985-88 (percent)	1985	1988*
Extreme poor	2,092	1,055	-50	5.4	1.8
Mid-poor	3,655	2,725	-25	3.6	2.6
Nonpoor	9,267	6,424	-31	2.8	2.5
Abidjan	14,462	10,430	-28	3.6	3.4
Other cities	8,814	6,521	-26	3.8	3.5
East Forest	7,257	4,017	-45	4.0	2.5
West Forest	6,272	3,227	-49	2.6	2.3
Savannah	1,660	837	-50	1.1	0.7
All	7,898	4,881	-38	3.1	2.5

* Average of shares calculated at the household level.

Health

Table 4.4 presents information on several health indicators. As shown in Part A, the rate at which ill people consulted modern health personnel fell by about 10 percent between 1985 and 1988. However, consultations among the nonpoor actually increased (by 10 percent), so that the drop in the use of modern health facilities was concentrated entirely among the mid-poor and especially the extreme poor. Consultations among ill women from extremely poor households dropped by almost 50 percent, so that less than one ill woman in five sought care in a modern health facility in 1988. The regional breakdown confirms the picture further. Progress in access to modern health care occurred only in Abidjan and other cities. In all rural areas, the rate of consultations declined, but most heavily in the Savannah.

The picture of preventive consultations, primarily for prenatal care and vaccinations, is more positive (Table 4.4.B). The rate increased substantially between 1985 and 1988, from 22.3 to 32.8 percent. Here, the increase was actually highest among the mid-poor and the extreme poor, higher among women than among men, and highest in the two poorest regions, West Forest and the Savannah. Since preventive health care is usually delivered by special programs set up by both government and nongovernmental organizations, the results clearly indicate that these programs were well targeted.[4]

An important element of maintaining health is access to safe water. The CILSS results indicate that only about one in five persons in Côte d'Ivoire had access to tap water in 1988 – a figure that is essentially the same as it was in 1985 (Table 4.4.C). However, the most striking feature here is not the pattern over time but the huge gap between the poor and the nonpoor. Access to tap water among extremely poor persons was only one tenth of the rate among nonpoor and one fourth of the rate among mid-poor.[5] It is also clear that access to tap water in Côte d'Ivoire is strictly an urban benefit. In West Forest and the Savannah, less than two percent of rural residents have access to tap water. Even in urban areas, the availability of tap water became worse between 1985 and 1988, except in Abidjan.

Beyond the health implications from the lack of access to safe water, the poor must often spend more time to fetch water. This seems to be the case in Côte d'Ivoire, but the differences between the poor and nonpoor are small (Table 4.4.D). The average distance to the nearest water source increased from 264 meters to 294 meters between 1985 and 1988, but this distance is still not excessive. The distance did increase more among extremely poor households than among others, but the difference is small (in 1985, the average distance for the poor was actually less than for the nonpoor). Clearly, the policy priority for the Ivorian government is not to bring nontapped sources of water supply closer to households, but to expand the coverage of

Table 4.4
Health indicators, by poverty status and region

Poverty status/region	1985	1986	1987	1988
A. Percentage of ill people who consulted a doctor or nurse				
Extreme poor				
- Male	31.2	30.8	20.0	19.1
- Female	30.2	28.0	15.5	16.2
Mid-poor				
- Male	36.9	30.0	37.4	32.8
- Female	36.2	30.6	34.0	31.3
Nonpoor				
- Male	48.6	47.7	46.2	52.6
- Female	50.8	51.8	48.4	54.8
Abidjan	62.5	63.6	61.1	70.5
Other cities	53.9	55.8	53.5	56.5
East Forest	43.8	47.1	47.4	42.7
West Forest	39.6	39.0	26.9	34.6
Savannah	30.3	22.1	22.1	18.1
Côte d'Ivoire	45.8	43.9	40.6	41.3
B. Percentage of people having preventive consultations				
Extreme poor				
- Male	14.2	21.9	19.9	40.0
- Female	15.6	27.2	26.1	47.3
Mid-poor				
- Male	17.1	21.9	29.7	31.4
- Female	18.1	23.6	33.3	35.9
Nonpoor				
- Male	23.5	29.2	29.9	26.0
- Female	25.8	30.7	37.2	32.8
Abidjan	33.2	22.4	32.9	27.5
Other cities	27.0	42.6	39.0	37.9
East Forest	23.9	33.5	30.2	27.4
West Forest	16.5	14.7	25.4	34.1
Savannah	9.3	18.6	30.6	36.9
Côte d'Ivoire	22.3	27.9	32.1	32.8

(Table 4.4, cont.)

Table 4.4
Health indicators, by poverty status and region

Poverty status/region	1985	1986	1987	1988
C. Percentage of people with access to tap water				
Extreme poor	1.5	4.4	3.1	2.9
Mid-poor	7.9	7.7	4.0	11.4
Nonpoor	28.7	29.4	31.6	31.2
Abidjan	47.3	48.5	57.8	57.5
Other cities	46.5	46.8	42.2	37.6
East Forest	8.5	7.2	4.2	10.3
West Forest	-	-	-	0.7
Savannah	1.8	2.9	2.4	1.7
Côte d'Ivoire	21.8	22.7	21.9	20.9
D. Average distance (in meters) to water supply (if not tap water)				
Extreme poor	237	318	348	336
Mid-poor	237	311	264	273
Nonpoor	276	254	242	294
Côte d'Ivoire	264	269	258	294

tapped water to rural areas and to stem the slipping coverage in urban areas outside Abidjan.

Table 4.5 reports on the availability of two other facilities important for hygiene – toilets and garbage removal. Their health implications may be less direct than in the case of access to safe water, but the lack of toilets and garbage removal does contribute to the spread of disease and to generally unsanitary living conditions. For the country as a whole, the percentage of households that had a flush toilet or a pit latrine and the percentage of those who benefited from garbage removal by truck did not change much between 1985 and 1988. Both features are entirely urban in Côte d'Ivoire and significantly more available to nonpoor households. They also declined sharply among the extremely poor, while they remained the same or improved slightly among other groups – a trend we have observed thus far for almost all basic needs components of the level of living.

As for education, we tabulated the proportion of expenditures that households devote to health care (Table 4.6). As with education, expenditures for health declined between 1985 and 1988 by more than the decline in total

124

expenditures. But there are two differences between health and education. First, the absolute per capita amount spent on health by households exceeded government spending per capita (for education, government per capita outlays were two to three times those of household expenditures). This disparity means that the cuts in household spending are relatively more critical to total resources devoted to health care than was the case with household spending on education. Second, the cutbacks are largest among nonpoor households. However, the absolute amount spent on health care by poor households was so low – the equivalent of less than $2 annually per person among extremely poor households – that there would appear to be little room for decline.

Table 4.5
Access to toilet facilities and garbage disposal,
by poverty status

Poverty status/region	1985	1986	1987	1988
A. Percentage of households with flush toilet or pit latrine				
Extreme poor	37.7	34.2	30.3	25.9
Mid-poor	46.8	42.4	45.5	42.9
Nonpoor	60.5	58.7	65.7	62.9
Côte d'Ivoire	56.8	55.0	59.3	53.7
B. Percentage of households with garbage removal by truck				
Extreme poor	7.0	13.6	9.4	5.5
Mid-poor	8.8	15.0	16.6	17.0
Nonpoor	33.6	34.3	42.5	38.1
Côte d'Ivoire	27.9	30.2	35.1	29.1

The general picture of health care provision in Côte d'Ivoire is that the use of curative health consultations and the use of such amenities as tap water and toilets remained the same or declined slightly. Among the extreme poor, however, the use of amenities declined sharply; for amenities for which it has not, such as access to tap water, it remains at such pitifully low levels (three percent) that any change would not make much difference. The one bright spot is the use of preventive health care, primarily vaccinations, which have increasingly reached the extreme poor. As with education, outcomes at the micro level bear little relation to the evolution of public expenditures (see Table 4.1).

Table 4.6
Household expenditures on health,
by poverty status and region

Poverty status/region	Real per capita expenditures (1985 CFAF per year)			Share of household expenditures* (percent)	
	1985	1988	Change: 1985-88 (percent)	1985	1988
Extreme poor	598	526	-12	1.0	0.9
Mid-poor	3,318	2,998	-10	3.3	2.8
Nonpoor	11,332	8,091	-28	3.1	3.0
Abidjan	16,956	8,985	-47	3.6	2.7
Other cities	9,036	9,793	+8	3.0	4.8
East Forest	6,214	4,661	-25	2.6	2.2
West Forest	13,346	3,510	-74	5.2	2.0
Savannah	1,871	2,913	+56	1.0	1.9
All	9,345	5,947	-36	3.0	2.7

* Average of shares calculated at the household level.

Housing

The distribution of home ownership in Côte d'Ivoire is unusual when compared with elsewhere in Africa. Home ownership in Abidjan is much lower than what is recorded in other major African cities, and it is not a status that is associated with high income (Grootaert and Dubois, 1988). In fact, high-income households tend frequently to be renters (Table 4.7.A). The reasons may pertain to the extreme concentration of land and building ownership in urban areas, especially in Abidjan, and the traditional availability of subsidized rental housing to workers in the civil service and in the formal private sector. This tradition, however, came to an end during the structural adjustment program, when the government phased out SICOGI and SOGEFIHA, the two agencies that were responsible for providing public housing. The housing units were sold (at below market prices) to existing tenants. Subsidies paid to civil servants in private housing were also curtailed. The CILSS results show that virtually no renters in public housing were poor (less than one percent in 1985). Among the nonpoor however, public housing was quite important; in 1985, 33 percent of all renters in Abidjan and 14 percent of all renters in other cities lived in public housing (rural areas do not contain public housing). The phasing out of public housing was fairly effective, and in 1988 these figures were reduced to 17 percent and four percent, respectively. Clearly, the government's withdrawal from the housing market was a measure that did not have direct implications for the poor.

As indicated in Table 4.7.A, the slight decline in home ownership between 1985 and 1988 was experienced equally in each of the three poverty categories. However, these figures are dominated by rural areas, where home ownership is above 90 percent. A further examination of the distribution of home ownership within Abidjan revealed that home ownership rose in middle- and high-income districts – which could well be due to the sale of public housing units – while it fell sharply in low-income districts. It is not clear whether this trend is due to the fact that people actually lost the title to their home as economic hardship set in or to the increase of squatting settlements in low-income areas (or to both).

As a measure of the quality of housing, Table 4.7.B and C shows the percentage of people who have access to electricity and the available floor space per person. For the country as a whole, access to electricity improved slightly until 1987, and then regressed. However, the trends in individual regions were very different. Significant improvements occurred in Abidjan and in East and West Forest, while access declined in other cities and Savannah. Obviously, these trends are not related to the general economic trends in these areas, and probably reflect the continuation of an independent investment program by Côte d'Ivoire's public utility. Nevertheless, one trend is again clear: the most severe deterioration occurred among the extreme poor. The quality of the housing of the extreme poor also declined according to the amount of floor space available to them. For the other groups, there was no significant change.

Finally, Table 4.8 shows the main source of fuel used for cooking. The preferred fuel is of course electricity, which as we just saw is significantly more available to the nonpoor. The least desirable source is wood, which was used by almost all extremely poor households (by all of them in 1988) and by 90 percent of the mid-poor. Due to the deterioration in welfare, the percentage of households that gathered wood (as opposed to buying it) rose between 1985 and 1988 – from 78 to 87 percent. In 1988, 95 percent of extremely poor households gathered their own wood, for which they had to travel an average distance of 2.9 km. This distance actually declined since 1985, raising an environmental concern that closer woods (perhaps previously bypassed because they were still too young or otherwise not ideal for harvesting) are now being cut down.

In summary, housing was the one basic needs provision that was addressed explicitly by the structural adjustment program. The government's withdrawal from the housing market eliminated a benefit for the better-off (although the below market price sale of units created a one-time windfall profit for them) and left the poor largely untouched. Changes in rates of home ownership and the quality of housing between 1985 and 1988 were small, but the evidence indicates that whatever unfavorable changes did occur affected almost solely extremely poor households.

Table 4.7
Housing indicators, by poverty status and region

Poverty status/region	1985	1986	1987	1988
A. Percentage of people living in owned home				
Extreme poor	92.2	89.4	90.4	84.9
Mid-poor	87.5	83.2	85.6	80.6
Nonpoor	63.1	64.4	58.4	57.7
Abidjan	28.1	25.4	23.4	25.3
Other cities	48.3	53.6	47.5	46.4
East Forest	88.9	90.5	86.7	82.5
West Forest	96.6	94.7	94.7	92.5
Savannah	97.3	94.4	92.5	93.3
Côte d'Ivoire	70.9	70.4	68.4	68.8
B. Percentage of people with access to electricity				
Extreme poor	14.1	6.1	8.4	10.9
Mid-poor	19.4	23.7	21.0	29.2
Nonpoor	46.9	47.7	53.6	53.3
Abidjan	74.8	73.5	88.9	91.1
Other cities	77.0	77.3	74.5	71.8
East Forest	15.5	16.4	19.2	23.4
West Forest	0.1	-	2.2	4.4
Savannah	14.4	15.9	12.2	10.4
Côte d'Ivoire	38.1	39.4	41.2	39.7
C. Average floor area per person (square meters)				
Extreme poor	7.6	5.4	6.4	6.1
Mid-poor	7.2	6.6	7.4	7.0
Nonpoor	9.6	10.7	10.4	10.2
All	8.9	9.4	9.3	8.6

Table 4.8
Use of wood as fuel, by poverty status

Poverty status/region	1985	1986	1987	1988
A. Percentage of households using wood as kitchen fuel				
Extreme poor	98.2	95.3	95.8	100.0
Mid-poor	95.3	90.4	93.1	89.5
Nonpoor	66.4	67.7	61.6	59.9
Côte d'Ivoire	73.1	72.7	70.1	72.0
B. Percentage of households gathering wood				
Extreme poor	88.6	91.0	89.8	95.2
Mid-poor	86.4	87.6	85.3	87.6
Nonpoor	4.9	77.3	77.7	84.4
Côte d'Ivoire	78.4	80.2	80.8	87.1
C. Average distance (km) to source of wood				
Extreme poor	4.2	4.4	2.7	2.9
Mid-poor	3.9	3.6	3.2	3.0
Nonpoor	3.5	3.4	3.1	2.9
Côte d'Ivoire	3.7	3.5	3.1	3.0

Conclusion

This chapter has shown that during structural adjustment as well as destabilization in the 1980s, the poorest population groups in Côte d'Ivoire suffered deep setbacks in their fulfillment of basic needs, even though the government maintained the overall level of social expenditures. Our results suggest that at least in the short and medium run there was little relation between the level of government expenditure devoted to health and education and achievement or use-of-service indicators in those sectors, due to suboptimal intrasectoral allocation of resources.

On a countrywide basis, most basic needs indicators (literacy, school enrollment, use of health care facilities, access to safe water, housing amenities) changed little over the period 1985-88. This is an encouraging finding, in that the deterioration in expenditure-based welfare and the concomitant rapid rise in poverty over the period was not matched by a deterioration in the fulfillment of basic needs. Even those indicators which did decline did not do so nearly to the same degree as the monetary indicators. This underscores the importance of looking separately at the different dimensions of the level of living since they clearly need not all move in the same direction.

However, the countrywide results mask very wide differences between the poor and nonpoor. Basic needs indicators declined systematically for the poorest households, almost regardless of the average trend of a given indicator. In very poor households, net primary school enrollment for girls fell from 22.4 percent to 16.7 percent, and the number of children one year or more behind their age-appropriate grade doubled to 64 percent for boys and 53 percent for girls. The rate of medical consultations of ill women in very poor households fell from 30 percent to 16 percent. The rate of home ownership of the very poor declined from 92 percent to 85 percent and their access to electricity fell from 14 percent to 11 percent. In addition, the amount of expenditures which very poor households devote to education and health care fell by 50 percent and 12 percent respectively. The sole exception to this pattern of deteriorating basic needs fulfillment occurred in health care: the rate of preventive consultations rose for very poor households and more so than the countrywide average. (Access to tap water also improved, but in 1988 it was still at a dismal three percent.)

The declines in education indicators were more severe after the adjustment program was abandoned, but for other indicators declines occurred both in the adjustment and destabilization phases. The cause must thus likely be sought in the general economic decline of the 1980s in Côte d'Ivoire and the concomitant deterioration in supply and delivery of public services. The shift in the functional allocation towards salaries and away from material inputs was certainly related to this. On the demand side, very poor households faced tighter budget constrains which reduced household resources available for health and education.

The results in this chapter support the argument that the focus of policy reform, and of indicators to monitor its social impact, should not be on aggregate levels of public spending. Instead the focus should be on the intrasectoral and functional allocation, but even more so on the distribution of service delivery. Both increases and decreases of public spending, at the sectoral and intrasectoral level, are compatible with improvement or deterioration in the use of services and the satisfaction of basic needs by the poor. The Côte d'Ivoire case shows that steady or even improving overall basic needs indicators can hide alarming declines in the situation of the poorest.

It must be recognized of course that in practice policy reform to change the intrasectoral and functional allocation of public expenditure is not always easy, particularly in the context of a stagnant or shrinking budget. There are technological obstacles, e.g. facilities and personnel trained for higher level of education and health care cannot usually be converted to primary care, or, where they can, it may involve high marginal cost. There are often political obstacles, such as vocal trade unions of teachers. Lastly, it is not straightforward to determine what the 'optimal' allocation is, even purely theoretically. The first two obstacles certainly played a role in the case of Côte d'Ivoire during the eighties. The theoretical consideration was probably not relevant because the functional allocation was so extremely lopsided that reallocation away from salaries would have continued to be an efficiency improvement over a wide range.

Finally, the chapter's results confirm the importance of not considering the poor as a homogeneous group. This is the implicit assumption when poverty analysis uses only one poverty line. The main finding of this chapter, viz the relative deterioration of the condition of the very poorest, would have been entirely missed if only one poverty line had been used. By the same token, the policy recommendations are distinctly different, since the very poor represent a more urgent target group. Policies like selected subsidies for school meals and books may be needed for the poorest but may not be appropriate for the poor as a group, if for no other reason than the forbidding total cost.

In most countries achievement or use-of-service social indicators are not kept by poverty category because the underlying household-level data are not available. Poverty alleviation programs should, therefore, include the establishment of such monitoring systems if programs aim to be targeted effectively. We have argued elsewhere (Grootaert, 1993b, Grootaert and Marchant, 1991) that the data needed to do this are actually quite limited in scope and can be collected easily, rapidly, and cheaply. Such data collection is not a statistical luxury but an essential ingredient in the overall effort to enhance the livelihood and well-being of the poor.

Notes

1   This chapter is a revised version of 'Poverty and Basic Needs Fulfillment in Africa During Structural Change: Evidence from Côte d'Ivoire,' by Christiaan Grootaert, which appeared originally in *World Development*, Vol. 22, No. 10, 1994, pp. 1521-1534. The material is used with the kind permission of Elsevier Science Ltd., The Boulevard, Langford Lane, Kidlington OX5 1GB, UK.

2   For that reason, Table 4.3 shows the average of shares calculated at the household level, since the share has meaning as a household-level variable. In this respect, Table 4.3 differs from Table 3.21 which shows the composition of aggregate nonfood expenditures. The figures in Table 3.21 are ratios of sums; for example, for education,

the table shows total educational expenses by a given poverty group as a percentage of the total nonfood expenses of that group. It is clear that the ratio of sums need not equal the mean of household ratios.

3   There appears to be a substitution effect with food expenditure. The share of food in total expenditure for the very poor rose from 52 percent to 60 percent between 1985 and 1988, while the food share for the nonpoor remained steady at 47 percent.

4   One reason that preventive care figures show such a marked improvement for the poor relative to the nonpoor may be the pent-up demand among the poor. A large part of preventive care is quite literally of the 'one-shot' variety – vaccinations. If the nonpoor routinely have their children vaccinated, then their rate of preventive care consultations should be roughly stable over time which is indeed what the data show. The rate among the poor would increase sharply when programs are launched and in a short period of time vaccinate many children, including those who should have been vaccinated in the course of the past several years. In the longer run, preventive health care rates should stabilize.

5   Because the CILSS reports access to tap water as a *household* feature, we cannot show differences between men and women.

5 The lucky few amidst economic decline: distributional change as seen through panel data

With Ravi Kanbur[1]

As the previous chapters have shown, the second half of the 1980s was a period of drastic economic decline for Côte d'Ivoire, as per capita GDP fell by 28 percent. The incidence of poverty increased from 30 percent in 1985 to 35 percent in 1987. This increase in poverty accelerated dramatically in 1988 to 46 percent. As shown in Chapter 3, the income distribution in 1988 was uniformly worse than in 1987, as measured by first-order dominance. Thus, poverty would be higher in 1988 than in 1987 according to *any* poverty measure that satisfies reasonable conditions (Ravallion, 1992).

The economic decline in Côte d'Ivoire and its consequences for poverty are not to be doubted. But how widespread was the collapse in welfare? Did a lucky few escape the decline? And what were the characteristics of those who did? In order to answer these questions, we need information on the welfare level of the *same* individuals for at least *two* periods of time. The CILSS allows us to construct three such panels, for 1985-86, 1986-87 and 1987-88. For about 700 households in each panel, we can track consumption over a two-year period. But because each panel consists of a different set of households, we do not have information on the same households over four years. Nevertheless, the availability of panel data sets for Côte d'Ivoire is a rare occurrence among the countries in Africa, and among developing countries in general. Alessie et al. (1992) and Deaton (1992) have used the 1985-86 panel to explore labor market behavior and savings, but the full set of three panels have not yet been used to examine poverty dynamics in the second half of the 1980s.

Chapter 2 provided details on how we constructed the three panels from the CILSS. In this chapter, we discuss how we used our welfare and poverty measures to track poverty in Côte d'Ivoire over the three panels. The results indicate that the broad trends discussed in Chapter 3 with annual data from 1985 to 1988 are confirmed. However, we also extend the analyses to an investigation of the 'lucky few' who improved their circumstances amid the general decline. Actually, the results indicate that the lucky 'few' were not so few! And, surprisingly, a significant number of the poorest of the poor *improved* their status over the two years of the panel data, despite a dramatic downturn in fortunes on average.

Poverty in Côte d'Ivoire: 1985-86, 1986-87, and 1987-88

To analyze poverty in this chapter, we have retained household expenditures per capita as the measure of welfare. As discussed in Chapters 2 and 3, we have defined two poverty lines: 128,600 CFAF/year, which classifies 30 percent of the population as poor in 1985, and 75,000 CFAF/year, which cuts off the bottom 10 percent of the distribution in 1985 to classify people in extreme poverty. Both lines are held constant in real terms for longitudinal analysis. Tables 5.1 and 5.2 summarize the evolution of poverty and extreme poverty in Côte d'Ivoire between 1985 and 1988, based on the P-alpha class of poverty measures (the P-alpha index was detailed in Chapter 2).

Table 5.1
Poverty in Côte d'Ivoire:
full samples for 1985, 1986, 1987, and 1988

	P_o	P_1	P_2
1985	0.300	0.098	0.045
1986	0.299	0.082	0.032
1987	0.348	0.101	0.043
1988	0.459	0.142	0.063

Source: See Chapter 3.

Table 5.2
Extreme poverty in Côte d'Ivoire:
full samples for 1985, 1986, 1987 and 1988

	P_o	P_1	P_2
1985	0.100	0.027	0.011
1986	0.064	0.013	0.004
1987	0.091	0.023	0.008
1988	0.141	0.035	0.013

Source: See Chapter 3.

The cross-sectional analysis underlying Tables 5.1 and 5.2 shows that between 1985 and 1986 the incidence of poverty in Côte d'Ivoire did not change, but that the depth of poverty declined. Among the extreme poor both the incidence and depth of poverty declined. The trend changed after 1986, when the incidence and depth of poverty among all poor began to increase. The largest increase occurred in 1988, when the incidence of poverty rose from 34.8 percent to 45.9 percent and the incidence of extreme poverty rose from 9.1 percent to 14.1 percent.

Tables 5.3 and 5.4 show the P-alpha index for poverty and extreme poverty, respectively, as calculated from the panel data sets. The panel results confirm the pattern of poverty observed from the cross-sectional data. The first panel records the improvements in the incidence and depth of poverty (with the curious exception of P_0 for 1986 in Table 5.3, which is probably due to sample attrition). The improvement is still reflected in the first year of the second panel, after which all index figures rise, with a notable acceleration in the third panel.

Table 5.3
Poverty in Côte d'Ivoire as measured by panel data
for 1985-86, 1986-87, and 1987-88

		P_0	P_1	P_2
Panel (1)	1985	0.288	0.100	0.048
	1986	0.336	0.091	0.035
Panel (2)	1986	0.261	0.073	0.028
	1987	0.324	0.085	0.033
Panel (3)	1987	0.363	0.109	0.048
	1988	0.507	0.164	0.075

When the same individual's level of welfare changes over time, it can be argued that taking each time period separately to evaluate poverty is incorrect. The outcomes should be combined in some way to measure the overall level of living during the relevant period, and poverty should be assessed relative to this measure. Atkinson and Bourguignon (1984) provide general argument in this direction, in the context of social welfare requirements. In our specific case, a convenient way to apply these ideas is to take a discounted sum of per capita expenditures and compare it with a discounted sum of poverty lines in the two years of the panel (with the same discount rates for the two calculations).

Table 5.4
Extreme poverty in Côte d'Ivoire, as measured by panel data
for 1985-86, 1986-87, and 1987-88

		P_0	P_1	P_2
Panel (1)	1985	0.128	0.036	0.016
	1986	0.070	0.014	0.005
Panel (2)	1986	0.055	0.012	0.005
	1987	0.075	0.015	0.005
Panel (3)	1987	0.098	0.028	0.010
	1988	0.208	0.056	0.021

This type of calculation for constructing a two-period poverty index from panel data raises two new considerations, beyond those associated with cross-sectional calculations. First, the size of each panel household may change from one year to the next. Since poverty is calculated over individuals, there is a choice to be made as to which household size to use for deriving the distribution of expenditures per capita over the individuals that form the basis of the poverty index. We selected the initial year. (Note that the welfare measure – expenditures per capita – was of course calculated in each year with the corresponding household size in that year.) Second, the sampling weights to be applied to the CILSS data also change from year to year. Since only one set of weights can be applied to calculate within-panel poverty, only one year can be chosen for the calculation. Again, we selected the initial year.

Table 5.5 shows the results for two-period poverty with a discount rate of 10 percent.[2] As shown, the broad conclusions about *trends* continue to hold. However, the more interesting conclusion is that 'two-period' poverty is generally less than the larger of the two snapshot poverty figures for each panel. In fact, in some cases, two-period poverty is less than *both* snapshot figures. And it is certainly less than the full sample snapshots provided in Table 5.1 and Table 5.2. These findings suggest that mobility in the panels is considerable, particularly across poverty classes. For example, if a very rich household falls to just below the poverty line in the second period, or one just below the poverty line becomes very rich in the second period, it would register as being poor in one of the two snapshots, but not necessarily in the two period comparison. From the standpoint of welfare, this result indicates that conventional measures of poverty, may yield overestimates. From the standpoint of positive analysis, the results call for a more in-depth investigation of the extent and nature of this mobility.

Table 5.5
Two-period poverty and extreme poverty
in the three panels

	P_0	P_1	P_2
(A) Poverty			
Panel (1)	0.281	0.077	0.030
Panel (2)	0.267	0.060	0.021
Panel (3)	0.401	0.118	0.051
(B) Extreme poverty			
Panel (1)	0.100	0.020	0.005
Panel (2)	0.038	0.007	0.002
Panel (3)	0.146	0.034	0.012

The lucky 'few'

Chapter 3 demonstrated that, by and large, poverty in Côte d'Ivoire increased during the second half of the 1980s. This result was confirmed by the three panels. However, the finding does not of course mean that *all* households lost out. Table 5.6 presents information on households whose welfare did or did not improve. (In this section, the basic unit of analysis is the household, given that the panels are *household* panels and there is no need here to convert the data into individual-level data in order to calculate poverty indexes).

For Côte d'Ivoire as a whole, a minimum of 30 percent of households *improved* their level of living, even during the precipitous decline at the end of the period under consideration. And this figure persists throughout the regions and throughout the period. The regional pattern varies, of course, and is influenced by which pair of years we use. Thus, in 1985-86 only 13.2 percent of Abidjan households experienced an increase; in 1986-87, as many as 43.3 percent of households in West Forest improved their level of living. However, the general message is loud and clear: the lucky 'few' are not so few!

Of course, the improvements may have been very small – so small that they can be attributed to measurement error. Tables 5.7.A, B, and C provide figures that show the movement of households across poverty classes: the extreme poor (those below the extreme poverty line), the mid-poor (those between the poverty line and the extreme poverty line), and the nonpoor (those above the poverty line). Each table presents raw frequencies (the fractional households are due to weighting procedures) and percentages.

Table 5.6
Frequencies of the change in
per capita expenditures (percent)

	1985-86	1986-87	1987-88
Côte d'Ivoire			
Increase	39.2	44.6	30.2
Decrease	60.8	55.4	69.8
Abidjan			
Increase	13.2	54.7	38.7
Decrease	86.8	45.3	61.3
Other cities			
Increase	40.8	42.4	31.4
Decrease	59.2	57.6	68.6
East Forest			
Increase	51.9	38.8	33.9
Decrease	48.1	61.2	66.1
West Forest			
Increase	33.0	43.3	22.1
Decrease	67.0	56.7	77.9
Savannah			
Increase	56.5	44.5	25.0
Decrease	43.5	55.5	75.0

Let us start with Table 5.7.C, which reports the results of the analysis with the third panel, for changes between 1987 and 1988. As shown, 69.1 percent of households remained in their class, and 30.9 percent changed classes. More important, 6.3 percent of households *improved* their class, moving from the extreme poor to mid-poor or nonpoor categories, and from mid-poor to nonpoor. In all, 26.7 percent of households that started as extreme poor improved their class, as did 19.3 percent of households that started as mid-poor. Thus, even in the midst of the general decline, there was a significant probability that a poor household could become nonpoor. These results are confirmed by the 1986-87 and 1985-86 panels. In 1986-87, 8.5 percent of households improved their poverty class, and the probability that an extremely poor household would improve its poverty class was a staggering 64.8 percent. In fact, the probability that an extremely poor household would jump two classes to become nonpoor was 23.2 percent. These results are based only on a small number of households (only 3.3 percent of households were very poor in 1986), but similar probabilities are observed in the 1985-86 panel where 8.2 percent of households were very poor. Here the probability for the very poor to rise one poverty category is 43.3 percent and the probability to rise two poverty categories is 26.9 percent. To check whether such movements are statistically significant relative to the expected probabilities of being in a poverty class (as represented by the row and column totals in Table 5.7), we ran chi-square tests on each panel of Table 5.7. Each of the three tests indicated statistical significance of the movements across poverty classes. The same result obtained when we repeated the test on a 2 x 2 condensed version of Table 5.7 distinguishing only poor and nonpoor. The panel data thus indicate that in Côte d'Ivoire in the second half of the eighties there was considerable mobility counter to the general trend of immiserization.

This mobility has at least two implications for the analysis of poverty. First, it raises questions about *who* these lucky 'few' are. Second, it indicates that poverty measures based on snapshots may be inappropriate, and that 'two-period' poverty measures may be more appropriate. The second question was addressed in the previous section. The remainder of this section addresses the first.

Table 5.7
Changes in poverty status,
as measured by the three panels

A. Panel (1)

		1985			
		Extreme poor	Mid-poor	Nonpoor	All
1986	Extreme poor	17.6	11.0	4.8	33.5
		(2.4)	(1.5)	(0.7)	(4.6)
		52.6	32.9	14.4	
		29.7	9.9	0.9	
	Mid-poor	25.7	50.4	75.9	152.0
		(3.5)	(7.0)	(10.5)	(21.0)
		16.9	33.1	49.9	
		43.3	45.3	13.7	
	Nonpoor	16.0	49.7	472.2	537.9
		(2.2)	(6.9)	(65.3)	(74.4)
		3.0	9.2	87.8	
		27.0	44.7	85.4	
	All	59.4	111.1	552.9	723.4
		(8.2)	(15.4)	(76.4)	(100.0)

(Table 5.7, cont.)

Table 5.7
Changes in poverty status,
as measured by the three panels

B. Panel (2)

		1986			
		Extreme poor	Mid-poor	Nonpoor	All
1987	Extreme poor	7.6	18.3	15.4	41.3
		(1.2)	(2.8)	(2.3)	(6.3)
		18.4	44.4	37.2	
		35.1	16.6	2.9	
	Mid-poor	9.0	50.5	88.1	147.6
		(1.4)	(7.7)	(13.4)	(22.5)
		6.1	34.2	59.7	
		41.6	45.8	16.8	
	Nonpoor	5.0	41.4	419.8	466.2
		(0.8)	(6.3)	(64.1)	(71.2)
		1.1	8.9	90.0	
		23.2	37.6	80.2	
	All	21.7	110.2	523.3	655.2
		(3.3)	(16.8)	(79.9)	(100.0)

C. Panel (3)

		1987			
		Extreme poor	Mid-poor	Nonpoor	All
1988	Extreme poor	41.7	51.6	14.4	107.6
		(5.8)	(7.2)	(2.0)	(15.0)
		38.7	47.9	13.3	
		73.2	33.3	2.9	
	Mid-poor	11.7	73.6	109.3	194.7
		(1.6)	(10.3)	(15.3)	(27.2)
		6.0	37.8	56.2	
		20.6	47.5	21.7	
	Nonpoor	3.5	29.9	379.2	412.6
		(0.5)	(4.2)	(53.0)	57.7
		0.8	7.2	91.9	
		6.1	19.3	75.4	
	All	56.9	155.1	502.9	714.9
		(8.0)	(21.7)	(70.3)	(100.0)

Note: The cells in this table contain:
  -absolute frequency of households (fractional numbers are due to weighting)
  -relative frequency in parentheses
  -row percentage
  -column percentage

As a first cut at identifying the lucky few, consider Table 5.8. Of all households that improved their poverty status, the majority were to be found consistently in the Savannah and East Forest. The contrast between Abidjan, the richest region, and the Savannah, the poorest, is striking. In each panel, the number of households in the Savannah that improved their poverty status is several times the corresponding number for Abidjan, despite the fact that the total number of households in the panels from the two regions is about the same. The detailed analysis of mobility for the Savannah for 1987-88 shows that 7.2 percent of households improved their poverty class, compared with only four percent among households in Abidjan. (The tables in Annex 1 provide the results of this more detailed analyses of regional poverty for the three time periods.) Table 5.9 shows the regional probabilities to move up one or two poverty classes. The probabilities decline as one moves from the first to the third panel, in line with the overall deterioration of economic conditions. The decline is most pronounced for mid-poor households. The regional pattern is quite diverse. In 1987-88, in the Savannah, the probability of a very poor household escaping its class was 12 percent and the probability of a middle-poor household escaping poverty was 17.8 percent. In other cities these probabilities were 42.9 and 15.6 percent.

Table 5.8
Poverty changes, by region, as measured
by the three panels (percent)

	Abidjan	Other cities	East Forest	West Forest	Savannah	Total
Panel (1)						
Improved poverty status	2.0	13.6	44.9	10.7	28.7	100.0
Worsened poverty status	20.3	12.7	21.9	23.7	21.3	100.0
Panel (2)						
Improved poverty status	7.7	16.4	30.8	11.1	34.0	100.0
Worsened poverty status	4.7	13.9	36.3	8.3	36.8	100.0
Panel (3)						
Improved poverty status	11.8	15.8	20.4	20.2	31.8	100.0
Worsened poverty status	1.0	14.8	19.5	25.3	39.4	100.0

Table 5.9
Probabilities to improve poverty class,
by region (percent)

	Abidjan	Other cities	East Forest	West Forest	Savannah
Panel (1)					
Extreme poor households	-	53.4	72.8	-	75.0
Mid-poor households	47.5*	41.6	43.1	75.6	36.8
Panel (2)					
Extreme poor households	33.3*	-	59.3	54.5*	77.3
Mid-poor households	54.7	45.9	32.1	41.3	35.8
Panel (3)					
Extreme poor households	-	42.9	49.1	42.9	12.0
Mid-poor households	49.4	15.4	17.9	17.4	17.7

* Based on fewer than five observations.

Table 5.10 is analogous to Table 5.8, but examines results for socioeconomic categories described earlier in Chapter 3. The relevant statistic here is the relative probability that poverty improved or deteriorated. The third panel shows that this relative probability is highest among private formal sector employees and lowest among food crop farmers. Export crop farmers have a higher relative probability than food crop farmers in all three panels, while the poverty status of the self-employed and public sector employees (with the exception of the latter in the first panel) is equally likely to have improved or deteriorated.

One problem with such tabulations based on only 700 households is 'small cells', and some of the erratic variations in the figures can be attributed to this problem. Nevertheless, the results confirm specific patterns among the lucky few that are worth investigating in the future.

Conclusion

This chapter was an exploratory exercise in using panel data sets to investigate the change in the distribution of poverty. It confirmed the existing evidence on declining welfare in Côte d'Ivoire during the second half of the 1980s, which relied on snapshots of the distribution of welfare during 1985-88. But the panels also allow us for the first time to highlight and quantify the mobility of the same households across poverty classes over time. The finding that 'two-

Table 5.10
Poverty changes by socioeconomic group, as measured by the three panels (percent)

	Export crop farmers	Food crop farmers	Public sector employees	Private formal sector employees	Informal sector employees	Self-employed	Other	Total
Panel (1)								
Improved poverty status	14.5	61.6	1.1	0.0	0.0	18.5	4.3	100.0
Worsened poverty status	11.0	50.3	3.6	9.2	2.9	14.2	8.8	100.0
Panel (2)								
Improved poverty status	21.7	46.6	1.4	5.2	3.8	16.9	4.4	100.0
Worsened poverty status	18.3	52.7	1.5	0.6	2.9	16.4	7.7	100.0
Panel (3)								
Improved poverty status	26.0	39.1	6.3	3.9	4.4	14.5	5.8	100.0
Worsened poverty status	17.9	56.9	6.7	0.9	1.5	12.8	3.3	100.0

143

period' poverty was generally less than poverty measured by single-period snapshots alerted us to the extent of this mobility. Thus, a lucky few must have bucked the trend and improved their welfare amid general decline. Our investigations revealed that the lucky few were fairly numerous, and the probability of escaping poverty was quite high even among the extreme poor. We found that these lucky few were distributed widely throughout the regions, although among some socioeconomic groups the poor had a greater chance of escaping poverty amid the general decline in levels of living. A more precise investigation of these characteristics is hampered somewhat by the small sample sizes of the panels, but it is hoped that future work will reveal additional patterns that will provide useful guidance for designing policy.

Notes

1   This chapter is a revised version of the article 'The Lucky Few Amidst Economic Decline: Distributional Change in Côte d'Ivoire as Seen Through Panel Data Sets, 1985-88' by Christiaan Grootaert and Ravi Kanbur, which appeared originally in *Journal of Development Studies*, Vol. 31, No. 4, 1995, pp. 603-619. The material is used with permission of Frank Cass & Co., Ltd.

2   We repeated the calculations with discount rates of three percent, five percent, and 15 percent. This produced only very slight differences from the results in Table 5.5 which in no case affected the conclusions.

Annex 1
Changes in poverty status, by region and panel: detailed analysis

The tables in this annex are regional breakdowns of Table 5.7. The cells in each table show absolute frequency of households (fractional numbers are due to weighting), relative frequency in parentheses, row percentage, and column percentage.

A. 1985-86

Abidjan

		1985			
		Extreme poor	Mid-poor	Nonpoor	All
1986	Extreme poor	-	0.2	-	0.2
		-	(0.2)	-	(0.2)
		-	100.0	-	
		-	6.4	-	
	Mid-poor	-	1.9	18.4	20.3
		-	(1.3)	(12.9)	(14.3)
		-	9.4	90.5	
		-	47.4	13.3	
	Nonpoor	-	1.9	119.7	121.6
		-	(1.3)	(84.2)	(85.5)
		-	1.5	98.5	
		-	46.1	86.7	
	All	-	4.0	138.1	142.2
		-	(2.8)	(97.1)	(100.0)

Other cities

		1985			
		Extreme poor	Mid-poor	Nonpoor	All
1986	Extreme poor	5.3	2.4	0.3	8.1
		(4.5)	(2.0)	(0.3)	(6.8)
		66.7	29.8	4.2	
		46.1	16.2	0.4	
	Mid-poor	2.6	6.3	9.0	17.9
		(2.2)	(5.3)	(7.5)	(15.0)
		14.6	35.2	50.1	
		22.5	42.4	9.7	
	Nonpoor	3.6	6.2	83.2	93.0
		(3.1)	(5.2)	(69.9)	(78.1)
		3.9	6.6	89.4	
		31.4	41.4	89.9	
	All	11.6	14.9	92.5	119.0
		(9.8)	(12.5)	(77.7)	(100.0)

145

(Annex 1, cont.)

Annex 1
Changes in poverty status, by region and panel: detailed analysis

East Forest

		1985			
		Extreme poor	Mid-poor	Nonpoor	All
1986	Extreme poor	7.3	5.0	3.1	15.4
		(4.1)	(2.8)	(1.7)	(8.6)
		47.4	32.3	20.3	
		27.4	9.8	3.0	
	Mid-poor	11.5	23.8	12.0	47.3
		(6.4)	(13.3)	(6.7)	(26.4)
		24.2	50.4	25.4	
		43.2	47.1	11.7	
	Nonpoor	7.8	21.8	87.3	116.8
		(4.3)	(12.1)	(48.6)	(65.1)
		6.7	18.6	74.7	
		29.4	43.0	85.2	
	All	26.5	50.6	102.4	179.5
		(14.8)	(28.2)	(57.0)	(100.0)

West Forest

		1985			
		Extreme poor	Mid-poor	Nonpoor	All
1986	Extreme poor	-	0.6	-	0.6
		-	(0.4)	-	(0.4)
		-	100.0	-	
		-	4.8	-	
	Mid-poor	0.3	2.4	21.2	23.9
		(0.2)	(1.5)	(13.7)	(15.4)
		1.2	10.0	88.8	
		34.4	20.0	14.9	
	Nonpoor	0.6	9.0	121.0	130.6
		(0.3)	(5.8)	(78.1)	(84.2)
		0.4	6.9	92.7	
		65.6	75.2	85.1	
	All	0.8	11.9	142.3	155.1
		(0.5)	(7.7)	(91.7)	(100.0)

146

(Annex 1, cont.)

Annex 1
Changes in poverty status, by region and panel: detailed analysis

Savannah

		1985			
		Extreme poor	Mid-poor	Nonpoor	All
1986	Extreme poor	5.0	2.8	1.4	9.2
		(3.9)	(2.2)	(1.1)	(7.2)
		54.2	30.8	15.0	
		24.4	9.5	1.8	
	Mid-poor	11.3	15.9	15.4	42.7
		(8.9)	(12.5)	(12.1)	(33.4)
		26.6	37.3	36.1	
		55.7	53.7	19.8	
	Nonpoor	4.0	10.9	60.9	75.8
		(3.2)	(8.5)	(47.7)	(59.4)
		5.3	14.4	80.3	
		19.8	36.8	78.4	
	All	20.4	29.6	77.7	127.7
		(15.9)	(23.2)	(60.8)	(100.0)

B. 1986-87

Abidjan

		1986			
		Extreme poor	Mid-poor	Nonpoor	All
1987	Extreme poor	1.6	-	1.6	3.2
		(1.2)	-	(1.2)	(2.4)
		49.9	-	50.1	
		66.9	-	1.3	
	Mid-poor	-	2.9	4.1	7.0
		-	(2.2)	(3.2)	(5.4)
		-	41.2	58.8	
		-	45.2	3.4	
	Nonpoor	0.8	3.5	115.8	120.0
		(8.6)	(2.7)	(88.9)	(92.2)
		0.6	2.9	96.4	
		33.0	54.8	95.3	
	All	2.4	6.4	121.5	130.2
		(1.8)	(4.9)	(93.3)	(100.0)

147

(Annex 1, cont.)

Annex 1
Changes in poverty status, by region and panel: detailed analysis

Other cities

		1986			
		Extreme poor	Mid-poor	Nonpoor	All
1987	Extreme poor	-	2.2	-	2.2
		-	(1.6)	-	(1.6)
		-	100.0	-	
		-	13.8	-	
	Mid-poor	1.0	6.4	14.8	22.1
		(0.7)	(4.7)	(10.9)	(16.4)
		4.3	28.9	66.8	
		50.0	40.6	12.6	
	Nonpoor	1.0	7.2	102.9	111.0
		(0.7)	(5.3)	(76.0)	(82.0)
		0.9	6.5	92.7	
		50.0	45.6	87.4	
	All	1.9	15.7	117.7	135.3
		(1.4)	(11.6)	(87.0)	(100.0)

East Forest

		1986			
		Extreme poor	Mid-poor	Nonpoor	All
1987	Extreme poor	3.4	9.0	3.2	15.6
		(2.1)	(5.6)	(1.9)	(9.7)
		22.0	57.8	20.1	
		40.3	24.2	2.7	
	Mid-poor	4.3	16.4	32.0	52.7
		(2.7)	(10.1)	(19.8)	(32.6)
		8.2	31.0	60.7	
		50.5	43.8	27.7	
	Nonpoor	0.8	12.0	80.4	93.2
		(0.5)	(7.4)	(49.8)	(57.7)
		0.8	12.8	86.3	
		9.2	32.0	69.6	
	All	8.6	37.4	115.6	161.5
		(5.3)	(23.1)	(71.5)	(100.0)

148

(Annex 1, cont.)

Annex 1
Changes in poverty status, by region and panel: detailed analysis

West Forest

		1986			
		Extreme poor	Mid-poor	Nonpoor	All
1987	Extreme poor	1.0	1.1	1.0	3.1
		(1.4)	(1.5)	(1.4)	(4.2)
		32.8	34.8	32.4	
		46.0	8.8	1.7	
	Mid-poor	1.2	6.1	8.1	15.4
		(1.6)	(8.3)	(11.0)	(20.9)
		7.7	39.8	52.5	
		54.0	50.4	13.6	
	Nonpoor	-	5.0	50.3	55.3
		-	(6.7)	(68.2)	(74.9)
		-	8.9	91.0	
		-	40.7	84.7	
	All	2.2	12.1	59.4	73.8
		(3.0)	(16.5)	(80.5)	(100.0)

Savannah

		1986			
		Extreme poor	Mid-poor	Nonpoor	All
1987	Extreme poor	1.6	6.0	9.6	17.3
		(1.0)	(3.9)	(6.2)	(11.2)
		9.1	35.0	55.8	
		23.8	15.7	8.8	
	Mid-poor	2.6	18.7	29.1	50.4
		(1.6)	(12.1)	(18.9)	(32.7)
		5.1	37.1	57.8	
		38.5	48.5	26.7	
	Nonpoor	2.5	13.8	70.4	86.7
		(1.6)	(8.9)	(45.6)	(56.2)
		2.9	15.9	81.2	
		37.7	35.8	64.5	
	All	6.6	38.5	109.2	154.3
		(4.3)	(25.0)	(70.7)	(100.0)

Annex 1
Changes in poverty status, by region and panel: detailed analysis

C. 1987-88

Abidjan

		1987			
		Extreme poor	Mid-poor	Nonpoor	All
1988	Extreme poor	-	-	-	-
		-	-	-	-
		-	-	-	
		-	-	-	
	Mid-poor	-	4.4	1.8	6.2
		-	(3.3)	(1.3)	(4.7)
		-	71.4	(28.6)	
		-	50.0	1.4	
	Nonpoor	0.9	4.4	121.4	126.7
		(0.7)	(3.3)	(91.3)	(95.3)
		0.7	3.5	95.8	
		100.0	50.0	98.6	
	All	0.9	8.9	123.2	133.0
		(0.7)	(6.7)	(92.7)	(100.0)

Other cities

		1987			
		Extreme poor	Mid-poor	Nonpoor	All
1988	Extreme poor	5.2	1.9	2.6	9.7
		(3.8)	(1.4)	(1.9)	(7.1)
		53.3	20.0	26.7	
		57.1	9.4	2.4	
	Mid-poor	3.9	15.6	21.4	40.9
		(2.9)	(11.4)	(15.7)	(30.0)
		9.5	38.1	52.4	
		42.9	75.0	20.1	
	Nonpoor	-	3.2	82.4	85.6
		-	(2.4)	(60.5)	(62.9)
		-	3.8	96.2	
		-	15.6	77.4	
	All	9.1	20.8	106.4	136.2
		(6.7)	(15.2)	(78.1)	(100.0)

Annex 1
Changes in poverty status, by region and panel: detailed analysis

East Forest

		1987			
		Extreme poor	Mid-poor	Nonpoor	All
1988	Extreme poor	2.6	11.8	3.9	18.4
		(1.8)	(8.0)	(2.7)	(12.5)
		14.3	64.3	21.4	
		50.0	32.1	3.7	
	Mid-poor	2.6	18.4	18.4	39.5
		(1.8)	(12.5)	(12.5)	(26.8)
		6.7	46.7	46.7	
		50.0	50.0	17.5	
	Nonpoor	-	6.6	83.0	89.6
		-	(4.5)	(56.2)	(60.7)
		-	7.4	92.6	
		-	17.9	78.7	
	All	5.3	36.9	105.4	147.5
		(3.6)	(25.0)	(71.4)	(100.0)

West Forest

		1987			
		Extreme poor	Mid-poor	Nonpoor	All
1988	Extreme poor	5.2	10.4	-	15.6
		(5.2)	(10.4)	-	(15.6)
		33.3	66.7	-	
		57.1	34.8	-	
	Mid-poor	2.6	14.3	33.8	50.7
		(2.6)	(14.3)	(33.8)	(50.6)
		5.1	28.2	66.7	
		28.6	47.8	55.3	
	Nonpoor	1.3	5.2	27.3	33.8
		(1.3)	(5.2)	(27.3)	(33.8)
		3.8	15.4	80.8	
		14.3	17.4	44.7	
	All	9.1	29.9	61.2	100.2
		(9.1)	(29.9)	(61.0)	(100.0)

(Annex 1, cont.)

Annex 1
Changes in poverty status, by region and panel: detailed analysis

Savannah

		1987			
		Extreme poor	Mid-poor	Nonpoor	All
1988	Extreme poor	28.7	27.4	7.8	63.8
		(14.5)	(13.8)	(3.9)	(32.2)
		44.9	42.9	12.2	
		88.0	46.7	7.3	
	Mid-poor	2.6	20.8	33.9	57.3
		(1.3)	(10.5)	(17.1)	(28.9)
		4.5	36.4	59.1	
		8.0	35.6	31.7	
	Nonpoor	1.3	10.4	65.1	76.9
		(0.7)	(5.3)	(32.9)	(38.8)
		1.7	13.6	84.7	
		4.0	17.8	61.0	
	All	32.6	58.6	106.8	198.0
		(16.4)	(29.6)	(53.9)	(100.0)

6 Regional price differences and poverty measurement

With Ravi Kanbur[1]

As we discussed in Chapter 2, different households in any one country face different costs and prices according to the region in which they live. Thus, in using household expenditures as our measure of the incidence and depth of poverty, we must account for these differences by using an appropriate cost of living index. The theory behind cost of living indexes is well established. Deaton and Muellbauer (1980) describe the concepts and principles involved in the theoretically ideal price index, and how these pertain to the standard usage of the Laspeyres and Paasche indexes. In practice, applying this theory requires information on both the prices for and expenditures of households whose welfare is being evaluated, and this is where the problems begin. The information base in many developing countries, especially in Africa, does not provide sufficient coverage of household-level prices and expenditures. The Consumer Price Index (CPI) for many countries is based on prices and expenditure patterns only for the capital city, or only for urban areas. Rural areas are not covered in any systematic way. While inadequate at the best of times, these indexes are particularly inappropriate in the presence of structural adjustment policies, whose entire purpose is to alter price relativities, most of which have a significant effect on rural households.

This chapter expands on the discussion in Chapter 2 to estimate a regional price index for Côte d'Ivoire based on the strengths of two independent data sources: the CILSS and the International Comparisons Project (ICP). The CILSS has revolutionized analysis of household behavior in Côte d'Ivoire because it contains detailed information on household income, expenditures, employment, and other socioeconomic characteristics; yet its price data leave much to be desired. The ICP provides a more detailed account of regional variations in prices than does any other source for Côte d'Ivoire, but does not contain data on expenditure patterns or other socioeconomic variables.

Beyond showing how we combined these two sources to produce a regional price index, the key question addressed in this chapter is this: how estimated patterns of poverty are affected by the use of different price indexes. In the end, we argue that the regional price index based on the CILSS and the ICP is superior to indexes used previously to provide estimates of regional price differences in Côte d'Ivoire.

The CPI and previous regional price indexes in Côte d'Ivoire

Côte d'Ivoire has traditionally compiled two different CPI series: one for African households and one for European households. Since 1985, a further disaggregation has been available for African households, based on the occupation of the head of household; the African CPI series is now available for 'workers and traditional craftsmen' and for 'professional and managerial occupations.' But beyond the fact that this disaggregation is in fact unavailable for most African countries, this CPI – like many others in Africa– is inadequate because it excludes rural households. Even for urban households, the data cover only Abidjan and four main cities. Thus, this information base alone cannot be used to construct a regional price index.

Constructing a regional cost of living index requires information on prices and on expenditure patterns across the country. With this information, a common operational procedure is to construct a Paasche cost of living index:

$$C(p^X, p^A; q^X) = \frac{p^X q^X}{p^A q^X}$$

where X is the region under consideration, A is the reference region, p is the price vector, and q is the quantity vector. As is well known, dividing nominal expenditures in a region by this index will yield the consumption basket of that region evaluated at the prices of the reference region.

The CILSS was designed to collect information on expenditure patterns and on a host of other socioeconomic variables for a nationally representative sample of households. It thus satisfies one of the informational requirements for constructing a regional price index. However, the price data that it collects, while national in coverage, do not have adequate commodity coverage. Glewwe (1990) provides an excellent account of the problems that stem from the inadequacy of commodity-price coverage:

> The price data were recorded on a separate price questionnaire which was administered in the local markets of the sampling areas from which CILSS households were drawn. Prices were obtained for 18 food items and four nonfood items... The prices of the four nonfood items (domestic cloth, plastic sandals, enamel bowl and menthol)

154

varied widely, and further investigation led to the conclusion that [they were] unusable for the construction of a price index... Since variation in the price of nonfood items is largely due to transportation costs, it seemed advisable to use some of the food items which were relatively nonperishable and found throughout the country. The only food item to meet these criteria was canned tomato paste. Thus the price of cans of tomato paste are used as a proxy for the prices of nonfood items.

Glewwe (1987, 1990) and Kanbur (1990) used the Glewwe index to analyze poverty and welfare in Côte d'Ivoire. The problems with the index should be obvious. A more recent attempt by McKay (1992) to derive a regional price index addresses the problem simply by excluding nonfood items and focusing only on food items, hardly a satisfactory solution.

The only way to resolve the inadequacy of commodity price coverage in the CILSS is to utilize a database with adequate geographical *and* commodity coverage of prices. The ICP data make this possible.

ICP data and an alternative regional price index

Data collection for the ICP was carried out in Côte d'Ivoire in 1985 (Eurostat, 1989). The localities for price data collection were selected on the basis of the same sampling frame as was used in the CILSS. Price collection covered both urban and rural areas in all major regions of the country. A total of more than 20,000 prices were collected, covering 912 product codes. The first challenge in using these data was to establish a correspondence chart between these product codes and the expenditure categories distinguished in the CILSS. This correspondence chart is provided in Annex 1.

A characteristic feature of ICP data collection is the very specific and well-defined product descriptions. This specificity ensures the international comparability needed for ICP's purposes. The drawback for applying the data at the local or regional level is that not all items will be found in all parts of the country. Establishing a within-country regional price index requires that the same product be found in all regions which need to be distinguished. For our purposes, this requirement reduced the number of ICP prices that were available. Nevertheless, we had a total of 260 product categories for calculating the regional price index, and we matched them with 27 food categories and 25 nonfood categories derived from the CILSS. (The detailed expenditure shares derived from the CILSS for these categories are shown in Annex 2.)

Two restrictions slightly hampered our application of the ICP data. First, very few nonfood items were available for rural Savannah. We made the assumption that, in view of the low population density of the Savannah, many nonfood items would be available only in the urban centers of the region, and so we used prices in urban Savannah to impute their values for rural Savannah. Second, the prices for a few products that we felt were important representatives for a given expenditure category were not available for all regions. In this case, we made some imputations; for example, if prices for rural West Forest were unavailable, we imputed them on the basis of prices in rural East Forest. This type of imputation affected only a very small number of prices.

Having established the correspondence chart and the price ratios between the regions and Abidjan, we manually inspected these ratios and omitted a small number of individual prices because they appeared to be outlying or erroneously recorded values. In most cases, we could trace these anomalies to units that differed from the reference product description.

The new regional price index (N) is shown in Table 6.1 with Abidjan set equal to 100. For purposes of comparison, we have reproduced the Glewwe (G) and McKay (M) indexes discussed in the previous section.

Table 6.1
Regional price indices, 1985

	N	G	M
Abidjan	100.0	100.0	100.0
Other cities	92.8	86.7	70.2
East Forest	87.0	84.0	65.5
West Forest	78.2	81.8	61.2
Savannah	76.0	85.1	54.0

Note that the differences between the Glewwe and the McKay indexes are striking. Glewwe finds not more than an 18 percent price difference with Abidjan in any region, while McKay finds price differences of 30 percent or more in all regions, reaching almost 50 percent for the Savannah. It seems reasonable to assume that the McKay index overestimates regional price differences because it is based only on food items. Indeed, in Côte d'Ivoire many food items are produced locally in rural areas and are likely to be more expensive in the cities (due to transport costs.) Yet many nonfood items are either imported or produced in Abidjan and are thus more likely to be more expensive in rural areas. An index relying only on food prices would thus overestimate price differences and underestimate regional welfare differences.

With the new index, N, the figures show that prices in other urban areas are about eight percent below those in Abidjan on average. In rural areas, price differences are greater; the largest difference is for the Savannah – about 25 percent below Abidjan. The figures of the N index thus largely confirm our suspicion that the G index would tend to underestimate urban-rural price differences, while the M index would tend to overestimate them. In any event, the comprehensive commodity coverage of the N index gives us greater confidence in its validity.

Using the new regional price index to estimate poverty

We have already discussed in Chapter 2 the conceptual considerations associated with measuring poverty and the problems associated with operationalizing measures of the 'standard of living' from household income and expenditure surveys (Kanbur, 1987, provides a more in-depth discussion). As we mentioned, a common procedure for measuring the welfare of an individual is to calculate real per capita expenditures of the household (with suitable imputation for such items as home-produced consumption) in which he or she lives. When a single snapshot is being considered, the term 'real' refers to adjustments of nominal expenditures by a regional price index. As a reminder, the analysis so far has used two poverty lines: 128,600 CFAF per person annually in 1985 Abidjan prices (which classifies 30 percent of the population as poor), and 75,000 CFA per person annually (which classifies the bottom 10 percent of the population as extremely poor). However, these thresholds are not paramount for the discussion of this chapter; the critical issue is how the estimated pattern of poverty is affected by using different regional price indexes.

Table 6.2 shows average nominal household expenditures per capita for each of the regions in Côte d'Ivoire, deflated with the N, G, and M indexes. For the country as a whole, average real expenditures per capita are very close according to the N and G indexes, but the M index generates a 23 percent overestimate relative to the N index. However, larger differences are revealed in the estimates by region and by socioeconomic group. The Glewwe index generates underestimates for West Forest and the Savannah and for food crop farmers (who are concentrated in the Savannah). Real expenditures for other groups and regions are slightly overestimated (by one to seven percent). In contrast, the McKay index generates a significant overestimate of expenditures for all regions, but especially for the Savannah (41 percent). Among the socioeconomic groups, the overestimates are most pronounced for food crop farmers (34 percent) and export crop farmers (31 percent). Among the primarily urban-based groups, the overestimates are in the order of 10 to

Table 6.2

Household expenditures per capita deflated with alternative regional price indexes

Region and socioeconomic group	Nominal	N	G	G/N	M	M/N
Abidjan	376,108	376,108	376,108	1.00	376,108	1.00
Other cities	252,387	271,864	291,104	1.07	359,526	1.32
East Forest	143,104	164,472	170,362	1.04	218,479	1.33
West Forest	187,120	239,134	228,753	0.96	305,751	1.28
Savannah	115,910	152,573	136,204	0.89	214,648	1.41
Export crop farmers	162,761	194,418	194,371	1.00	254,312	1.31
Food crop farmers	139,209	171,802	165,692	0.96	230,656	1.34
Public sector employees	412,795	431,171	445,083	1.03	503,620	1.17
Formal private sector employees	354,478	364,835	371,294	1.02	403,111	1.10
Informal sector employees	220,088	230,593	236,341	1.02	265,560	1.15
Self-employed	219,258	234,910	239,728	1.02	279,657	1.19
Inactive	242,515	253,049	257,824	1.02	287,152	1.13
Unemployed	303,553	306,624	309,658	1.01	320,447	1.04
Côte d'Ivoire	213,634	237,853	238,389	1.00	291,799	1.23

20 percent (except for the unemployed). This comparison underlines the importance of adequate commodity coverage in a regional price index, and, specifically, the magnitude of the biases that can result from noninclusion of information on nonfood prices.

It stands to reason that any poverty index based on household expenditures will similarly be affected by the of cost of living index used. In Table 6.3, we show three poverty indexes derived from the P-alpha class of measures (again, these calculations are explained in Chapter 2).

The N index yields an estimate of the incidence of poverty in Côte d'Ivoire of 30 percent in 1985. Although the G index generates slightly higher average real household expenditures per capita, it affects the distribution in such a way that it generates a higher estimate of poverty (this is true for P_0, P_1, and P_2). While the difference is marginal at the national level, the G index has a greater impact on the regional and socioeconomic pattern of poverty. For example, the G index underestimates poverty (P_0) in urban areas other than Abidjan by 14 percent, and overestimates it in the Savannah by 13 percent. This bias is not necessarily constant over poverty measures. For example, P_2 in the Savannah is overestimated by 26 percent. In general, the G index generates underestimates of urban poverty and overestimates of rural poverty when compared with the new index.

Ideally, of course, the M index should be used only to deflate food expenditures, and thence to calculate 'food poverty' with a 'food poverty line'. But we would like some idea of the consequences of using this index, in the absence of other information, for the calculation of broad poverty with a poverty line defined over all expenditures. With the M index the incidence of poverty in Côte d'Ivoire is estimated at only 17.6 percent – 41 percent less than the incidence estimated with the N index. The difference even widens when P_1 and P_2 are considered. Regional and socioeconomic patterns are also very different. For example, the M index estimates poverty in West Forest at only 6.2 percent, while with the N index it is 17.8 percent. It yields a P_0 of 14.7 percent for export crop farmers, compared with an N index estimate of 36.6 percent.

Such differences in poverty estimates can obviously have a profound impact on policy decisions about the need for poverty alleviation interventions, where they should be targeted, and the amount of resources that are required. The main lesson from this exercise is that what may appear to be a relatively simple academic choice – how the prices of nonfood items should be captured by a price index – can have a major impact on estimates of poverty that form the basis for important policy decisions.

Table 6.3
Poverty measures based on alternative price indices

Region and socioeconomic group	P_0			P_1			P_2		
	N	G	M	N	G	M	N	G	M
Abidjan	0.034	0.034	0.034	0.009	0.009	0.009	0.004	0.004	0.004
Other cities	0.236	0.204	0.119	0.075	0.064	0.042	0.037	0.033	0.022
East Forest	0.479	0.463	0.285	0.155	0.144	0.076	0.069	0.063	0.032
West Forest	0.178	0.214	0.062	0.036	0.043	0.015	0.013	0.015	0.006
Savannah	0.502	0.591	0.322	0.183	0.221	0.093	0.088	0.111	0.037
Export crop farmers	0.366	0.366	0.147	0.094	0.095	0.042	0.038	0.039	0.015
Food crop farmers	0.434	0.468	0.263	0.144	0.156	0.071	0.065	0.072	0.028
Public sector employees	0.049	0.038	0.003	0.007	0.004	0.001	0.001	0.001	0.000
Formal private sector employees	0.071	0.070	0.023	0.014	0.012	0.005	0.005	0.004	0.002
Informal sector employees	0.262	0.225	0.225	0.075	0.069	0.037	0.028	0.024	0.008
Self-employed	0.262	0.260	0.185	0.104	0.103	0.067	0.058	0.058	0.038
Inactive	0.183	0.191	0.152	0.075	0.072	0.053	0.043	0.040	0.030
Unemployed	0.041	0.041	0.041	0.005	0.005	0.005	0.001	0.001	0.001
Côte d'Ivoire	0.300	0.314	0.176	0.098	0.102	0.050	0.045	0.048	0.022

Disaggregated price indices

For certain policy purposes, it may be useful to have a price index that covers only a subset of the consumption basket (for example, food or nonfood only) or that covers the entire basket but pertains only to certain groups of households (for example, farmers or the poor). The detailed price information in the ICP, combined with the detailed expenditure shares available from the CILSS, made it possible to construct such disaggregated price indexes. This section provides some examples.

Perhaps the most useful breakdown of the consumption basket is between food and nonfood. This breakdown is relevant for poverty analysis, in view of Engel's law. Moreover, many food items are subsidized in developing countries – and these subsidies must often be eliminated under structural adjustment programs. Addressing nutritional concerns requires a further breakdown of types of food. Table 6.4 shows regional price indexes for three food categories and five nonfood categories. Note that, conceptually, this disaggregation requires the assumption that consumer preferences are separable – that the prices for items outside the sub-index do not affect the consumption of items included in the sub-index (see Deaton and Muellbauer, 1980). Clearly, this assumption becomes less tenable as the disaggregation becomes finer.

Table 6.4 shows that, in general, food items display a wider regional price variation than do nonfood items. Food is significantly cheaper in rural areas than in Abidjan, and more so than is nonfood. Several nonfood categories are in fact more expensive in some rural areas than in Abidjan. This finding directly confirms our earlier hypothesis that the omission of nonfood prices in a price index (as with the McKay index) will lead to overestimates of regional price differences.

In the context of structural adjustment, the distinction between tradeable and nontradeable goods and services is important, since adjustment programs seek to change relative prices in favor of tradeables (World Bank, 1990). Table 6.4 also shows the regional price index for food and nonfood items, broken down by tradeability. Food items show no systematic pattern: in some regions, the price differential for tradeable food exceeds that for nontradeable food, but in other regions it is the reverse. Tradeable nonfood items, however, are priced lower in rural areas than in Abidjan, with the largest differentials in East Forest and Savannah. Nontradeable nonfood items are priced the same or higher in rural areas than in Abidjan (except in the Savannah), which may reflect their higher production costs in rural areas.

As we mentioned earlier, the government of Côte d'Ivoire produces two series for the CPI, depending the occupation of the head of household. The two series reflect the fact that expenditure patterns differ across

161

socioeconomic categories in the population. With the CILSS, it is possible to distinguish more than two groups. Table 6.5 shows the cost of living index recalculated for eight socioeconomic groups, accounting for the expenditure pattern of each group. In general, the differences are fairly minor (ignoring the cells with a small number of observations). The main differences are that the regional cost of living differential appears somewhat larger for farmers. The other groups, which are primarily urban based, display smaller regional variations. In particular, employees in both the private and public formal sector show smaller than average cost of living differences between Abidjan and other cities.

Table 6.4
Regional price index, by expenditure category

	Abidjan	Other cities	East Forest	West Forest	Savannah
Food	100.0	86.7	85.5	66.7	72.6
- Grains and bread	100.0	96.6	111.1	74.4	64.8
- Roots and vegetables	100.0	75.4	82.7	43.1	82.1
- Other food	100.0	88.6	80.9	87.2	71.6
Nonfood	100.0	99.8	89.2	101.9	87.6
- Clothing	100.0	105.8	80.2	106.2	66.0
- Home and furniture	100.0	93.9	106.4	92.9	79.1
- Transport and communications	100.0	108.3	76.2	114.4	109.6
- Education and health	100.0	89.4	116.2	99.6	79.1
- Other nonfood	100.0	95.4	100.2	90.4	90.4
Tradeable food	100.0	86.2	104.8	76.1	62.6
Nontradeable food	100.0	87.0	80.8	62.5	79.6
Tradeable nonfood	100.0	99.8	79.5	97.8	84.8
Nontradeable nonfood	100.0	99.9	115.5	110.4	94.7

The data also permit us to calculate a cost of living index by poverty status, and here the differences are more pronounced (Table 6.5). The cost of living differential between Abidjan and other cities narrows as total expenditures rise: for the extreme poor it is 14 percent, for the nonpoor, it is only seven percent. In contrast, the differential in rural areas widens as expenditures rise; for example, in West Forest, the price differential for the extreme poor is seven percent, but for the nonpoor it is 12 percent. This differential implies that the extreme poor – who are located primarily in rural areas – do not benefit from the lower cost of living in rural areas as much do other groups. It also means that using a single index to deflate expenditures will lead to underestimates of real expenditure levels for urban poor and overestimates for rural poor. By implication, if real expenditures are used as a welfare measure to estimate poverty (as we have done earlier), the simple index will overestimate urban poverty and underestimate rural poverty.

The cost of living differences reflected in Table 6.5 are of course only those that are generated by the different expenditure patterns across the groups. The ICP data permit us to estimate regional price differences only on an average basis, since the prices are collected from selected points of sale without capturing the characteristics of actual purchasers. Cost of living differences could also exist if unit prices differed systematically across socioeconomic or poverty groups. In particular, it has been argued that the poor pay higher prices for many food items than do the nonpoor, because they have to buy in small quantities. Moreover, price differences may occur if the poor and nonpoor buy at different types of outlets or markets, and if prices differ systematically across these markets. Such differences cannot readily be captured by conventional price data collection, but are best relegated to household surveys. Questions on prices actually paid can then be related to the household's socioeconomic characteristics as captured in the survey.

Table 6.5
Cost of living index, by
socioeconomic group and poverty status

Socioeconomic group and poverty status	Abidjan	Other cities	East Forest	West Forest	Savannah
Export crop farmers	(100.0)	88.0	87.4	78.2	70.2
Food crop farmers	(100.0)	88.9	87.8	76.7	75.6
Public sector employees	100.0	93.7	83.7	(96.5)	(80.1)
Formal private sector employees	100.0	94.6	(88.8)	(84.0)	(77.5)
Informal sector employees	100.0	92.7	(81.3)	(75.0)	(118.1)
Self-employed	100.0	93.1	83.2	85.4	80.6
Unemployed	100.0	(97.7)	-	-	-
Inactive	100.0	92.3	88.2	(83.5)	(79.5)
Extreme poor	100.0	86.3	99.7	93.1	77.0
Mid-poor	100.0	90.9	89.7	78.3	76.1
Nonpoor	100.0	93.1	85.9	78.1	75.8
Côte d'Ivoire	100.0	92.8	87.0	78.2	76.0

Note: Numbers in parentheses indicate cells that contain fewer than 10 observations.

Conclusion

Regional price variations can generate different estimates of poverty. Analysts should use the best and most comprehensive *combinations* of available information sets to construct these indexes. In this chapter, we have shown how the CILSS and the ICP can be combined to produce a regional price index that provides superior coverage to that in previous indexes. And we have shown that this is not merely statistical exercise – that estimates of the levels and patterns of poverty are altered significantly when the improved index is used.

Notes

1   This chapter is a revised version of the article 'A New Regional Price Index for Côte d'Ivoire Using Data from the International Comparisons Project' by Christiaan Grootaert and Ravi Kanbur, which appeared originally in *Journal of African Economies*, Vol. 3, No. 1, 1994, pp. 114-141. The material is used with the permission of Oxford University Press.

Annex 1
Correspondence chart: CILSS expenditure categories and ICP product codes

CILSS Expenditure category	ICP Product description
1. Food and beverages consumed away from home, and takeout food	Meal local restaurant Meal food kiosk/hawker Ricard in a bar Beer in a cafe Breakfast in worker's cafeteria
2. Cigarettes, tobacco, and cola nuts	Cigarettes dark tobacco Cigarettes light tobacco Marlboro Kola nut
3. Commercial or home-made soap	Household soap 72% Household soap 72% 650-800 g Household soap 60%
4. Other personal care and health products	Hairdresser w/o own establishment Toothbrush European comb Razor blades
5. Home maintenance products (brooms, detergents, toilet paper, etc.)	Toilet tissue Washing powder packet 100 g. Bleach Javel Lacroix
6. Charcoal	Domestic charcoal
7. Wood	Firewood
8. Other fuel for cooking, lighting	Paraffin
9. Shoes	Men's boots Ladies' plastic shoes
10. Fabric for clothing	Fabric wax print Fabric wax block monochrome
11. Adult clothing	Men's brief 100% cotton Men's br. 2/3 polyamide 1/3 cotton Women's brief 100% cotton Brassiere Men's handkerchief Women's handkerchief

Annex 1
Correspondence chart: CILSS expenditure categories and ICP product codes

CILSS Expenditure category	ICP Product description
12. Children clothing	Boys' jeans
	Boys' shorts
	Boys' t-shirt monochrome
	Boys' t-shirt printed
	Zip fastener
13. Purchase of cars, bikes, and other transport	Renault R4 L
	Renault R5 GTL
	Renault R9 GTL
	Renault R9 GTC
	Mazda 323
	Peugeout 305 normal
	Peugeout 305 GR
	Peugeout 505 GL
	Peugeout 505 GL diesel
	Peugeout 504 normal
	Toyota Corolla 1300 L
	Toyota Corolla GL
	Toyota Corolla GLS
	Toyota Corolla 2000 GLE
	Toyota Corolla 1800 XL
	Nissan Sunny 1-3 std
	Nissan Sunny 1-3 DX
	Fiat Panda 45
	Fiat Uno 55
	Bicycle ladies' town
	Bicycle men's town, Raleigh
	Bicycle men's town other makes
	Motorcycle Peugeout 153 LSX
	Motorcycle Peugeout 103 SPB
	Motorcycle Motoconfort
	Motorcycle Yamaha
	Motorcycle Suzuki
	Motorcycle Honda 185 S
	Motorcycle Honda 125 S
	Motorcycle Honda CG 125
	Motorcycle Suzuki A 100
	Motorcycle Suzuki TS 125
	Motorcycle Yamaha YB 100

Annex 1
Correspondence chart: CILSS expenditure categories
and ICP product codes

CILSS Expenditure category	ICP Product description
14. Car repair and other expenses (gasoline, motor oil, etc.)	Motor bicycle tire Peugeot
	Bicycle tube
	Motor bicycle tire Suzuki
	Car tire Michelin 165 SR 13
	Car tire 175 SR 14
	Car tire 175 SR 14 retread
	Car tire 165 SR 13
	Car tire 165 SR 13 retread
	Car tire 155 SR 14
	Car tire 155 SR 14 retread
	Car tire 155 SR 13
	Car tire 155 SR 13 retread
	Motorcycle tire 2.75
	Motorcycle tire 2.60
	Motorcycle tire 3.50
	Motorcycle tire 4.10
	Battery locally manufactured 30ah
	Battery locally manufactured 45ah
	Imported battery 38ah
	Imported battery 44a.m.
	Sparking plug Champion
	Sparking plug Bosch
	Brake cable
	Tire tube 175 SR 14
	Tire tube 165 SR 13
	Tire tube 155 SR 14
	Tire tube 155 sr 13
	Distributor points r4 1
	Distributor points r9 gtl
	Distributor points Mazda 323
	Oil change & greasing official dealer
	Oil change & greasing not official dealer
	Replace water pump official dealer
	Replace water pump not official dealer
	Replace shock absorbers official dealer
	Replace shock absorbers not official dealer
	Engine tuning official dealer
	Engine tuning not official dealer

Annex 1
Correspondence chart: CILSS expenditure categories
and ICP product codes

CILSS Expenditure category	ICP Product description
14. (cont.)	Replace brake linings/pads official dealer
	Replace brake linings/pads not official dealer
15. Public transport, taxis, etc.	Taxi journey
	Collective taxi journey
	Bus journey minimum fare
	Bus journey maximum fare
	Bus fare student
	Bus fare adult
	Informal sector journey 4 km
	Train journey 2nd class
	Rail journey express
	Train journey round trip
	Bus journey
	Journey by motorcoach
	Journey by car or station wagon
	Journey by mini bus
16. Home expenses (repairs, painting, insurance, etc.)	Portland cement
	Painting of room w/whitewash
	Repair of a house roof
	Replacement of top formica
17. Educational expenses	School fees nursery
	School fees Koran
	School fees private vocational
	School fees private primary
	School fees private secondary
	Exercise book
	Pencil ordinary
	Ruler
18. Medical expenses	Aspirin upsa
	Flavoquine 12 tablets
	Nivaquine
	T A O
	Mercurochrome bottle 20-30 ml
	Mercurochrome bottle 125 ml

Annex 1
Correspondence chart: CILSS expenditure categories
and ICP product codes

CILSS Expenditure category	ICP Product description
19. Kitchen tools (cups, forks, plates, saucepans, etc.)	Tumblers Soup plate Saucepan Knife Soup spoon
20. Furniture (beds, tables, cupboards, chairs, rugs, etc.)	Mattress 190x140¾low density Mattress without springs Ordinary chair
21. Linen (sheets, towels, blankets, etc.)	Bed sheet polyester Bed sheet 100% cotton Hand towel Bath towel
22. Envelopes, writing paper, stamps	Ordinary envelopes Notepaper pad
23. Telephone, telegram, etc.	Telephone call public tel. box Telephone call subscriber Monthly rental of one telephone Telephone calls Telegram
24. Jewelry, watches	Gold ring 18 carat Gold ring 14 carat Men's wrist watch Men's digital wrist watch Watch maintenance
25. Entertainment (novels, newspapers, cinema, sports, records, tapes, toys, etc.)	Gramophone record Gramophone record pop music Unrecorded cassette 60 min. Unrecorded cassette 90 min. Unrecorded cassette other brands Tennis balls Building set ref. No. 10 Building set ref. No. 045

Annex 1
Correspondence chart: CILSS expenditure categories and ICP product codes

CILSS Expenditure category	ICP Product description
25. (cont.)	Bag of marbles
	Children's ball
	Film black and white
	Film color 20 exposures
	Film color 36 exposures
	Slides
	Services color TV technician
	Sports ground
	Photographic development and printing
	Novel detective
	Novel not detective
	Newspaper
	Magazine weekly
	Magazine monthly
26. Rice	Long-grained rice loose
	100% broken rice
27. Maize (cob, grain, or flour)	Yellow maize
	White maize
28. Millet, fonio, sorghum (grain or flour)	Sorghum
	Small millet souna variety
	Small millet sagno variety
29. Bread	Fresh bread
	Fresh bread baguette type
30. Cassava	Cassava fresh
	Cassava dried
31. Macaroni	Spaghetti prepacked 500 g
	Spaghetti prepacked 250 g
	Egg noodles 500 g
	Macaroni
32. Cookies and cake	Biscuits sweet tea
	Biscuits marie

Annex 1
Correspondence chart: CILSS expenditure categories
and ICP product codes

CILSS Expenditure category	ICP Product description
33. Yam	Yams fresh
34. Plantain (raw or flour)	Plantain Plantain green
35. Taro, sweet potato, potato	Taro (cocoyam) Sweet potatoes fresh
36. Peanuts (roasted, raw, or butter) and palmnuts	Peanut butter Ground-nuts dry roasted shelled
37. Other grains and nuts (avocado, coconut, nere, ouleoule, etc.) fresh/dried	Avocado Coconut without topshell
38. Fish and shellfish	Crabs Herring
39. Chicken, duck, pigeon, turkey, or other poultry	Live local chicken
40. Beef, mutton, goat, pork, other domesticated meat	Beef fresh with bone with offal Beef fresh with bone no offal Ox feet fresh Beef tripes and offal
41. Eggs	Chicken eggs commercial fresh
42. Palm oil, shea butter, and other oils	Palm oil unrefined Palm oil refined loose Shea nut butter
43. Butter, margarine	Margarine
44. Fruit	Lemon Bananas Mango not grafted

Annex 1:
Correspondence chart: CILSS expenditure categories
and ICP product codes

CILSS Expenditure category	ICP Product description
45. Sugar, candy, honey, sugarcane	Sugar cubes cardboard packet Sugar cubes 10 lumps Sugar refined white granulated in cellophane Acid fruit drops prepacked Chewing gum Wrigley Chewing gum other makes
46. Salt	Salt coarse kitchen
47. Alcoholic beverages	Wine red bottle 1 litre Beer Guinness Beer local other
48. Nonalcoholic beverages (tea, coffee, soft drinks, bouillon, etc.)	Ginger Juice Coffee beans roasted robusta Coffee soluble instant Tea black prepacked 20 bags Tea black prepacked 100 bags Natural mineral water Soda water Fanta orange bottle 33 cl
49. Tomato paste	Tomato puree 70 g
50. Leafy and other vegetables	Okra fresh Egg plant green fresh
51. Milk products	Milk sterilized homogenized long life Milk powdered skimmed 450 g Milk sweetened condensed
52. Other foods	[average of all food items]

Annex 2
Detailed expenditure shares used in calculating
regional price index, 1985 (ratio)

CILSS Category	Abidjan	Other cities	East Forest	West Forest	Savannah
1.	0.05995	0.05109	0.03024	0.04609	0.02599
2.	0.01145	0.01284	0.01409	0.01705	0.01698
3.	0.02211	0.02494	0.02149	0.01844	0.02242
4.	0.00659	0.00847	0.00347	0.00362	0.00288
5.	0.00351	0.00467	0.00071	0.00036	0.00053
6.	0.02188	0.01259	0.00160	0.00030	0.00000
7.	0.00611	0.01424	0.00241	0.00072	0.00011
8.	0.01262	0.01231	0.01822	0.01755	0.02185
9.	0.05416	0.08392	0.03954	0.01367	0.02941
10.	0.02623	0.02243	0.02238	0.03228	0.01619
11.	0.06637	0.07335	0.08325	0.10844	0.02402
12.	0.00755	0.01044	0.00839	0.01148	0.00509
13.	0.01326	0.01476	0.02178	0.01491	0.00522
14.	0.00000	0.00289	0.01016	0.00358	0.02646
15.	0.05665	0.05174	0.04356	0.05279	0.04057
16.	0.01215	0.00875	0.02005	0.02082	0.00892
17.	0.05751	0.05392	0.04510	0.02534	0.01451
18.	0.04980	0.03694	0.03046	0.04693	0.01432
19.	0.00875	0.00796	0.00766	0.01030	0.00489
20.	0.00388	0.01098	0.00452	0.00602	0.00000
21.	0.00787	0.01129	0.01082	0.00799	0.00323
22.	0.00152	0.00314	0.00204	0.00244	0.00117
23.	0.00613	0.00236	0.00101	0.00138	0.00007
24.	0.00985	0.00685	0.00251	0.00917	0.00069
25.	0.00948	0.00926	0.00146	0.00185	0.00053
26.	0.04968	0.06292	0.05963	0.11620	0.10184
27.	0.00733	0.01291	0.02194	0.02521	0.07456
28.	0.00261	0.00177	0.00001	0.00018	0.02465
29.	0.02310	0.02028	0.01435	0.01468	0.01398
30.	0.02270	0.02609	0.04252	0.06390	0.04269
31.	0.00295	0.00159	0.00078	0.00097	0.00052
32.	0.00387	0.00585	0.00534	0.00906	0.01083
33.	0.01628	0.03059	0.08399	0.01967	0.14410
34.	0.02353	0.02571	0.06037	0.03213	0.01290
35.	0.00416	0.00335	0.01633	0.00723	0.01652
36.	0.02103	0.01844	0.01477	0.02081	0.03739
37.	0.00241	0.00210	0.00103	0.00048	0.00078
38.	0.06340	0.05813	0.06899	0.05949	0.05297
39.	0.01861	0.01908	0.02845	0.03394	0.02170
40.	0.06759	0.57540	0.02245	0.02539	0.03366
41.	0.00681	0.00401	0.00132	0.00040	0.00246
42.	0.02100	0.01771	0.01646	0.01472	0.01807
43.	0.00498	0.00344	0.00037	0.00043	0.00007

(Annex 2, cont.)

Annex 2
Detailed expenditure shares used in calculating regional price index, 1985 (ratio)

CILSS

Category	Abidjan	Other cities	East Forest	West Forest	Savannah
44.	0.00948	0.00516	0.00467	0.00830	0.01582
45.	0.00786	0.00783	0.00632	0.00582	0.01057
46.	0.00173	0.00237	0.00480	0.00393	0.00553
47.	0.01175	0.01415	0.02766	0.02298	0.02226
48.	0.01881	0.01539	0.13333	0.01184	0.01104
49.	0.00760	0.00582	0.00227	0.00169	0.00211
50.	0.03195	0.02221	0.03250	0.02314	0.03580
51.	0.01326	0.00328	0.00229	0.00367	0.00106
52.	0.00017	0.00013	0.00013	0.00021	0.00006

Note: For CILSS category description, see Annex 1.

7 A poverty alleviation strategy for Côte d'Ivoire

The evolution of poverty during the 1980s

In its first 15 years of independence, Côte d'Ivoire achieved an average annual real GDP growth rate of 7.4 percent, or 3.6 percent per capita. The double challenge for the country was to sustain this economic success and to divide the benefits evenly over the population. In fact, the distribution of welfare became more unequal during the boom years – especially the share of the richest 20 percent increased – and the economic growth came to an abrupt halt in 1979, following the collapse of world prices of coffee and cocoa. Economic reform was attempted in 1981, when Côte d'Ivoire became one of the first African countries to start a structural adjustment program supported by the World Bank and the IMF. While poverty reduction was not an explicit objective of the reforms, they did aim to reduce urban-rural income gaps, by freezing public sector wages, and increasing producer prices to farmers. During the first half of the eighties, income distribution did become more equal and poverty was reduced. In 1985-86, 30 percent of the Ivorian population had an expenditure level below the poverty line of 128,600 CFAF per year.

The poverty situation changed dramatically in 1987, when the economy went into an accelerated decline following a sharp appreciation of the real effective exchange rate and a deterioration of the country's international terms of trade. Household consumption declined – by over 20 percent in two years (in real per capita terms) – and poverty rose sharply. By 1988, the number of poor people in Côte d'Ivoire had increased to almost five million. Of those, about one-third third lived in extreme poverty (less than 75,000 CFAF per year). Between 1989 and 1992, household consumption declined by an additional 24 percent and poverty incidence rose to approximately 60 percent. The average shortfall of a poor person's expenditure level also increased from 30 to 38 percent of the poverty line. The magnitude of these figures make it clear that poverty alleviation in Côte d'Ivoire can no longer be approached through redistribution of existing resources – growth has become the essential precondition for sustained poverty reduction.

Falling consumption levels are not the only characteristic of rising poverty – equally important is the decline of basic needs fulfillment among the poor, and especially among the poorest. The government of Côte d'Ivoire has protected the share of its budget going to education and health, but has let the share of salaries rise and that of other inputs (textbooks, medication) fall to a degree that serious internal inefficiencies exist. Little has been done to reorient the intrasectoral allocation towards primary education and primary health care, and to reduce the pro-urban bias in social infrastructure. Households have also reduced the share of their expenditures allocated to education and health, so that the total amount of resources going to education and health has declined. As a result, primary and secondary school enrollment, educational progress, use of modern health care, access to sanitary facilities, access to electricity all declined for the poorest households. In the case of education, the enrollment and educational progress gap between boys and girls increased. This happened even though some basic needs indicators did not change much in the aggregate – which means that for some groups, such as the nonpoor and urban households, the situation improved. Retargeting basic needs services towards the poorest and towards rural areas is thus a high priority in a poverty alleviation strategy.

Although basic needs services have been protected more in urban areas, the incidence of poverty increased much more rapidly in urban areas than in rural areas. The share of the urban poor in total poverty increased from 19 percent in 1985 to about 25 percent in 1988. This was due in part to the freeze of public service salaries which affected more than proportionately lower skill employees – the higher-level civil servants partly circumvented the freeze by an increase in benefits. In the private modern sector, adjustment to the economic crisis was largely done through employment reductions, which again befell mostly lower-skill employees, while wages of those who kept a job were maintained. This has resulted in a rising unemployment rate and a more than doubling of the size of the informal sector. The latter contains the highest incidence of urban poverty, particularly among those not able to set up their own enterprise and who have to work for wages in other small enterprises. They constitute a particularly vulnerable group. The informal sector is also the main source of employment for urban women, so that poverty and vulnerability in the sector have an important gender dimension.

Rural areas still contain the bulk of the poor in Côte d'Ivoire – about 70 percent – but the regional distribution has changed markedly. The situation has deteriorated most in West Forest due to falling yields and sales of cocoa and especially coffee, and, after 1989, due to the halving of producer prices for these crops. The Savannah, however, is still the poorest region, containing about one-third of all poor and one-half of all very poor in the country. Both regions should be the focus of an intense program to diversify the sources of income by growing a wider variation of crops and by increasing the role of nonfarm income, and to increase agricultural productivity by an improved extension service.

Table 7.1
Key poverty indicators

Poverty status		1985	1988	1992 (estimate)
Extreme poor		10%	14%	25%
Mid-poor		20%	32%	35%
Nonpoor		70%	54%	40%

		Poverty incidence	Share of all poor
Targeting priorities*	Savannah	65.2%	31.4%
	West Forest	55.3%	18.6%
	Food crop farmers	59.0%	52.4%
	Export crop farmers	54.8%	17.7%
	Informal sector employees	54.2%	1.6%
	Informal sector self-employed	46.2%	14.8%

Basic needs priorities for the poor*	Extreme poor	Mid-poor	Nonpoor
Net primary school enrollment rate			
- Male	31.0%	54.3%	74.1%
- Female	16.7%	41.9%	57.7%
Age-grade mismatches in primary school (as % of total enrollment)			
- Male	63.9%	48.7%	37.3%
- Female	52.9%	47.9%	37.7%
Net secondary school enrollment rate			
- Male	3.5%	14.8%	33.6%
- Female	1.2%	9.0%	21.1%
Use of modern health care			
- Male	19.1%	32.8%	52.6%
- Female	16.2%	31.3%	54.8%
Access to tap water	2.9%	11.4%	31.2%
Access to electricity	10.9%	29.2%	53.3%

* Based on 1988 figures.

Amid this bleak picture of poverty in Côte d'Ivoire, there is one bright spot: much poverty is of transitory nature and even in a time of rising poverty many poor – as much as 30 percent each year – succeed in escaping poverty on their own. This represents a major positive dynamic force which must be strengthened by policy. This means e.g. facilitating the creation of employment in the informal sector by a comprehensive package of support which complements the poor's own resources. Care will have to be taken that programs, especially transfers, do not undermine the spirit of self-help and reliance on networks of mutual support which exist among the poor. Employment creation focused on the informal sector is the policy intervention with the greatest potential of stimulating growth and alleviating poverty at the same time.

The analysis of the evolution of poverty during the eighties has clearly shown that the cause of rising poverty was the absence of economic growth. Changes in the distribution of welfare in fact contributed to reducing poverty. The remedy must thus in the first place lie in the generation of sustainable growth in such a way that all groups in Ivorian society participate. The encouraging lesson of the early part of the eighties is that even when growth is moderate, it is possible to improve the conditions of the poor. Improvements can again be realized as soon as positive growth returns. Nevertheless, there should be no illusion about the duration of the process: even under optimistic growth scenarios, significant reduction of poverty in Côte d'Ivoire will take a generation. Effective commitment to this goal by government thus requires a long term perspective and framework for action.

Ten orientations for a poverty strategy

Côte d'Ivoire's growth and poverty experience suggests that the following ten orientations should be embodied in an effective poverty strategy.

1   The key factor in the rise of poverty in the eighties was the absence of economic growth. Poverty alleviation in the long run can only succeed if economic growth resumes.

The increase in poverty which occurred in Côte d'Ivoire in the 1980s was the net result of two effects: a fall in the mean level of household expenditure per capita and a change in the distribution. The analysis in Chapter 3 has measured the relative importance of each of these effects. The main finding was that, in the 1985-88 period, the changes in distribution which took place in Côte d'Ivoire contributed to *reducing* poverty. This means that the observed increase in poverty was entirely due to the negative growth in household expenditure. Had the latter remained the same, the incidence of poverty would have been reduced by 20 percent between 1985 and 1988. Moreover, the changes in distribution were such that they benefited the poorest most. This strongly underlines the role of the absence of economic growth in the generation of poverty. While in the short run redistributive policies can help the neediest among the poor, in the long run sustained economic growth is a precondition for sustained poverty alleviation in Côte d'Ivoire.

2   Poverty rose much faster during the destabilization phase of the late eighties than during the earlier adjustment phase. Managed structural change needs to be the underlying framework for effective poverty alleviation.

The evidence presented in this book suggests that in the first half of the eighties, when Côte d'Ivoire had an actively managed structural adjustment program under way, poverty declined and the urban-rural income gap decreased. This occurred even though, as Chapter 1 outlined, the adjustment program was not successful in every aspect. In 1985-86, when the economy showed a small positive growth rate, the incidence of extreme poverty fell by 35 percent and the depth of poverty also decreased. In contrast, in 1987-88, when the recession resumed in full force, and the country effectively entered a period of economic destabilization, the incidence of poverty rose by 50 percent.

While one cannot attribute full causality of these changes in poverty to the change in macroeconomic regime, it is clear that only managed structural change provided a suitable framework for poverty alleviation. This will continue to be the case for the future. However, it needs to be emphasized that such managed structural change will have to pay particular attention to the way in which economic growth is generated. Growth *per se* is a necessary but not sufficient condition for poverty reduction. The experience of Côte d'Ivoire's boom years in the sixties and seventies indicate that even fast growth can coincide with increases in poverty. Côte d'Ivoire's growth strategy for the nineties will have to be based on three principles: increased productivity of agriculture, increased employment creation in the urban informal sector, and effective increases in human capital for the poor. These three principles underlay most of the remaining orientations for growth proposed below.

3   Rural areas contain the majority of the poor and almost all of the very poor, and must be the prime beneficiaries of poverty alleviation efforts.

179

Côte d'Ivoire is a relatively urbanized country: about 45 percent of the population lives in cities. However, the rural population contains far more than its proportionate share of poor people. In 1990, 70 percent of all poor lived in rural areas and close to 90 percent of all very poor. The bulk of poverty alleviation resources thus needs to be targeted towards the rural areas, whether in the form of transfers, efforts to increase incomes, or delivery of basic services to the rural population.

4   Priorities for targeting are the Savannah, where the poorest food crop farmers live, and West Forest, where many of the 'new poor' among export crop farmers live.

During the 1980s, important shifts occurred in the relative position of the three regions – East Forest, West Forest, and Savannah – which make up Côte d'Ivoire's rural areas. In 1985, West Forest was still a well-to-do area, with a level of living almost 50 percent higher than that of other rural areas, mainly fueled by high farmer revenues from coffee and cocoa. In the second half of the eighties, area under production, yields and revenues from export crops all declined and many farmers in West Forest joined the ranks of the poor. The region suffered the largest economic decline of any part of Côte d'Ivoire and became worse off than East Forest. The Savannah, however, with a strong concentration of food farmers has remained Côte d'Ivoire's poorest region. In 1988, household expenditure per capita were only half of the country's average, and the region contained one third of all poor and almost one half of all very poor. It appears justified therefore to focus poverty alleviation resources on Savannah and West Forest.

5   Commodity-specific price supports (coffee and cocoa) are not effective in benefiting poor groups and should be abandoned, because there is too much leakage to nonpoor groups.

The key instrument which the government of Côte d'Ivoire has used to influence farm incomes is fixing the domestic producer prices of major crops, especially coffee and cocoa. Throughout the seventies these prices rose sharply, in line with increases in world prices for these commodities. Domestic producer prices for coffee and cocoa peaked in 1985 (well after the peak in world prices). They were held steady at this peak level until 1989, at which time they were cut by 50 percent. One objective of this price maintenance was to prevent increases in poverty among farmers. As the figures in Chapter 3 indicate this objective was not achieved (although one could argue that poverty increases may well have been higher had prices not been maintained). However, throughout the 1980s, domestic prices exceeded world prices, so that the price maintenance scheme was a significant fiscal drain on government resources. Apart from the fact that poverty among export crop farmers rose during the price support period (due to falling area under production and yields) about two thirds of the benefit occurred to nonpoor farmers. This is because in Côte d'Ivoire there is only a weak association between cropping pattern and poverty status among farmers. Only cotton is grown predominantly by poor farmers, and there is a strong regional effect here, because cotton is grown only in the Savannah. With the possible exception of cotton, therefore, general price support schemes for specific crops will benefit nonpoor farmers more than poor farmers, and are an expensive and inefficient way to help poor farmers in Côte d'Ivoire.

6   Aid to poor farmers must consist of a complete package aimed at promoting diversification and increasing productivity.

The high dependence of Ivorian farmers on one or two export crops, of which the prices tend to fluctuate greatly, implies the need for more diversification. As we have seen, a pure price support system largely benefits nonpoor farmers. Assuming that farmgate prices cannot be differentiated according to farm size or income level, a poor-oriented strategy will have to focus on the delivery to poor farmers of a package of extension services, geared to a wide variety of crops and including support in the procurement and use of inputs, and support in sales and marketing. This will have to be supplemented by government efforts to introduce cash crops such as rubber, oil palm, coconut, pineapple, etc. Such programs are not new in Côte d'Ivoire – they existed in the seventies, and were revamped in the eighties as part of the structural adjustment programs.

With respect to food crop farmers, sight should not be lost of the fact that they have lower incomes than export crop farmers. Price policies are much less important here since no single crop dominates income, with the possible exception of rice. A poverty-oriented strategy towards food crop farmers will have to focus on extension services which can effectively reach smallholders, and promote diversification towards cash crops such as fruit and vegetables, and support in the procurement of inputs.

With two-thirds of the economically active population in Côte d'Ivoire working in agriculture, and more than two thirds of the poor living in rural areas, it is clear that efforts to increase the productivity of agriculture will have to be a cornerstone of a poverty-oriented growth strategy. Crop diversification programs and effective extension serve to contribute to both growth and poverty alleviation objectives.

7   A growing share of resources has to go to alleviating urban poverty. Support to the informal sector will be the key to this.

In Abidjan and in Côte d'Ivoire's other cities poverty rose faster than the national average during the second half of the 1980s. However, the basis from which this increase occurred was quite small, since in 1985 the incidence of poverty in cities, especially Abidjan, was still low. The share of urban poverty in the total rose from about 20 percent in 1985 to about 30 percent in 1992. Moreover, the urban population continues to grow more rapidly than the national average (although less so now than during most of the eighties), so that the urbanization process will continue. Urban poverty has now reached a critical mass and poverty in Côte d'Ivoire can no longer be considered just a rural phenomenon. Growing attention, and resources, will have to go to addressing the plight of the urban poor.

The nature of the needed interventions must take into account the dramatic changes which occurred in the urban labor market. During the 1980s, modern sector employment fell by 14 percent, employment in the informal sector more than doubled and unemployment tripled. In 1980, the informal sector was smaller than the modern sector, but in the early nineties it had become almost three times the size of the modern sector, accounting for three quarters of urban employment. Much of informal sector employment is characterized by low wages and productivity. In view of the continued rapid population growth in Côte d'Ivoire, the annual influx of new labor market entrants is so high that the informal sector will have to absorb an increasing share of them. A policy to promote this sector will thus have to be the urban cornerstone of growth policy, and play a vital role in the alleviation of urban poverty.

8   The delivery of public services (education, health, tap water) needs to be targeted better to the very poor households who are rapidly falling behind in the fulfillment of basic needs.

In Côte d'Ivoire, like in most countries, the poor have less access to basic services, whether it is in education, health, water supply, sanitation or others. However, one of the most disturbing observations of the impact of the economic recession of the eighties has been that the poor, and especially the poorest, have fallen further behind in the fulfillment of basic needs. This was especially the case in the latter part of the decade, during the destabilization phase, and it occurred almost regardless of the average trend of a given indicator: in very poor households, net primary school enrollment for girls fell from 22.4 percent to 16.7 percent; the number of children one year or more behind their age-appropriate grade doubled to 64 percent for boys and 53 percent for girls; the rate of medical consultations of ill women fell from 30 percent to 16 percent; the rate of home ownership declined from 92 percent to 85 percent; access to electricity fell from 14 percent to 11 percent. In addition, the amount of expenditures which very poor households devote to education and health care fell by 50 percent and 12 percent respectively. The sole exception to this pattern of deteriorating basic needs fulfillment occurred in health care: the rate of preventive consultations rose for very poor households and more so than the countrywide average. (Access to tap water also improved, but in 1988 it was still at a dismal three percent.)

The solution to this problem lies not in increased investment in social infrastructure, but in an explicit shift in targeting priorities of existing and new programs. Regional targeting, and a more balanced distribution of resources between urban and rural areas are starting points, but successful targeting will have to go further and seek out poor villages or districts in cities, and the poorest households within them. The setting of priorities among the different needed services should occur with the participation of the intended beneficiaries.

9   Improvements in the intrasectoral allocation of education expenditures are a priority. Transfer payments (scholarships) need to be targeted on a needs basis, with priority given to girls.

The share of Côte d'Ivoire's government budget devoted to education stayed above 40 percent throughout the decade – this is one of the highest shares in the world. The issue is thus clearly not the level of government resources available for education, but rather their allocation. The share going to primary education rose slightly towards the end of the decade, but it is doubtful that this will have had a pro-poor redistributive effect, since 95 percent of current expenditure for primary education went to salaries of teachers. Less than one percent was available for materials such as textbooks. For the education sector as a whole, the ratio of personnel to nonpersonnel expenditure stood at about 10:1 in the period 1986-88. Such imbalanced functional allocation of government expenditure constitutes a very serious internal inefficiency in the education system, and is a key obstacle to achieving a favorable redistributive effect from public expenditure. Efforts to shift the allocation of resources towards the primary level are needed but will achieve little if the share of non-salary inputs is not enhanced at the same time. The cost of education to the very poor needs to be reduced, if necessary, by selective subsidization of textbooks, and possibly school supplies and uniforms. This is especially important after the devaluation since most textbook and many other supplies are imported. Scholarships need to be reallocated to primary and secondary students based on a need criterion; priority should be given to girls. This can be financed by improved cost recovery in teacher and tertiary education.

10   In the area of health, increased delivery of health care and, in urban areas, of tap water to the very poor are the top priorities.

The share of health in the government's budget rose from seven percent to 7.8 percent over the course of the eighties. As in the case of education, the allocation of these expenditures is excessively skewed towards salaries, which accounted for 77 percent of recurrent expenditure in 1990. More than half of recurrent expenditure was devoted to tertiary level care, mainly large urban hospitals. Making the government's expenditure on health benefit the poor more, will require a simultaneous shift towards primary care and towards better provision of medication and other nonpersonnel inputs. Subsidies for essential medication need to be introduced, targeted towards the poor (this is especially important after the devaluation of the CFAF, since most medication is imported). Cost recovery needs to be improved at the secondary and tertiary levels. The favorable experience with the delivery of preventive care (mainly vaccinations) to the poor indicates that successful targeting in the delivery of health services is possible.

In urban areas, a top priority is to improve the access of the poor to tap water (house connections or outdoor standpipes). The availability of safe water overall has declined in urban areas, except in Abidjan. Related to this is inadequate sanitation and garbage removal. Here too the situation of the urban poorest has deteriorated. These priorities need to be taken into account in projects which aim to upgrade urban slums or squatter areas.

A poverty strategy for Côte d'Ivoire

These ten orientations can be combined into an effective long term strategy to reduce poverty in Côte d'Ivoire. The key ingredient is the generation of sustainable economic growth. This will create the necessary employment growth and provide the resources to the government to tackle the needed improvements in basic needs fulfillment. The poverty strategy proposed here contributes towards creating income and employment growth by focusing on the sectors with the greatest potential – agriculture in rural areas and the urban informal sector. The realities of population growth in Côte d'Ivoire are such that even in the most optimistic scenario for economic recovery in the modern sector, it will only be able to absorb a small fraction of new labor markets entrants. By the same token, the successful restructuring of the public sector entails that it forgoes its role of employer of the last resort and abandons the policy of assuring jobs for graduates from the formal education system.

The poverty strategy needs to be three-pronged: income generation for the poor is combined with a more targeted delivery of those basic needs services most lacking to the poor, and with the provision of selected safety nets to the most destitute.

Income generation for the poor

Urban areas In urban areas, employment creation in the tradeable goods sectors needs to be promoted. This effort will involve aid to restructuring for the formal sector, but the lead needs to be taken by the informal sector. This is where almost all of the poverty impact will be situated. The approach to program design is to channel appropriate information to existing and prospective entrepreneurs about new opportunities, and to take a pro-active role in stimulating the creation of new enterprises and the upgrading of the urban informal sector labor force. At the same time, the urban infrastructure serving informal enterprises needs to be upgraded. Actions include:

- creation of a credit facility to provide small loans to set up small enterprises producing tradeable goods or to expand existing ones;

- an information program based on marketing research to communicate to prospective and existing entrepreneurs what sectors and product lines holds promise for production and exports, and what government support measures are available;

- an export assistance program;

- retraining for unemployed workers and for entrepreneurs whose enterprises close down;

- informal education classes which are accessible to apprentices and which focus on complementary skills (enterprise management, marketing, accounting) and transfer of new technologies;

- a pilot program for 'model' small enterprises and a concomitant urban extension service to provide general support (marketing, management, and technology transfer);

- construction of small plots for microenterprises in accessible locations selected by local communities and entrepreneurs, and provided with a minimum service level;

185

- increased provision of urban infrastructure (roads, sewage systems, etc.) through labor intensive techniques with employment targeted to low-income households; and

- selection of urban infrastructure projects which give priority to those of direct benefits to the poor.

Rural areas Rural programs need to be geared towards promoting more diversification in the export crops grown, which will be more profitable following devaluation, and by providing a full support package for farmers through an enhanced extension system. The latter should be reoriented towards enhancing productivity of the farming system as a whole rather than focusing on selected crops. While this approach is applicable to all rural areas, the poverty impact will be maximized by focusing on smallholders and on the Savannah and West Forest zones. Measures include:

- creation of a rural credit facility for smallholders who wish to adopt new export or domestic cash crops;

- a marketing and export assistance program for smallholders;

- enhancing the quality of rural extension services which need to be focused more on smallholders and women farmers;

- a pilot export crop diversification program in West Forest;

- a review of the cotton support program in Savannah and a pilot diversification program.

Targeted basic needs improvements

Education Long terms efforts to enhance the participation of the poor in education are preconditioned on reallocation of public expenditures towards the primary level and towards complementary inputs such as textbooks and other education materials, away from salaries. In the meantime, several concrete actions can be taken to help the poor:

- enhance cost recovery for the secondary and tertiary levels by increasing fees; limit cost recovery efforts at primary level;

- reduce scholarships to teacher and tertiary education and reallocate them to primary and secondary students based on a needs criterion; priority should be given to girls;

- provide needs-targeted subsidies for textbooks, uniforms and school meals at the primary level.

Health Long term efforts to improve the access of the poor to health services require a fundamental reorientation of Côte d'Ivoire's health system away from urban-based curative facilities toward more rural and primary care. Recurrent expenditures need to be reallocated especially towards medications. This is especially important following the devaluation since most medication is imported. Improved access to safe water at a reasonable cost for the urban poor is a priority. Specific measures to help the poor include:

- continuation of a pro-poor targeting of preventive medicine, especially prenatal care and vaccinations; the level of such programs needs to be increased and internalized in the regular health care system;

- enhance number and quality of rural primary health care centers;

- provide needs-targeted subsidies for medical fees and medication;

- strengthen policy to promote generic drugs in public and private hospitals and pharmacies;

- improve cost recovery in urban hospitals;

- enhance the program to provide social house-connections and public standpipes to provide drinking water to the poorest urban households; increase the share of the program going to interior cities;

- reduce the cost of water available from 'paying' standpipes; allow hookup costs for house connections to be paid over two to three year period as part of regular bills and shorten billing period for low-income households; allow use of central meter for several households to reduce hookup cost per household;

- continue the program to provide motorized pumps for wells in rural areas.

Housing The main element in the strategy is to promote regularization of home ownership in squatting areas and to increase access to home ownership by the poor in urban areas. Measures include:

- regularize land ownership in urban squatting areas; upgrade drainage and waste removal facilities;

- set up credit program targeted towards poor urban home owners for upgrading the quality of the home and towards poor urban renters for obtaining loans to purchase a home.

Income transfer programs and safety nets

Consideration needs to be given to reviewing existing income transfer programs with a view to reforming them. A program of cash transfers could be considered oriented towards the most destitute households who lack the means to take advantage of the income generation programs (households with disabled persons, the elderly, etc.).

Since the creation of employment will take time, efforts to launch labor-intensive public works might be accelerated. Programs should be self-targeted to the poor by low wages, as a temporary measure. Such works could be used to improve both urban and rural infrastructure.

Modalities of implementation

Regulatory reform

Several of the actions proposed for Côte d'Ivoire's poverty alleviation strategy will be helped greatly by regulatory reform. This is especially the case for actions to promote the urban informal sector and those to improve the poor's access to urban services. Excessively complicated procurement rules effectively keep small enterprises out of the bidding for government contracts. Regulations which distort the labor market, red tape which makes it very difficult to set up an enterprise, etc., all discourage prospective entrepreneurs. A critical review and subsequent rationalization and simplification of regulations affecting the functioning of enterprises and the delivery of urban services would create a more enabling environment for the poverty alleviation strategy. The guiding principle should be to recognize that the public sector and the private sector are not competitors in this strategy, but can work together and achieve a constructive interaction between market forces and government intervention.

Financing poverty alleviation

A number of policies proposed above can be managed with full cost recovery. This is especially the case with the provision of services. In the case of services such as water supply, the willingness to pay by the poor is already demonstrated (given that the poor now pay higher prices than the nonpoor). For many services, government should permit and encourage the use of low-cost solutions which are often developed spontaneously by the local populations (e.g., community-organized garbage removal, reselling of water to neighbors, etc.). Often, this will make possible full cost recovery even from poor beneficiaries. For education and health services, the burden of cost recovery needs to be shifted towards tertiary-level services and towards the nonpoor. The poorest households may well continue to benefit from selective subsidization. As we discussed in Chapter 4, the level of government expenditure and the current skewness in their intrasectoral allocation is such that the proposed pro-poor reallocation can be achieved without increases in total costs. In fact, one could well argue that efficiency improvements contain much scope for resource savings.

Other poverty alleviation actions will however require additional resources, e.g., promotion of informal enterprises, improved rural extension services, labor-intensive public works. These efforts need to remain centrally financed, although the implementation can often be delegated to local government, provided of course that a matching transfer of funds takes place.

Decentralization

For more than a decade now, Côte d'Ivoire has been engaged in a process of decentralization – transferring responsibilities for service delivery from central authorities to cities and (large) villages. The main difficulty so far has been that a corresponding transfer of resources and fiscal authority has not yet fully taken place. Local governments should be given an increasing responsibility for poverty alleviation, especially in areas of public works and targeting of services and infrastructure. Commensurate with this increase in responsibilities, financial transfers from central to local government need to increase. Such effective decentralization is likely to be a pro-poor event.

By increasing the total amount of resources going to smaller cities, where there are more poor people, relative improvements for the poor should result (even if within-city targeting is not improved). The decentralization process must thus be seen as an important ingredient of poverty alleviation policy.

Popular participation

The implementation of all aspects of the poverty alleviation strategy discussed so far will be rendered more effective if the level of popular participation is increased. Decentralization shifts responsibilities to local governments, who are typically closer to the people than a central government. However, within each city, large or small, local government needs to interact more with the local communities. This can be channeled through a variety of organizations, such as NGOs, church groups, chambers of commerce, volunteer groups, etc. The important point is that local government needs to send out the message that it welcomes a dialogue with its constituency on a wide range of issues pertaining to the management of the community.

To the extent possible, community organizations should be involved in all stages of the decisionmaking process, not just at the end, so that there is a sense that their participation can make a real difference. For selected services (e.g., garbage removal), community management can be encouraged. In programs to upgrade urban squatters or low-income areas, priorities for improvements should be determined by residents. In all this, a special effort will be needed to ensure that the poorest are not excluded from local groups.

Poverty monitoring

The results presented in this book indicate the crucial importance of annual monitoring of poverty. Year-to-year changes in Côte d'Ivoire were drastic (see Chapter 3), and there is no reason to think that such changes could not occur in other countries as well. Moreover, this study's results, especially those in Chapter 4, show that it is insufficient to monitor social indicators at the national level only. This is the current practice in the majority of developing countries because the underlying household-level data are not available, which would make possible cross-tabulations by poverty status. Yet, one of the main findings of this study was that the basic needs fulfillment of the poorest households had deteriorated significantly in spite of often steady or even rising trends of national-level indicators. Such information is critical for making correct policy decisions regarding the allocation of funds for social programs as well as for the targeting of these programs. Data collection to monitor poverty is thus not a statistical luxury, but an essential ingredient on the overall effort to enhance the livelihood and well-being of the poor.

This does not mean, however, that the annual undertaking of complex integrated surveys, such as the Côte d'Ivoire Living Standards Survey is the only way to proceed. The CILSS was a difficult and expensive undertaking, and, in the case of Africa, only a few countries have been able to successfully run this type of survey. Effective poverty monitoring can be done with simpler surveys. We have argued elsewhere (Grootaert 1993b; Grootaert and Marchant, 1991) that the data needed to do this are actually quite limited in scope and can be collected easily, rapidly, and cheaply.

What then is the key information needed for poverty monitoring? Our research results suggest that both household expenditure and basic needs information are needed, since neither is able to provide by itself a full picture of welfare. In contrast, income data are much less useful. As we have argued, household expenditure is a preferred welfare indicator conceptually and it is easier to collect. The analysis of the full current account of households, including savings is, in our view, not the top priority for welfare and poverty analysis in a poor country. However, what is important to link macroeconomic change to welfare is the *composition* of income and changes in it. This can be established through a series of qualitative questions which are much simpler than the literally hundreds of questions needed to build up the *level* of income. We recognize the potential importance of an integrated living standards survey to provide a baseline data set and to permit in-depth analysis of household behavior and response. For those reasons, such a survey might be undertaken every five years or so (at least if the country has the necessary analytic capacity). Apart from that, the monitoring of poverty should occur annually, or even more frequently if the country undergoes rapid economic change. This can be achieved by a simpler survey focusing only on household expenditure and selected basic needs variables of the sort used in the analysis in this book. This approach is likely to yield results much faster and thus to be of more interest and use to policy makers. If this then leads to better policy, data collection will indeed have helped the poor.

Lessons for other African countries

Côte d'Ivoire's macroeconomic experience is not unique in Sub-Saharan Africa. Between 1965 and 1974, GDP per capita grew by an average of 2.6 percent a year in the region, but in the late seventies and eighties, most countries experienced declines. Many countries eventually had a lower GDP per capita than before independence some 20 years earlier (World Bank, 1994). The root causes of Côte d'Ivoire's economic crisis of the eighties were also shared by many other African countries: an overvalued exchange rate and budget deficits undermined the macroeconomic stability needed for long term growth; lack of diversification of the export base, government monopolies and heavy taxation of agricultural exports reduced competition and caused volatile export receipts, thus complicating macroeconomic management (World Bank, 1994). These and other factors have been well documented for many countries, but as we argued in the introduction of this book, the empirical investigation of the social impacts of this process and its implications for poverty and basic needs fulfillment is largely nonexistent. And this provided the raison d'être for this book.

While we hope that future studies will document clearly the experience of other African countries, in the meantime we would argue that several lessons from the Côte d'Ivoire case should guide policy in other countries as well.

First, one of the most striking findings of this study is the speed with which the recession/destabilization in Côte d'Ivoire in 1987-88 'trickled down' to households, and the magnitude of the effect. There is no reason to assume that such effect could not occur in other countries experiencing similar declines in macroeconomic performance. The explanation probably includes the standard argument that reductions in aggregate demand 'bite' much faster than supply incentives and price realignments. The contrast with the adjustment years provides dramatic evidence of the costs in terms of increased poverty that can stem from even one or two years of unchecked economic decline or destabilization. The important lesson is that it is much more feasible to protect the poor with a managed adjustment program than under conditions of destabilization.

Second, the decomposition of the changes in poverty demonstrated that the overriding cause of the increase in poverty was the negative economic growth. Changes in distribution which occurred over the period contributed to reducing poverty. The phenomenon at work could have been a 'Kuznets curve' in reverse: when the economy contracts, the distribution of income gets better before it gets worse. This reemphasizes of course that the policy priority is to generate economic growth.

A third general lesson pertains to the fulfillment of basic needs. On the positive side, the Côte d'Ivoire experience highlights the possibility to protect, on the average, the fulfillment of basic needs even in conditions of rapid economic decline. On the negative side, the CILSS data underline the danger that the very poor may suffer serious setbacks in basic needs fulfillment, even when average conditions remain the same or even improve. Indeed, during 1985-88, for Côte d'Ivoire as a whole, the fulfillment of basic needs did not suffer precariously, but the very poor bore almost the entire burden of whatever declines did occur. It would appear that the reasons behind this phenomenon may occur in other countries too: the very poor are often marginal users of health and educational services and any deterioration in supply or demand causes them to relinquish using the service. In the case of a supply reduction, the opportunity cost may become too high, and in the case of falling income the very poor may no longer be able to afford the monetary outlays. Clearly, the lesson for other countries is that it is not sufficient to monitor basic needs trends at the national level, but that disaggregation by region, socioeconomic group and welfare level are essential. By the same token, separate targeting and policy design for the very poor may well be essential.

As a corollary to the previous point, a fourth lesson is that basic needs should be monitored *directly*, and not by looking at aggregate levels of public spending. The focus of policy reform should be on the intrasectoral and functional allocation. In the case of Côte d'Ivoire, aggregate spending levels painted a rosy picture, which revealed neither the growing inefficiencies in service delivery due to a growing share of wages in public expenditure, nor the deterioration in access by the very poor.

Fifth, this study's results confirm the importance of not considering the poor as a homogeneous group. This is the implicit assumption when poverty analysis uses only one poverty line. One of the main findings of this study, viz the relative deterioration of the condition of the very poorest would have been entirely missed if only one poverty line had been used. By the same token, the policy recommendations are distinctly different, since the very poor represent a more urgent target group. Policies like selective subsidies for school meals and books may be needed for the poorest but may not be appropriate for the poor as a group, if for no other reason than the forbidding total cost.

Lastly, and most generally, our use of a multidimensional poverty profile in combination with a decomposable poverty index proved to be an effective tool to link macroeconomic change to the change in welfare of households and individuals. The decomposition over socioeconomic groups was especially useful, given that those groups were defined according to source-of-income and sectoral criteria – which could be linked directly to policy measures (e.g., relating to public sector, export crops, etc.). We do not claim to have proved causality formally, as perhaps we could have done with a full-fledged economywide model. However, the flexibility and ease of use of our analytic tool provides, in our view, an ample tradeoff for the loss of formal causality. It seems clear that the possibility of widely applying this type of analysis in most African countries is far greater than that of economywide models.

Bibliography

Ainsworth, M. (1989), 'Socioeconomic Determinants of Fertility in Côte d'Ivoire', Living Standards Measurement Study Working Paper, No. 53, The World Bank: Washington, DC.

Ainsworth, M. and Munoz, J. (1986), 'The Côte d'Ivoire Living Standards Survey – Design and Implementation', Living Standards Measurement Study Working Paper, No. 26, The World Bank: Washington, DC.

Alessie R., Baker, P., Blundell, R., Heady, C., and Meghir, C. (1992), 'The Working Behavior of Young People in Rural Côte d'Ivoire', *The World Bank Economic Review*, Vol. 6, No. 1.

Atkinson, A. (1987), 'On the Measurement of Poverty', *Econometrica*, Vol. 55.

Atkinson, A. and Bourguignon, F. (1984), 'The Comparison of Multi-dimensional Distributions of Economic Status', *The Review of Economic Studies*, Vol. 49.

Berthélemy, J.C. and Bourguignon, F. (1992), 'Growth and Crisis in Côte d'Ivoire', Delta (Joint Research Unit CNRS-ENS-EHESS): Paris (processed).

Boateng, O., Ewusi, K., Kanbur, R., and McKay, A. (n.d.), 'A Poverty Profile for Ghana, 1987-88', Social Dimensions of Adjustment Working Paper, No. 5, The World Bank: Washington, DC.

Boughton, J. M. (1992), 'The CFA Franc: Zone of Fragile Stability in Africa', *Finance and Development*, Vol. 29, No. 4.

Boughton, J. M. (1991), 'The CFA Franc Zone: Currency Union and Monetary Standard', IMF Working Paper No. 133, International Monetary Fund: Washington, DC.

Chamley, C. and Ghanem, H. (1991), 'Fiscal Policy with Fixed Nominal Exchange Rates: Côte d'Ivoire', World Bank Policy Research Working Papers, No. 658, The World Bank: Washington, DC.

Corbo, V., Fischer, S. and Webb, S.B. eds., (1992), *Adjustment Lending Revisited: Policies To Restore Growth*, The World Bank: Washington, DC.

Cornia, G.A., Jolly, R. and Stewart, F. eds., (1987), *Adjustment with a Human Face: Protecting The Vulnerable and Promoting Growth*, Oxford University Press: New York.

Daho, B. (1992), 'La Qualité des Données de l'Enquête Permanente Auprès des Ménages de Côte d'Ivoire', Poverty and Social Policy Division, Africa Technical Department, The World Bank: Washington, DC (processed).

Deaton, A. (1992), 'Saving and Income Smoothing in Côte d'Ivoire', Discussion Paper, No. 156, Research Program in Development Studies, Woodrow Wilson School of Public and International Affairs; Princeton University: Princeton.

Deaton, A. and Benjamin, D. (1988), 'The Living Standards Survey and Price Policy Reform – A Study of Cocoa and Coffee Production in Côte d'Ivoire', Living Standards Measurement Study Working Paper, No. 44, The World Bank: Washington, DC.

Deaton, A. and Muellbauer, J. (1980), *Economics and Consumer Behavior*, Cambridge University Press: Cambridge.

Demery, L. (1993), 'Income and Expenditure Aggregates: Estimates from the Côte d'Ivoire Living Standards Surveys', Poverty and Social Policy Division, Africa Technical Department, The World Bank: Washington, DC (processed).

Demery, L. and Grootaert, C. (1993), 'Correcting for Sampling Bias in the Measurement of Welfare and Poverty in the Côte d'Ivoire Living Standards Survey', *The World Bank Economic Review*, Vol. 7, No. 3.

Demery, L., Ferroni, M. and Grootaert, C. eds., (1993), *Understanding the Social Impact of Policy Reform*, The World Bank: Washington, DC.

Den Tuinder, B.A. (1978), *Ivory Coast – The Challenge of Success*, Johns Hopkins University Press (for The World Bank): Baltimore.

Devarajan, S. and de Melo, J. (1987), 'Adjustment with a Fixed Exchange Rate: Cameroon, Côte d'Ivoire and Senegal', *World Bank Economic Review*, Vol. 1, No. 3.

Edwards, S. (1989), *Real Exchange Rates, Devaluation and Adjustment: Exchange Rate Policy in Developing Countries*, The Massachusetts Institute of Technology Press: Cambridge.

Eurostat (1989), *Comparison of Price Levels and Economic Aggregates 1985: The Results of 22 African Countries*, Luxembourg.

Ferroni, M. and Kanbur, R. (1990), 'Poverty-Conscious Restructuring of Public Expenditure', Social Dimensions of Adjustment Working Paper, No. 9, The World Bank: Washington, DC.

Foster, J. (1984), 'On Economic Poverty: A Survey of Aggregate Measures', *Advances in Econometrics*, Vol. 3.

Foster, J., Greer, J., and Thorbecke, E. (1984), 'A Class of Decomposable Poverty Measures', *Econometrica*, Vol. 52, No. 1.

Foster, J. and Shorrocks, A. (1988), 'Poverty Orderings', *Econometrica*, Vol. 56.

Glewwe, P. (1990), 'Investigating the Determinants of Household Welfare in Côte d'Ivoire', Living Standards Measurement Study Working Paper, No. 71, The World Bank: Washington, DC.

Glewwe, P. (1987), 'The Distribution of Welfare in the Republic of Côte d'Ivoire in 1985', Living Standards Measurement Study Working Paper, No. 29, The World Bank: Washington, DC.

Grootaert, C. (1993a), 'The Evolution of Welfare and Poverty Under Structural Change and Economic Recession in Côte d'Ivoire, 1985-88', Policy Research Working Paper, No. 1078, The World Bank: Washington, DC.

Grootaert, C. (1993b), 'How Useful Are Integrated Household Survey Data for Policy-Oriented Analyses of Poverty? Lessons from the Côte d'Ivoire Living Standards Survey', Policy Research Working Paper, No. 1079, The World Bank: Washington, DC.

Grootaert, C. (1992), 'The Position of Migrants in the Urban Informal Labor Markets in Côte d'Ivoire', *Journal of African Economies*, Vol. 1, No. 3.

Grootaert, C. (1987), 'Côte d'Ivoire's Vocational and Technical Education', Policy, Planning and Research Working Paper, No. 19, The World Bank: Washington, DC.

Grootaert, C. (1986), 'Measuring and Analyzing Levels of Living in Developing Countries: An Annotated Questionnaire', Living Standards Measurement Study Working Paper, No. 24, The World Bank: Washington, DC.

Grootaert, C. (1983), 'The Conceptual Basis of Measures of Household Welfare and Their Implied Survey Data Requirements', *The Review of Income and Wealth*, Series 29, No. 1.

Grootaert, C. and Dubois, J.L. (1988), 'Tenancy Choice and the Demand for Rental Housing in the Cities of the Ivory Coast', *Journal of Urban Economics*, Vol. 24.

Grootaert, C. and Kanbur, R. (1990), 'Policy-Oriented Analysis of Poverty and the Social Dimensions of Structural Adjustment: A Methodology and Proposed Application to Côte d'Ivoire, 1985-88,' Social Dimensions of Adjustment Working Paper, No. 1, The World Bank: Washington, DC.

Grootaert, C. and Marchant, T. (1991), 'The Social Dimensions of Adjustment Priority Survey - An Instrument for the Rapid Identification and Monitoring of Policy Target Groups', Social Dimensions of Adjustment Working Paper, No. 12, The World Bank: Washington, DC.

Haddad, L. and Kanbur, R. (1989), 'How Serious is the Neglect of Intra-Household Inequality?' Discussion Paper, No. 95, Development Economics Research Centre; University of Warwick: Coventry.

Johnson, M., McKay, A. and Round, J. (1990), 'Income and Expenditure in a System of Household Accounts – Concepts and Estimation', Social Dimensions of Adjustment Working Paper, No. 10, The World Bank: Washington, DC.

Kakwani, N. (1990), 'Testing for Significance of Poverty Differences with Application to Côte d'Ivoire', Living Standards Measurement Study Working Paper, No. 62, The World Bank: Washington, DC.

Kanbur, R. (1990), 'Poverty and the Social Dimensions of Structural Adjustment in Côte d'Ivoire', Social Dimensions of Adjustment Working Paper, No. 2, The World Bank: Washington, DC.

Kanbur, R. (1987), 'Measurement and Alleviation of Poverty', *IMF Staff Papers*, Vol. 34, No. 1.

Kravis, I., Heston, A. and Summers, R. (1982), *World Product and Income – International Comparisons of Real Gross Product*, Johns Hopkins University Press: Baltimore.

Lane, C. (1989), 'Monetary Policy Effectiveness in Côte d'Ivoire', ODI Working Paper, No. 30, ODI: London.

Levy, V. and Newman, J. (1989), 'Rigidités des Salaires – Données Microéconomiques sur l'Ajustement du Marché de Travail dans le Secteur Moderne', Living Standards Measurement Study Working Paper, No. 55, The World Bank: Washington, DC.

Mahieu, F. (1990), *Les Fondements de la Crise Economique en Afrique*, Logiques Economiques, L'Harmattan: Paris.

McKay, A. (1992), 'Estimation of a Regional Cost of Living Index for Côte d'Ivoire, 1985-88', Development Economics Research Centre; University of Warwick: Coventry (processed).

Oh, G.T. and Venkataraman, M. (1992), 'Construction of Analytic Variables and Data Sets from the Côte d'Ivoire Living Standards Survey, 1985-88: Concepts, Methodology and Documentation', Poverty and Social Policy Division, Africa Technical Department, The World Bank: Washington, DC (processed).

Ravallion, M. (1992), 'Poverty Comparisons: A Guide to Concepts and Methods', Living Standards Measurement Study Working Paper, No. 88. The World Bank: Washington, DC.

Ravallion, M. and Datt, G. (1991), 'Growth and Redistribution Components of Changes in Poverty Measures – A Decomposition with Applications to Brazil and India in the 1980s', Living Standards Measurement Study Working Paper, No. 83, The World Bank: Washington, DC.

Ruenda-Sabater, E. and Stone, A. (1992), 'Côte d'Ivoire: Private Sector Dynamics and Constraints', Policy Research Working Paper, No. 1047, The World Bank: Washington, DC.

Sahn, D. and Bernier, R. (1993), 'Evidence from Africa on the Intra-Sectoral Allocation of Social Sector Expenditures', Cornell Food and Nutrition Policy Program: Washington, DC.

Sen, A. (1987), *The Standard of Living,* Cambridge University Press: Cambridge.

Serageldin, I., Elmendorf, E. and El Tigani, E. (1993), 'Structural Adjustment and Health in Arica in the 1980s', Africa Technical Department, The World Bank: Washington, DC (processed).

Schiff, M. and Valdes, A. (1992), 'The Political Economy of Agricultural Pricing Policy', Vol. 4, *A Synthesis of the Economies in Developing Countries,* John Hopkins University Press: Baltimore.

Srinivasan, T. (1981), 'Malnutrition: Some Measurement and Policy Issues', World Bank Staff Working Papers, No. 373, The World Bank: Washington, DC.

Stolber, W. and Vagenas, C. (1992), *The Future of the CFA Franc – A Case for Currency Adjustment or More?*, Union Bank of Switzerland Occasional Paper: Zurich.

van der Gaag, J. and Vijverberg, W. (1989), 'Wage Determinants in Côte d'Ivoire: Experience, Credentials and Human Capital', *Economic Development and Cultural Change*, Vol. 37, No. 2.

World Bank (1994), *Adjustment in Africa: Reforms, Results and the Road Ahead,* Oxford University Press: Oxford.

World Bank (1990), *Making Adjustment Work for the Poor – A Framework for Policy Reform in Africa,* The World Bank: Washington, DC.